PSYCHIATRY – THEORY, APPLICATIONS AND TREATMENTS

PSYCHOTHERAPY: NEW RESEARCH

Psychiatry – Theory, Applications and Treatments

Additional books in this series can be found on Nova's website under the Series tab.

Additional E-books in this series can be found on Nova's website under the E-books tab.

Psychology Research Progress

Additional books in this series can be found on Nova's website under the Series tab.

Additional E-books in this series can be found on Nova's website under the E-books tab.

PSYCHIATRY – THEORY, APPLICATIONS AND TREATMENTS

PSYCHOTHERAPY: NEW RESEARCH

AUGUSTUS J. LANCASTER
AND
OLEN SHARPE
EDITORS

Nova Science Publishers, Inc.
New York

For permission to use material from this book please contact us:
Telephone 631-231-7269; Fax 631-231-8175
Web Site: http://www.novapublishers.com

NOTICE TO THE READER

Additional color graphics may be available in the e-book version of this book.

Library of Congress Cataloging-in-Publication Data
Psychotherapy : new research / editors, Augustus J. Lancaster and Olen Sharpe.
p. cm.
Includes index.
ISBN 978-1-61942-611-5 (hardcover)
1. Psychotherapy. I. Lancaster, Augustus J. II. Sharpe, Olen.
RC475.P79 2011
616.89'14--dc23
2011050991

Published by Nova Science Publishers, Inc. † New York

CONTENTS

PREFACE

This book explores new research in psychotherapy including dyadic developmental psychotherapy and its primary components; hope-focused couple enrichment (HFCE) analysis; body-psychotherapy and trancework; the effect of perceived parental bonding on patients' attitudes towards psychotherapy; culture and psychotherapy and spiritual group psychotherapy. (Imprint: Nova).

Chapter 1 – Psychological treatments are fully recognized as a relevant response to schizophrenia, but only as adjuncts to pharmacotherapy (Dixon, Dickerson, Bellack et al., 2010; Haddock, and Spaulding, 2011; Lemos Giráldez, Vallina Fernández, Fernández Iglesias et al., 2010; Tandon, Narsallah, and Keshavan, 2010). In general, there is no objection to recognizing the role of psychological therapy and including it in the integrated treatment of schizophrenia, given the quantity of aspects involved and the complexity of the problem, where every little helps. The inclusion of psychological therapy as an adjunct to medication is often justified in view of the limitations and problems drugs can involve: limited improvement of negative symptoms, of cognitive functioning, of social functioning and of quality of life, in addition to so-called drug-resistant symptoms, relapses due to lack of treatment compliance and side effects (including weight gain). However, we might reasonably raise a question of principle: whether the psychological approach may actually be where we should begin, without denigrating medication.

Chapter 2 – This chapter will describe Dyadic Developmental Psychotherapy, its primary components, and the differential use of those components in the different stages of treatment. The empirical research and other materials demonstrating the efficacy and evidence-base of this approach will be summarized. The use of this treatment with families who have children who have experienced complex trauma will be described. This approach was originally developed for use with adopted and foster children and has now been demonstrated as valuable as a general treatment model. The use of this model in residential treatment settings will also be described. Case examples and excerpts from treatment sessions will be used to illustrate the differential use of components in different phases of treatment and other aspects of this treatment.

Chapter 3 – Hope-focused couple enrichment (HFCE) has been evaluated as one of four empirically supported couple enrichment interventions (Jakubowski et al., 2004). The authors first review the essence of the hope-focused approach. The authors then review outcome research on HFCE and its components. We present and discuss four possible reasons for the efficacy of the non-religiously accommodated hope-focused approach. These include (a) a focus on hope, (b) a simple strategy with diverse techniques, (c) a focus on repairing damaged emotional bonds through forgiveness, and (d) reliance on systematic research on the components of the method. The authors hope to interest researchers and clinicians in the hope-focused approach as well as improve couple therapists' counseling.

Chapter 4 – After over nine years of Jungian analysis, Grace was shocked to discover repressed memories of sexual abusesurfacing shortly after commencing psychotherapy. The focus on body, the use of hypnosis, and a relational positioning are believed to have contributed to this emergent biography, which illuminated for Grace many of her dissociative and sexualizing tendencies. Co-written by psychotherapist and client (a psychotherapist herself), this chapter illustrates some clinical applications of relational-embodied hypnosis. Through exploring transferential and generative aspects of trance, the paper further introduces relational facets of hypnotic work, while explaining issues of touch, intimacy, regression, and influence. Moreover, this case material presents a psychotherapeutic dialogue with surrender: surrender to the edge of love, to the charge of erotic transference, and to an intersubjective third, which threatens to touch and change both parties deeper than they intended to.

Chapter 5 – Attachment theory originating from the work of John Bowlby and Mary Ainsworth has been an influential paradigm in psychoanalysis, developmental and general psychology over the last 50 years bridging the gap between academic and clinical psychology. Representing a lifelong developmental perspective and having a relational emphasis attachment theory has become a very fruitful ground for practice and research of psychotherapy as well. Early infant-caregiver relations are pivotal for attachment theory and are the source of transference in the process of psychotherapy. Although there are studies proving the effect of early childhood memories on transference and therapeutic relationship in general, the effect of perceived parental bonding on the therapeutic relationship has not been investigated yet in a systematic attachment perspective. Moreover, the possible effect of perceived parental bonding on patients' attitude toward psychotherapy has been ignored. In the study presented, psychotherapy patients (n=97) completed Parental Bonding Instrument, Attachment Avoidance in Therapy Scale and three items on attitude toward their psychotherapy in progress. Results show that a model consisting of six parental bonding scales, duration of psychotherapy and therapeutic attachment avoidance predicts 28 per cent of variance for attitude toward psychotherapy. Paternal care and therapeutic attachment avoidance proved to be significant predictors. Moreover, hierarchical linear modeling shows that paternal care and duration of psychotherapy have an indirect effect on patients' attitude mediated by attachment avoidance. The possible interpretations of this specific paternal contribution to experiencing psychotherapy relationship and attitude toward psychotherapy are discussed.

Chapter 6 – Terminally ill patients sometimes experience depression, anxiety, or psycho-existential suffering. Psycho-existential suffering is defined as pain caused by extinction of being and extinction of meaning of self due to the loss of relationships with others, loss of autonomy, or loss of a future[1.]In this model, psycho-existential suffering has the sense of meaning as a core concept. Because psycho-existential suffering is related to quality of life, good death, depression[2], desire for hastened death, hopelessness, and suicidal ideation[3], it is important to palliate psycho-existential suffering.

Chapter 7 – Despite the growing awareness of culture within psychology, critics contend that understandings of culture remain largely superficial. Hermeneutics is a way of thinking interpretively about cultural meanings and discerning their specific manifestations that helps to remedy this situation. Hermeneutics offers a comprehensive theory of culture that (a) details how the self is embedded in culture, (b) highlights culture's inherently moral nature, and (c) provides conceptual tools for approaching culture in specific encounters. It can be utilized by psychotherapists not only to help understand clients from different cultural backgrounds but also to better recognize how the dominant Western cultural outlook, individualism, influences psychotherapy theory, research, and practice. These concepts are applied to cross-cultural cases.

Chapter 8 – A large number of publications have previously shown spirituality/religiosity to crucially boosting the mental resilience and curing the psychiatric illness. Religiosity and spirituality can be defined broadly as any feelings, thoughts, experiences, and behaviors that arise from a search for the "sacred", with the former implying group or social practices and doctrines and the latter tending to refer to personal experiences and beliefs. The present study aimed to develop a novel spiritual group psychotherapy based on the Four True Paths; Love, Wisdom, Self-reflection, and Progress, and to evaluate the efficacy in a randomized controlled trial with 26 Japanese out-patients suffering from mood disorders or neurotic, stress-related, and somatoform disorders. The treatment participants (n=14) at 3-6 people per group took part in five 90-minutes sessions at one-week intervals, while the delayed-treatment control patients (n=12) only received a usual care including medication. Their mental status was assessed before and after the intervention by the Profile of Mood States and the Positive Negative Affect Schedulescale. The authors found that the depressive symptom was significantly improved in the trial group, compared with the control group. In conclusion, the currently developed group psychotherapy might have an unyielding effectiveness on thedepressive symptom, which further needs to be confirmed by a large randomized controlled trial.

In: Psychotherapy
Editors: A. J. Lancaster and O. Sharpe

ISBN 978-1-61942-611-5

Chapter 1

From Neurochemistry to Interpersonal Chemistry: Towards a Psychotherapy of Schizophrenia

Marino Pérez-Álvarez[1], and José M. García-Montes[2]
[1]Universidad de Oviedo, Spain
[2]Universidad de Almería, Spain

Psychological treatments are fully recognized as a relevant response to schizophrenia, but only as adjuncts to pharmacotherapy (Dixon, Dickerson, Bellack et al., 2010; Haddock, and Spaulding, 2011; Lemos Giráldez, Vallina Fernández, Fernández Iglesias et al., 2010; Tandon, Narsallah, and Keshavan, 2010). In general, there is no objection to recognizing the role of psychological therapy and including it in the integrated treatment of schizophrenia, given the quantity of aspects involved and the complexity of the problem, where every little helps. The inclusion of psychological therapy as an adjunct to medication is often justified in view of the limitations and problems drugs can involve: limited improvement of negative symptoms, of cognitive functioning, of social functioning and of quality of life, in addition to so-called drug-resistant symptoms, relapses due to lack of treatment compliance and side effects (including weight gain). However, we might reasonably raise a question of principle: whether the psychological approach may actually be where we should begin, without denigrating medication.

First of all, the very heterogeneity of schizophrenia makes the homogeneity with which medication is prescribed somewhat suspicious. The systematic and "compulsive" application of medication, as a treatment of first response, entails three problems. The first is that it can unintentionally condemn the patient to a "psychiatric career" from which it will not be easy to escape. Medication "marks" a destiny. It suggests from the outset that there is an illness in need of medication, if indeed it is not directly explained that this is the case, as proposed by the vulnerability-stress model. Medication thus becomes the subject of the interactions with the clinician (maintaining it, increasing it, reducing it, etc.), reducing the disorder to set of symptoms, in accordance with the procedure of listening to the drug (Pérez-Álvarez and García-Montes, 2007), in this case *listening to Olanzapine*, rather than to the actual person. Another problem is that medication is merely symptomatic, ignoring the *causes* of psychotic crises, which commonly occur in adolescent. Patients' experience of medication involves feeling indifference toward the symptoms and toward everything (Healy, 1989; Mizrahi, Bagby, Zipursky, and Kapur, 2005). Medication does not exactly produce an experience of recovery of the sense of self and of normal contact with reality. Even when the clinician asks questions and gives the person the opportunity to talk about what happened, etc., it is not the same if there is medication involved. If the patient is taking antipsychotic medication, it is not easy for either the clinician or the patient to take the psychological approach *seriously*. And the third problem is that psychological help becomes "corrupted" in the context of medication. The state of indifference to the symptoms gets in the way of psychological therapies that try to explore, confront and understand the psychotic experiences. Indeed, the aim of psychotherapy is not necessarily to eliminate the symptoms, but to change one's relationship with them and develop an understanding of their meaning.

But these potential problems with medication are not the only reasons for raising what is in fact a *question of principle*, related to the use of psychological therapy from the outset. The main reason concerns the very nature of schizophrenia, as a disorder of the self, in line with the phenomenological perspective developed by, among others, American psychologist Louis Sass (Nelson, Sass, Thompson et al., 2009; Pérez-Álvarez, García-Montes and Sass, 2010; Sass, 2007; Sass and Parnas, 2003). According to this conception, the most appropriate approach would be a psychological therapy focusing on the alterations of the self which are at the root of the schizophrenic condition, without *spurning* antipsychotic medication, but without its inevitable application. In the context of psychological therapy, medication would be not a compulsive protocol-based procedure, but rather an optional resource to give support to a therapeutic approach based on the person, on finally *listening to the person*. In the words of a patient: "People talk about chemical imbalance. Well, [my friend] and I, [together we made] a chemical balance." (Davidson, 2003, p. 170). *Interpersonal chemistry*, in the clinical relationship, for example, may actually be of more help in the recovery of one's sense of self than interneuronal chemistry.

Before proposing a psychological therapy for schizophrenia or psychotherapy*of* schizophrenia, we must ask ourselves whether it is reasonable to even think about it. Wouldn't it be madness to consider psychotherapy of schizophrenia without beginning with medication? From the prevailing orthodoxy, this could involve two ethical problems at the same time. Wouldn't it be unethical to *not* prescribe antipsychotic medication from the outset? And similarly, is it not already a matter of ethics to apply evidence-based treatments such as those endorsing antipsychotics, which are "the only effective therapeutic agents currently available"? This is the argument of, for example, Keshavan, Nasrallah and Tandon (2011).

In response to these alleged ethical failings we might consider the Hippocratic principle, *primum non nocere* ("First, do no harm"). Protocol-based compulsive antipsychotic medication, as currently established, can do the unintended harm of predestining a patient to a psychiatric career (chronification), with all the acknowledged limitations and disadvantages, as outlined above. Bentall and Morrison (2002) and Whitaker (2004) have argued and shown that compulsive medication can do *more harm than good*. Moreover, we must take into account the *collateral damage* from what is left out by beginning with medication: everything related to the personal meaning of the symptoms, and indeed, everything psychological. And this is not to mention the advantages of medication-free research, including the possibility of assessing the effects of psychological interventions (Bola, 2006; Carpenter, 1997).

First of all, we look at the question of what really happens if we use a first response other than medication. In these times of antipsychotics, are there such things as drug-free, psychologically-treated cases? We continue by proposing a form of psychotherapy of schizophrenia, with its basis in phenomenology. Finally, we consider some of the challenges faced by such a psychological approach.

PSYCHOLOGICAL THERAPIES FOR SCHIZOPHRENIA - AS FIRST-RESPONSE TREATMENT

Psychoanalysis – What Became of It?

Prior to the introduction of neuroleptics in the 1950s, psychoanalytical psychotherapy was the treatment most widely applied for schizophrenia (Fenton, 2000; García Cabeza, 2008). In general, its results have been disappointing, and it does not in fact figure among the recognized psychological treatments in schizophrenia (Dixon, Dickerson, Bellack et al., 2010; Haddock and Spaulding, 2011; Lemos Giráldez, Vallina Fernández, Fernández Iglesias et al., 2010). Freud himself warned of the inadequacy of psychoanalysis for schizophrenia, in view of the difficulty for establishing a transference relationship, etc. Subsequently, research would show that investigative psychotherapy, focused on personality change, was no more effective than support psychotherapy, more focused on the current crisis (Fenton, 2000).

However, the psychoanalytical psychotherapy perspective has made substantial contributions to psychological therapy for schizophrenia. It is worth recalling three of them. One is the interpersonal psychiatry paradigm developed by Harry Stack Sullivan in the 1920s, based on observation and the idea of the importance of mutual trust for psychotherapeutic help. Another contribution has to do with the emphasis psychoanalysis places on relations and interactions from early childhood ("object relations," "basic trust," "affective bonds," "identification figures", "ambivalence of relations," "limits of the self," etc.) in the formation of the self, and in turn, the alterations that can lead to the development of schizophrenia. Even though Frieda Fromm-Reichmann's hypothesis of the "schizophrenogenic mother" cannot be sustained, it suggests the relevance of family communication patterns, including those that can "drive people mad" (Searles, 1959).

A further contribution directly concerns the structure and functioning of psychotherapy. In relation to the crucial importance of the "therapeutic alliance," the psychodynamic approach highlights the tasks of psychotherapy in helping patients to recognize, endure and put into perspective their feelings and life experience (Fenton, 2000). Although psychoanalytical or psychodynamic psychotherapy is not acknowledged in the dominant school of psychological therapies in schizophrenia, it still prevails, constituting an important part of integrated perspectives (Cullberg, 2007; Hinglay, 2006/2008), as well as being recognized by the *International Society for the Psychological Treatments of the Schizophrenias and other Psychoses* (ISPS), which dates from the 1950s (Alanen, Silver and González de Chavez, 2006; García Cabeza, 2008) – coincidentally, the same decade in which neuroleptics were introduced. Whilst history shows that neuroleptics, as Whitaker (2004) points out, may be doing more harm than good, the truth is that the fifty years of humanistic treatment of psychosis is humanizing the treatment of people with schizophrenia, referring to ISPS.

As regards schizophrenia cases approached psychoanalytically prior to the arrival of antipsychotic medication, worthy of note are those of Renée, the subject of "Diary of a schizophrenic" and treated by the Swiss psychoanalyst Marie-Anne Sechehaye (2003), and that of Joanne Greenberg, treated by Frieda Fromm-Reichmann and famous for her autobiographical novel (Green, 1974).

Cases of Psychological Therapy for Schizophrenia, without Medication

Finding cases of schizophrenia treated psychologically is not easy these days, given the extent to which antipsychotic medication is established in clinical practice. Medication is the order of the day not only on the basis of a neurobiological conception, but also in line with ethical imperatives, related to its consideration as the best treatment available or to "defensive practices" against what patients might do to themselves or others (suicide, assault, etc.), which could be blamed on lack of medication (control). Nevertheless, there are indeed cases of schizophrenia treated psychologically and without medication, and not just anecdotal cases, but cases involving systematic study, such as those outlined below.

Carpenter, McGlashan and Strauss (1977) set out expressly to investigate whether the withdrawal of medication in the context of a psychological treatment has an unfavourable influence on the course of acute schizophrenia. The study shows that the *non*-use of neuroleptics during acute psychotic episodes, psychological therapy being used in its place (in this case with a psychodynamic approach), does not necessarily lead to an unfavourable course or outcome, and can indeed bring some advantages. The advantages of non-medication here would include, in addition to the possible avoidance of side-effects, a lower probability of rehospitalization compared to those using the normal medication. The authors use their data for arguing against the established opinion (even as early as 1977) that the schizophrenic patient should be treated with medication, and that failing to do so is unethical (Carpenter, McGlashan and Strauss, 1977).

Morrison (2001) presents four cases of patients who, for various reasons, were not on medication (failure to respond to medication, adverse reaction and refusal to take it), of whom two improved significantly with regard to the hallucinations, which were the target of the applied cognitive therapy. The author stressed the viability of cognitive therapy as an alternative to medication for auditory hallucinations. Christodoulides, Dudley, Brown et al. (2008) also report three cases of patients with non-medicated schizophrenia who improved in negative symptoms, as well as in other general psychopathology, with cognitive-behavioural therapy. Although the patients improved with this therapy, two of them started taking antipsychotic medication again, to the astonishment of the therapists themselves and the authors of the study, despite the fact that the therapy addressed the management of the symptoms and not compliance with the prescribed medication (Christodoulides, Dudley, Brown et al., 2008, p. 205). This circumstance raises a question that is more institutional than clinical. Patients improve with psychological therapy, but the least "opportunity," which may be a relapse (relapses form part of the normal course of many clinical conditions, including schizophrenia), rather than providing the cue to turn back to psychological help or seek more "doses" of psychotherapy, serves, as we said, as an excuse for returning to medication. This highlights the need for coherence on the part of the clinical team, particularly doctors or psychiatrists, who must be capable of recognizing improvements due to factors other than medication, in this case psychological therapy, and of accepting their own unease and "nervousness" with the patient's symptoms.

In relation to this problem, it is worth citing the case reported by García-Montes and Pérez-Álvarez (2001). The authors applied Acceptance and Commitment Therapy (ACT), which places the emphasis on the acceptance of unpleasant experiences (such as hearing voices – ceasing to be dependent on what they say), as well on the solution of "problems in living", with a commitment to act in line with values that are significant for the person, instead of being subject to their self-experiences. The patient, a 21-year-old man, improved with regard to both the distress caused by the voices and the resolution of his life problems. In fact, in view of these improvements and in agreement with his psychiatrist, the patient was reducing the dose of medication. However, certain setbacks triggered a crisis with exacerbation of symptoms, and hence the psychiatrist's "relapse" into increasing the medication and the consequent loss of the case for psychological therapy. The application of the same therapy to another case in which there was better collaboration with the clinical team (and, it must be said, there was no inopportune crisis) permitted an improvement in relation to the voices, the patient's reorientation in his everyday life, and a gradual decrease in the amount of medication (Veiga-Martínez, Pérez Álvarez and García Montes, 2008).

The same authors, García-Montes and Pérez Álvarez (2010), were involved in helping another patient to "get on with his life." The patient in question was a 28-year-old man, diagnosed with schizophrenia and in treatment, who was "stuck" in his bodily sensations, devoid of initiative, and overwhelmed by others' judgements of him, as though they were going to break the "internal" and "external" barrier, and thus define his identity, "without having any right to do so." He led a life that was, in his own words, "totally unproductive," given the way he was absorbed in his sensations and in music; he spent three whole months just staying in his bedroom in the dark, scarcely eating or moving, due to the distress caused by the sensations. At the time of the psychological therapy, when he was 28, he was taking no medication, after having taking it without improvement from age 17 to 20. Given the failure of the medication, he had withdrawn into himself, into his solitude and nihilism, without initiative, more likely to make another suicide attempt than to get back to having a "productive" life. The case was approached from the Acceptance and Commitment Therapy (ACT) perspective and re-appraised in existential terms, focusing, for example, on his rejection of aspects constitutive of the human condition, such as the "condemnation to freedom," relations with others and one's dependence on them, as well as one's own bodily experiences. The acceptance of and orientation toward values, aspects emphasized in ACT, were situated in an existential perspective, taking as references the ideas of Spanish philosopher Ortega y Gasset and Jean-Paul Sartre. The patient made gradual progress, concomitantly with the therapy received, with a steady increase over the 22 months of follow-up. The authors highlight the relevance of raising philosophical questions in the therapy, taking seriously some of the existential concerns often found in schizophrenia patients.

Romme, Escher, Dillon et al. (2009) report 50 stories of recovery from problems of hearing voices without the need for medication, and thanks to diverse types of help and strategies implemented by the persons themselves. Important aspects of the recovery were as follows: 1) finding someone (therapist or other hearer) who takes an interest in the hearer of the voices as a person and accepts them as real experiences; 2) becoming actively interested in one's own experience of the voices (e.g., relating them to one's life experiences); 3) changing the power structure between oneself and the voices, in various ways: offering them a space, challenging them, accepting them, etc.; 4) making decisions to seek help, friends, a job, etc., and 5) changing one's relationship with the voices, which may involve accepting them, learning to talk about them with others, using them as help, understanding their meaning, giving more importance to oneself than to the voices, and so on.

What it is important to stress, as do Romme, Escher, Dillon et al. (2009), is that none of this is possible according to the medical model, which assumes the voices to be an aberrant symptom of the brain that must be treated with medication. Moreover, their consideration as a symptom of an illness in need of medication may be more harmful than beneficial, especially when, as often occurs, attempts to eliminate them come to nothing, and without their meaning having been explored.

The voices, at least in some 70% of the 50 cases reported, are related to traumas or situations of impotence, failure or helplessness, which it would be better to try and understand; indeed, when treated in this way, patients improve (Romme, Escher, Dillon et al., 2009, p. 25).

Soteria Paradigm

An entire treatment model of schizophrenia without medication (or with minimum levels) is the "Soteria paradigm." The Soteria paradigm (from the Greek: salvation, protection) was founded in the early 1970s in the USA (San Francisco) by psychiatrist Loren Mosher, who was its director until its closure, due to lack of funds, in 1983. In 1984 it was refounded by the Swiss psychiatrist Luc Ciompi in Berne (Soteria Berne), where it still operates, and whence it has spread to other European countries, mainly Germany. Mosher's original project, reminiscent of moral treatment, found its most immediate inspiration in therapeutic communities, in Sullivan's interpersonal psychiatry, and in phenomenology and existentialism, especially as regards the "being-with" principle. Mosher maintained that close human relations with psychotic patients ("being-with") in small, non-hospital communities for support and protection ("soteria") make it possible to achieve therapeutic effects similar to or better than those of traditional treatment based on hospitalization, and with scarcely any use of antipsychotic medication (Mosher, 1999).

The Soteria Berne model works according to 8 therapeutic principles (Ciompi and Hoffmann, 2004):

1. Small (6-8 patients), relaxing, stimulus-protecting and as "normal" as possible therapeutic community (e.g., in a house)
2. Continual personalized "being with" the patient
3. Personal and conceptual continuity over the whole period of treatment (few therapists in 48-hour shifts)
4. Continued close collaboration with family members and other important persons of reference for the patient
5. Clear and concordant information, for patients, family and staff
6. Elaboration of common and shared realistic goals and expectations for future housing and work
7. Consensual low dose neuroleptic strategies, where necessary
8. After-care and relapse prevention for at least two years

A systematic review of the numerous studies of its efficacy in comparison to the traditional procedure of hospitalization and medication led to the following conclusion: "the evidence does not appear to indicate that the Soteria paradigm was ineffective; rather it suggests that it seemed to be at least as effective as traditional hospital-based treatment, this being achieved without the use of antipsychotic medication as the primary treatment." (Calton, Ferriter, Huband, and Spandler, 2008, p. 186). As regards the question of medication, it should be noted that the Soteria paradigm, while refraining from a dogmatic "anti-medication" attitude, sets out to avoid the use of drugs, considering it as a possibility open to an informed voluntary decision, as opposed to the compulsion encountered in traditional clinical contexts, where medication is a first response. In the original study during Mosher's time, just 24% of the patients received medication in the first six weeks, and the majority at low doses, compared to the 100% of the hospitalized patients in the reference group, at standard doses. In a follow-up at 2 years, the percentage of Soteria patients taking medication had risen to 57%, at less than half the standard dose, compared to 97% of patients in the traditional paradigm at full doses (Calton, Ferriter, Huband, and Spandler, 2008, p. 187).

Another study set out to find research on the treatment of acute schizophrenia which did not use medication, such as the Soteria paradigm and other projects, with the aim of determining the possible long-term harm of the *non*-use of medication, on the assumption that a delay in its application would be prejudicial, not to mention its lack of application altogether (Bola, 2006). The conclusion is that no harm appears to derive from non-medication in early phases, or from the much-feared delay of treatment programmes. As Bola (2006) concludes: "In the absence of substantive evidence of long-term harm from short periods of medication-free research in schizophrenia, a categorical prohibition of medication-free research in early episode schizophrenia on the ethical grounds of harm to human subjects should probably be reconsidered" (p. 294).

Finnish Model

The Finnish model for the early treatment of schizophrenia also shows that medication is not indispensable, and that even in its absence things can improve (Alanen, Lehtinen, Lehtinen et al., 2002/2009). It is a model developed from several previous projects, and defined as an integrated treatment, adapted to patient needs, and based on psychodynamic individual therapy. The psychodynamic basis of the therapy refers to the process of understanding what has occurred and what is occurring to patients in their interpersonal context. One project compared a no-medication (or minimum-medication) experimental group with a standard-medication control group. The schedule of minimum neuroleptics use included, wherever possible, an initial period of three weeks without these drugs and their introduction at highly restricted dosage, and only if it were considered strictly necessary (Alanen, Lehtinen, Lehtinen et al., 2002/2009, p. 451). In the no-medication experimental group, 42% of the patients received no neuroleptics at all during the two-year follow-up period, including the initial phase, whilst in the standard-medication control group only 6% were not given drugs. On the other hand, almost all the patients received some form of psychological treatment, which suggests, from what we shall see below, that patients taking medication obtain less benefit from psychological therapy – undoubtedly for some of the reasons already mentioned (failure to take psychological therapy seriously, etc.).

"In general, the patients' situation, at the two-year follow-up, was relatively good, but the outcome was somewhat better in the experimental group than in the control group." This advantage of non-medication refers to fewer hospitalizations in two years, fewer psychotic symptoms and other improvements in general health. The most notable finding, according to Alanen et al., was the threefold presence of psychotic symptoms in the standard-medication control group compared to the no-medication experimental group (Alanen, Lehtinen, Lehtinen et al., 2002/2009, p. 451). "The use of neuroleptics," continued these authors, "in the treatment of patients diagnosed with first-episode schizophrenia-type psychosis does not appear to be essential, as has been thought. The outcome after two years in a non-selected group of patients, treated according to the Finnish model but avoiding neuroleptics in almost half of the patients was even somewhat better than that for the control group that had been given neuroleptics on a regular basis" (Alanen, Lehtinen, Lehtinen et al., 2002/2009, p. 452).

Another variant of the Finnish model is the Open Dialogue approach for acute psychoses developed by Jaakko Seikkula and cols. (Seikkula, Aaltonen, Alakare et al., 2006; Seikkula and Olson, 2003). Open Dialogue is characterized by a social and systemic constructivist framework, involving a focus on crisis intervention, in which listening to and accepting the psychotic experiences and symptoms are fundamental. Psychotic reactions are understood as attempts and efforts to express, make sense of and cope with overwhelming circumstances that prevent one from constructing a comprehensible narrative. Hence the importance Open Dialogue gives to the narrative in the process of restitution and recovery of the psychotic experience, a co-created dialogical narrative in the setting shared by the participants; a kind of "transformational dialogue". The aim is to work with a non-pathologizing discourse, in contrast to the case of, for example, the vulnerability-stress narrative.

The results of the Open Dialogue approach show, in a 5-year follow-up study, that 82% of the patients have no psychotic symptoms and 86% returned to their job or studies, 19% relapsed in the three years following the help received, and 29% used neuroleptic medication at some point in the treatment (Seikkula, Aaltonen, Alakare et al., 2006). These results are indeed slightly better than those of the integrated treatment proposed by the Finnish model proper (described above), which already emerged as markedly superior to the traditional medication model.

Australian Model

In the line followed here of highlighting cases and systematic programmes of psychological therapy for schizophrenia, without the use of medication – or at least without its compulsive application –, we should mention the Australian model of early intervention in psychosis (McGorry, 2002/2009; McGorry, Killackey and Yung, 2008). Even though the Australian model is among the leaders of the ultra-high-risk movement, and hence of the new syndrome of psychosis-risk, within the neurobiological community that advocates the avoidance of delay in treatment (medication), it has its basis in the interpersonal psychotherapy of Sullivan and in modern cognitive therapy. In any case, Patrick McGorry denounces the lack of a psychological and personal perspective in mental healthprofessionals, who have become "deskilled and ill-equipped to properly understand their patients and to respond with skill to their human and developmental needs," stressing at the same time "the central role of the person and the therapeutic relationship in the treatment process" (McGorry, 2002/2009, p. 465).

Without Medication, Patients Do Not Necessarily Fare Worse

At least one group of schizophrenia patients actually function better without antipsychotics, many of whom gave up the medication themselves (Harrow and Jobe, 2007). As these authors conclude: "the current data suggest that for the select subgroup of patients with schizophrenia who are not in clinic settings, who have gone off antipsychotics and did not immediately relapse, and stayed off them for a period of time, a surprising number experienced periods of recovery and continued to function well for a considerable period without antipsychotics. Clearly, the present longitudinal data suggest that not all patients with schizophrenia need to use antipsychotic medications continuously throughout their lives" (Harrow and Jobe, 2007, p. 413). The factors associated with good levels of functioning without medication have to do, according to the cited study, with certain patient characteristics such as better prognosis, internal-control personality style (less dependency on external help), higher self-esteem, greater resilience and less vulnerability (which is all, indeed, somewhat tautological, since these are factors which practically describe good functioning). What is relevant is that a group of patients functions well without medication. As the authors of the study point out, given that patients who do not need medication to function well do not spend much time in clinical contexts, professionals' view that all of them need drugs may be a biased one. Compulsive medication may be an iatrogenic route for some patients, subjected to the toxicity of medication and deprived of the possibility of psychological therapy.

We have considered a question of principle, about whether psychological therapy or psychotherapy might be used as a first-response therapy for schizophrenia, as would correspond to its conception as a disorder of the self. To this end, we have asked what would happen if medication were not given, and psychological therapy were used as a treatment of first response. Two findings were obtained:

a) Without medication, incipient schizophrenia does not seem doomed to progressive deterioration, and
b) With psychological therapy, schizophrenia seems to have a better prognosis: patients recover their sense of self and of life, "without rose gardens."

Towards a Phenomenologically-Oriented Psychotherapy of Schizophrenia

Having dispelled some of the doubts concerning the fearful consequences of *non-medication* from the outset, as well as showing the viability of psychological therapy, we now explore the possibility of a therapy in accordance with the consideration of schizophrenia as a disorder of the self. One might expect this to be a "phenomenological therapy", but there exists no such therapy distinguished from others with such a label. What phenomenology offers are foundations and principles for any kind of therapy that takes an interest in subjective experience and the life of people who have anomalous experiences of themselves and the world, such as those that occur in schizophrenia. But while phenomenology provides the principles for psychological therapy concerned with understanding what is happening to people and with helping them to recover their sense of themselves, it is not a concrete therapy with its own name. In fact, the therapies mentioned so far incorporate phenomenological aspects in one way or another, beginning with the emphasis all of them place on the therapeutic relationship, on making sense of the patient's experiences in the biographical context and on recovery rather than vulnerability. In this context, some therapies may reflect more or less phenomenological inspiration or be more or less phenomenologically informed.

Here, we shall propose an approach involving psychological therapy or phenomenologically-oriented psychotherapy, in whose framework one can recognize and integrate therapies inspired in other perspectives.

A psychotherapy of schizophrenia within the phenomenological perspective sets out to reconstruct the person's integrity. Patients themselves reveal that the recovery process involves the sense of self (Davidson, 2003; Davidson and Strauss, 1992). First of all, we shall describe the characteristics of a phenomenologically-informed psychotherapy of schizophrenia, highlighting within it the role of personal narrative. Finally, we shall include acceptance and action in the phenomenological perspective.

Phenomenological Framework for a Psychotherapy of Schizophrenia

The condition *sine qua non* in the psychotherapy of schizophrenia is a particular kind of therapeutic relationship. It is a question not simply of a good therapeutic alliance or collaborative relation, but rather of a genuine inter-personal encounter. This inter-personal encounter is more concerned with understanding the person's altered experience of being-in-the-world than in repairing the supposed malfunctioning of a mechanical system (Nelson, Yung, Bechdolf and McGorry, 2008, p. 283). What is important in the psychotherapy of schizophrenia is, as we said, the *chemistry* of the therapeutic relationship.

Phenomenology, according to Thomas Fuchs, offers a perspective that situates patients' disorders not in the hidden circuits of their brains, nor in the remote corners of their minds, but rather in the real world of their life with others, the world of life (*Lebenwelt*), which is, after all, the only world in which psychotherapy takes place (Fuchs, 2007, p. 423-4). The *Lebenwelt* is the place that human beings occupy and inhabit, where their experiences, thoughts, beliefs and actions makes sense, in accordance with their life course and the circumstances they find themselves in. Thus, the world offers different "valences", "relevances" or "availabilities," according to the person's motives or potentialities. In order to understand a person, we have to understand and glimpse their "horizon," in relation to which everything they do makes sense, including anomalous experiences such as those of a psychotic nature.

On this basis, the psychopathological disorder can be considered as a narrowing or deformation of the *Lebenwelt*, as a constriction of its possibilities (Fuchs, 2007, p. 428). Disorders result from disruption in the circuit of the corresponding activities, be it, for example, because of separation from shared common sense, because of the loss of contact with reality and with oneself, or due to the discrepancy between one's own potentialities and the valences and availabilities of the environment. Once established, the disorder can inhibit patients' activity, and in turn increase their rigidity and limit their contact with others and the pursuit of their own values. As Fuchs points out, the ecological niche becomes constrictive, fragmented and inadequate. Moreover, the environmental constrictions themselves, the efforts at adaptation, the symptoms and experiences, can bring cerebral alterations, which turn out to be more an effect of the "schizophrenic condition" than its presumed cause. This would be in line with a socio-developmental model – alternative to the current neuro-developmental model (Morgan and Hutchinson, 2010) – whereby, as we say, the possible brain alterations associated with psychological disorders are more likely to need explanation themselves than to provide an explanation (Pérez-Álvarez, 2011). In any case, phenomenology considers "mental illness" not as something mental, internal, but as an alteration in the form of being-in-the-world.

Phenomenology helps to explore the altered experience of the world and of oneself (in this case of schizophrenia) – experience which it would be difficult to understand based on data from the third-person perspective (signs, symptoms, neurochemical imbalances, defective neuronal circuits, etc.). The goal of the treatment is to expand the patient's horizon and increase his or her freedom. As the character "Furii" (the incarnation de Frieda Fromm-Reichmann) says in Joanne Greenberg's autobiographical novel *I never promised you a rose garden*: "I never promised you a rose garden. I never promised you perfect justice . . . and I never promised you peace or happiness. My help is so that you can be free to fight for all of those things. The only reality I offer is challenge, and being well is being free to accept it or not at whatever level you are capable. I never promise lies, and the rose-garden world of perfection is a lie . . . and a bore, too!" (Green, 1974, p. 125 of the Spanish edition).

From the phenomenological perspective, the principal agent of this proposal is the interactive context opened up by the encounter between patient and therapist. In contrast to traditional therapy, focused on changing the internal world through cognitive or interpretive interventions, phenomenologically-oriented psychotherapy is an interpersonal process. It involves the creation of meanings that emerge from "between" the patient and the therapist. The therapeutic process is more experiential than cognitive, oriented to insight, and sometimes referred to as "archaeological" (Fuchs, 2007).

An empathic bridge between the therapist and the patient forms the basis of a possible recovery from schizophrenia (Davidson, 2003). The space necessary for a person to emerge from their illness is opened through others' perceptions of the person as being more than their illness (Davidson, 2003, p. 173). Stanghellini and Lysaker (2007) have shown how this occurs in psychotherapy sessions, when the therapist repeatedly offers a second-person view, when one "you" addresses another "you", in contrast to a third-person view where we would be talking, for example, about the "illness" or about some supposed external mechanism of it, such as an underlying conflict or cognitive process. It is not so much a case of analyzing the content of the experience or disputing it, but more of recognizing it and validating it and offering the perspective of another "you." Stanghellini and Lysaker (2007) identify four principles of phenomenologically-informed psychotherapy.

1) Relevance of disturbances of inter-subjectivity. Inter-subjective difficulties are a *core aspect* of schizophrenia and *not* an epiphenomenon deriving from supposed neurobiological anomalies, psychodynamic conflicts or idiosyncratic cognitions (Nelson, Sass, Thompson et al., 2009). Thus, for example, if hallucinations are understood as actually being "human" voices in substitution of a world that has become uninhabitable, the therapeutic relation can provide a context from which to change the relationship with the voices (Pérez-Álvarez, García-Montes, Perona-Garcelán and Vallina-Fernández, 2008).

2) Establishment of a shared relationship. Here the focus is on establishing mutual recognition as people, a necessary condition for re-establishing the first-person perspective and thus re-appropriating one's own experiences. As Stanghellini and Lysaker (2007) point out, the process of a phenomenologically-informed psychotherapy takes place, not in an "internal" place, but rather, as we said, in an open, public place situated *between* therapist and patient.

3) *Focus on the here-and-now, on the you-and-I relation.* The goal is to re-establish the "intentional arc" which, as mentioned, connects the person with the present context and which, according to the phenomenological perspective, would be damaged in persons with schizophrenia. As Stanghellini and Lysaker (2007) state: "Psychotherapy may serve as a "dialogical prosthesis" to help re-establish the lost connection between bodily feelings (emotions) and interpersonal situations" (p. 174).

4) Construction of shared meaning. The second-person approach as a therapeutic method proposes the construction of narratives that help to reconstruct the sense of self, stories that must have both internal and external coherence. Whilst internal coherence is necessary for the patient to develop any meaningful understanding, external coherence concerns the interpersonal constrictions that make the narrative meaningful for others. The therapist acts as mediator, as catalyst and as a common-sense reference for meaningful narratives.

Stanghellini and Lysaker (2007) show through vignettes of therapeutic sessions that the "inter-subjective method" can help people with schizophrenia to develop the first-person perspective for themselves and the second-person perspective when they are with others, thus opening up the way to recovery. The possibility of recovery has its roots in the simple but profound notion that people who have been diagnosed with schizophrenia are *people*, and continue to be so.

The Role of the Narrative in Recovery

Within the consideration of schizophrenia as a disorder of the self, and in line with a phenomenologically-oriented therapy, the importance of narrative psychotherapy emerges (Pérez-Álvarez, García-Montes, Vallina-Fernández et al., 2011). Personal narratives are significant for recovery from psychosis at multiple levels (Roe and Lysaker, 2012).

First of all, the narrative of recovery is distinct from the usual narrative in biomedical terms (e.g., the theory of vulnerability-stress), which promotes a genetic-biological conception, a passive attitude in the patient toward the illness and medication for life to keep the symptoms in check, all of which is likely to produce chronification. The "narrative turn" in psychotherapy and in psychiatry (Brown, Nolan, Crawford and Lewis, 1996) involves listening to patients and taking their "stories" seriously, rather than "listening to the drug" (in this case, listening to olanzapine) and disregarding the personal meaning of the symptoms, on assuming them to be mere "outbreaks" of chemical imbalances or defective circuits. The narrative attitude, oriented toward recovery, can already be therapeutic even by the fact of at least jolting the person out of merely staring at their fate as a chronic patient and resituating them to face a new horizon of possibilities. Patients' recovery, as they themselves report, is characterized by a renewed sense of hope, the understanding of their own experiences, active participation in life, the resurgence of a sense of personal responsibility, the consideration of oneself as a person, and so on (Riggay, 2001).

The biomedical model of illness certainly does not facilitate such recovery. Quite apart from its conception that can promote chronicity, it focuses solely on clinical recovery, revolving around the reduction of symptoms. However, clinical recovery may be less important than social and psychological recovery (May, 2005). Social recovery involves the development of significant social relations and roles, of work activities, etc. For its part, psychological recovery refers to the process of understanding and managing the psychotic experience and to the recovery of some form of structure in one's life. These distinctions are relevant, since clinical care and research are too focused on clinical recovery. As May argues, if a person is able to recover at a social and psychological level, clinical recovery may be irrelevant to his or her quality of life (May, 2005). In any case, acceptance of the symptoms and changing one's relationship with them may be a more realistic clinical goal than trying to eliminate them (Pérez-Álvarez, García-Montes, Perona-Garcelán and Vallina-Fernández, 2008).

More specifically, the narrative can serve as a basis for the re-authoring of one's life. What is behind the symptoms is a tormented, disconnected, broken, diminished self. In the words of one patient, "Schizophrenia is ultimately a disorder of the self, a disturbance of one's subjective self-experience and the external or objective reality" (Kean, 2009, p. 1). The self can recover its meaning and position through personal narratives. Personal narratives are the stories one tells oneself and others in order to make sense of one's experiences and the vicissitudes of life. People's lives are based on stories, not statistics. The personal narratives appropriate for therapy are not fictions such as those that might be produced in a creative writing workshop or discourse that might emerge from conversations with a persuasive therapist, but living stories, constructed in the course of an interpersonal relationship, and constitutive of experiences, meanings and courses of action. Therapeutic narratives make sense of psychotic experiences, explaining the "symptoms" in the biographical context, linking affect and cognitions, confronting life events, proposing alternatives, opening up horizons, and so on. Narratives do not simply relate experience, they actually shape it, insofar as the functions of language and hermeneutics are not only expressive, but also constitutive of one's own experience and personal history (Ricoeur, 1996; Sass, 1988).

The key condition for this is the interpersonal context of a participative relationship, focused on the here-and-now and on the you-and-I interaction (Pérez Álvarez, García-Montes, Vallina-Fernández et al., 2011; Stanghellini and Lysaker, 2007). The narrative "sprouts" from the interpersonal relationship and is co-authored by the patient (client, consultant) and the therapist (clinician, consultant). It is not so much a cognitive endeavour, in which the person looks at him or herself in the third person (analyzing the symptoms, understanding them, etc.), as an experiential process, whose condition is to feel that he or she is in an interaction of equals and understood as a person. The interpersonal context and the narrative text form the basis for the recovery of the sense of agency and ownership of one's own experiences and actions and of membership of a shared world, given that the sense of self is constituted – and ruined – in social interaction. Naturally, this does not apply to just any type of narrative, such as a delusional one that a patient might adopt to make sense of his or her experience, but rather those that have internal coherence, for the person him/herself, and external coherence, for others.

The "narrative turn" is one of the most significant trends in the context of this renewed interest in the psychotherapy of schizophrenia (Pérez Álvarez, García-Montes, Vallina-Fernández et al., 2011). Narrative therapy can be conceived and articulated on the basis of different approaches and clinical schools (psychoanalytical, cognitive-behavioural, systemic-family, phenomenological-existential, etc.). Indeed, apart from serving the psychological integration of the individual, narrative can also serve the psychology of integration of different approaches. In any case, in accordance with a conception of schizophrenia as a disorder of the experience of oneself, or ipseity (Pérez-Álvarez, García-Montes and Sass, 2010; Pérez Álvarez, García-Montes, Vallina-Fernández et al., 2011; Sass and Parnas, 2003), the phenomenological perspective may be the most appropriate, insofar as ipseity is constituted in the world of inter-subjectivity (Zahavi, 2006) and the narrative is, so to speak, the natural form of constituting the identity in accordance with the necessary alterity (given by otherness and the other) that constitutes *oneself as another* (Ricoeur, 1996).

However, psychotherapy in the phenomenological perspective should not *be content* with simply accepting and working with the narrative that emerges in the therapeutic context, however focused on the person it might be. While it is undoubtedly important, as we have stressed, the narrative is not life itself: we cannot live just on narratives. Yes, our lives are based on stories, not on statistics, but above all, and when all is said and done, we live in the world. It is easy for a psychotherapy that emphasizes the narrative to fall into an excessive focus on the story, without giving equal consideration to action in the world. This is what happens, for example, in one of the most well-developed and prestigious therapeutic approaches, the Lysakers' dialogical model. Among its contributions is the definition of a narrative structure of schizophrenia, consisting in empty, cacophonous and monological selves (Lysaker and Lysaker, 2002) and in the development of scales that measure it (Lysaker, Taylor, Miller et al., 2006) and of specific therapeutic procedures for each altered structure (Lysaker and Lysaker, 2011). Numerous case studies show the effectiveness of the dialogical model in improving narrative structures and, in turn, quality of life (Lysaker and Lysaker, 2008; 2011). But while this is important, it is not all that a phenomenologically-informed psychotherapy of schizophrenia should have to offer.

Two aspects developed by other therapies are found wanting in a phenomenologically-based therapy. These are the acceptance of distressing experiences and the re-orientation toward values that are meaningful for one's personal life.

Not Just Narrative, but Also Acceptance and Action

These aspects constitute the essence of Acceptance and Commitment Therapy (ACT), an approach that has also been extended to the field of schizophrenia (Pérez Álvarez, García-Montes, Vallina-Fernández et al., 2011). Acceptance is an active attitude of understanding-based self-distancing, not of passive resignation, in the face of distressing experiences that one had up to now tried to avoid or control, with the paradoxical result of exacerbating one's distress in the long term. Acceptance is important in schizophrenia in relation to disturbing experiences such as voices, whose attempt to control is often more harmful than beneficial. In contrast to a fruitless attempt to eliminate the voices, a better objective is to change the relationship with them, one of the strategies for this being acceptance (Pérez-Álvarez, García-Montes, Perona-Garcelán and Vallina-Fernández, 2008). The point is that one can improve from a clinical condition without insisting on the elimination of the symptoms. Instead of fighting against them, it is a case of letting them flow past us, adopting active acceptance and involving ourselves in the important matters of life. This would be an example of psychological and social recovery, distinct from and perhaps more important than clinical recovery, defined by the elimination of symptoms. Acceptance is closely related to mindfulness, a concept applied more widely in psychosis, thanks above all to Paul Chadwick (Abba, Chadwick and Stevenson, 2008; Chadwick, 2006). Mindfulness basically consists in (1) learning to concentrate on private events (voices, thoughts, images, etc.) at the present moment, (2) letting these events come and go without a struggle and without reacting against them, and (3) reclaiming power through acceptance of psychosis and the self (Abba, Chadwick and Stevenson, 2008).

Acceptance and mindfulness are relevant to a phenomenological point of view involving the power of the self and self-distancing from one's own experiences, based on a kind of transcendental self which, instead of drifting and being subject to the vagaries of events, rises above them and holds firm its identity.

As far as commitment is concerned, it consists in the re-orientation toward values that are meaningful for one' s life, despite the fact that certain experiences persist and disturb, and one does not feel well. The commitment involves acting in the direction of values in spite of the symptoms. The point is not to wait to feel well enough for *going out* and *living*, but to act and rebuild one's life to feel well, or at least, to be on the way to something, rather than being locked inside oneself. This re-orientation of self-experiences towards values begins by finding and clarifying one's own values. When the values do not exist or are unclear, that is the problem, more than the symptoms themselves. Values are not concrete goals (such as a job or a relationship), but rather horizons of life, such as the person one wants to be, the fulfilment of responsibilities (as a citizen, parent, professional, etc.) or self-improvement, and which, like the geographical horizon, are for guiding us rather than for being reached, now or at any time. The point is that values can become more important than the symptoms.

From the phenomenological point of view, the re-orientation of life towards values, rather than self-experiences, can serve to reduce the hyper-reflexivity and intensified self-consciousness that characterize schizophrenia (Sass and Parnas, 2003; Nelson and Sass, 2009; Veiga-Martínez, Pérez-Álvarez and García-Montes, 2008). In any case, life oriented to a horizon and immersion in the world are inherent to phenomenology and existentialism, whose respective hallmarks, the world of life (*Lebenwelt*) and being-in-the-world, demand and underpin a therapy that helps one to transcend oneself (acceptance) and to reorient one's life beyond the illness, toward a horizon of values.

It is relevant to mention here that cognitive-behavioural therapy, the psychological therapy most widely applied today in schizophrenia, is moving away from a concern with the negative content of thoughts and schemas and a tendency for the elimination of symptoms, and turning towards the acceptance of experiences and immersion in practical activities for life (Tai and Turkington, 2009).

These aspects of acceptance and of life beyond the illness are incorporated in the therapy and rehabilitation promoted by Larry Davidson, on a phenomenological (Husserlian) basis, which gives an important role to the narrative in recovery. As Davidson points out, the primary focus of the treatment and efforts of rehabilitation needs to be "squarely on what the person with the illness is doing currently, on the consequences of those actions both for the illness and for the person's life in general, and what she or he could be doing instead in order to minimize the illness and maximize his or her chances for establishing and expanding a life outside of the illness." (Davidson, 2003, p. 207). The illness must not define the person or envelop him or her in its web of symptoms; rather it is necessary, by means of therapeutic help, to go beyond the illness, in spite of the suffering that persists. According to Davidson and cols., recovery involves: "A redefinition of one's illness as only one aspect of a multi-dimensional sense of self capable of identifying, choosing, and pursuing, personally meaningful goals and aspirations despite continuing to suffer the effects and side effects of mental illness" (Davidson, O'Connell, Tondora et al., 2005, p. 15).

Challenges for the Psychotherapy of Schizophrenia

The great challenge, of quixotic proportions, for these psychological therapies of schizophrenia is to make their mark in a world dominated by antipsychotic medication. In this scenario, psychotherapy has everything against it: the gene-centric and brain-centric *Zeigeist*, which explains everything, in reductionist fashion, in terms of genes, neurochemical imbalances and defective neuronal circuits, as well as the evidence-based practice approach, which subjects psychological treatments to randomized and protocolized studies that make abstractions from the particular case.

This gene-centric and brain-centric *Zeigeist* has to be confronted. Thus, it should be pointed out how epigenetics has shown in recent years that, far from there being *agene for everything*, it is actually the environment that regulates not only the expression of genes but also the activity of specific regions of the genome.

Epigenetics recovers for the environment what was usurped by genetics, and thus overcomes the genotype-phenotype and pathogeny-pathoplasty distinctions, redoubts of Cartesian dualism, and facilitates an understanding of trans-generational, non-genetic heredity (Nicolosi and Ruivenkamp, 2011; Zhang and Meaney, 2010). Likewise, brain plasticity reveals that the brain is acculturated, and therefore dependent on behaviour and culture, rather than being the supposed causal, etiological *agent*, as we might be seduced into thinking by neuroimaging (Gergen, 2010; Pérez-Álvarez, 2011).

For its part, *evidence-based practice* (and often, indeed, marketing-based practice), should give way to *practice-based evidence*, in our case the practice of psychological therapy, as presented here.

The factors that favour the psychological therapy of schizophrenia include, in addition to the above-mentioned practice-based evidence, the greater importance for patients of *interpersonal chemistry*, compared to inter-neuronal chemistry. Psychological therapy for schizophrenia is not a scientific issue, nor one of evidence, but rather an institutional and educational one. As Australian psychiatrist Patrick McGorry argues, the greatest problem for the appropriate application of psychological therapies in schizophrenia resides in the lack of training in health professionals (McGorry, 2002/2009). As a consequence of the bio-medical model that dominates in psychiatry, clinicians, beginning with psychiatrists themselves, know little else than the DSM, according to US psychiatrist Nancy Andreasen (2007), and follow no law, undoubtedly for reasons of convenience and personal benefit, than that of "evidence-based practice."

Scientifically, psychological therapy or psychotherapy for schizophrenia is founded on the conception of schizophrenia as a disorder of the self, of the subject or of the person, and for its part, the evidence is in the actual practice of psychotherapy, not anecdotal, but systematic. Thus, it has been seen that without medication, but with psychotherapy instead, patients fare no worse, and in general fare better. And this without the dogmatic proscription of medication, in contrast to its compulsive prescription in established clinical practice.

This consideration implies a need to review the sacrosanct nature of evidence-based practice, which could give way, as we said, to practice-based evidence. The institutional and educational problem refers above all to the training of clinicians: psychiatrists in the manner of medical interns and clinical psychologists in the manner of psychiatrists.

Both psychiatrists and psychologists are wasted with respect to what they could be doing, according to the traditions and knowledge of their disciplines, with particular reference to the phenomenological tradition, centred on the person.

Acknowledgment

This work was carried out with the help of Research Project PSI2009-09453, funded by the Spanish Ministry of Science and Technology.

References

Abba, N., Chadwick, P., and Stevenson, C. (2008). Responding mindfully to distressing psychosis: a grounded theory analysis. *Psychotherapy Research, 18*, 77-87.

Alanen, Y. O., Lehtinen, V., Lehtinen, K., Aaltonen, J. y Räkköläinen, V. (2002/2009). El modelo finlandés para el tratamientomprecoz de la esquizofrenia y psicosis afines [In spanish] En B. V. Martindale, A.Bateman, M. Crowe y F. Margison, eds., *Las psicosis. Los tratamientos psicológicos y su eficacia* (pp. 419-464). Barcelona: Herder.

Alanen, Y. O, Silver, A.-L- S and Gonzalez de Chavez, M., eds. (2006). *Isps and its symposia. Fifty years of humanistic treatment of psychoses. In honour of the history of Isps (1956-2006).* Madrid: Fundación para la investigación y el tratamiento de la esquizofrenia y otras psicosis.

Andreasen, N. C. (2007). DSM and the death of phenomenology in America: an example of unintended consequences. *Schizophrenia Bulletin, 33*, 108-112.

Bentall, R. P. and Morrison, A. P. (2002). More harm than good: the case against using anti-psychotic drugs to prevent severe mental illness. *Journal of Mental Health, 11*, 351-356.

Bola, J. R. (2006). Medication-free research in early episode schizophrenia: evidence of long-term harm? *Psychological Bulletin, 32*, 288-296.

Brown, B., Nolan, P., Crawford, P. and Lewis, A. (1996). Interaction, language and the "narrative turn" in psychotherapy and psychiatry. *Social Science and Medicine, 43*, 1569-1578.

Calton, T., Ferriter, M., Huband, N. and Spandler, H. (2008). A systematic review of the Soteria paradigm for the treatment of people diagnosed with schizophrenia. *Schizophrenia Bulletin, 34*, 181-192.

Carpenter, W. T. (1997). The risk of medication-free research. *Schizophrenia Bulletin, 23*, 11-18.

Carpenter, W. T., McGlashan, T. H. and Strauss, J. S. (1977). The treatment of acute schizophrenia without drugs: an investigation of some current assumptions. *American Journal of Psychiatry, 134*, 14-20.

Chadwick, P. (2006). *Person-based cognitive therapy for distressing psychosis*. Chitester, UK: Wiley.

Christodoulides, T., Dudley, R., Brown, S., Turkington, D. and Beck, A. T. (2008). Cognitive behaviour therapy in patients with schizophrenia who are not prescribed antipsychotic medication: A case series. *Psychology and Psychotherapy: Theory, Research and Practice, 81*, 199–207.

Ciompi, L. y Hoffmann, H. (2004). Soteria Berbe: an innovative milieu therapeutic approach to acute schizophrenia based on the concept of affect-logic. *World Psychiatry,* 3, 140-146.

Cullberg, J. (2006/2007). *Psicosis. Una perspectiva integrada* [In Spanish] Madrid: Fundación para la Investigación y Tratamiento de la Esquizofrenia.

Davidson, L. (2003). *Living outside mental illness. Qualitative studies of recovery in schizophrenia*. Nueva York: New York University Press.

Davidson, L., O'Connell, M. J., Tondora, J., Staeheli, M. and Evans, A. C. (2005). Recovery in serious mental illness: paradigm shift or shibboleth? In L. Davidson, C. Harding, and L. Spaniol, eds., *Recovery from Severe Mental Illnesses: Research Evidence and Implications for Practice* (pp. 5-26). Boston, MA: Center for Psychiatric Rehabilitation Sargent College of Health and Rehabilitation Sciences Boston University.

Davidson, L. and Strauss, J. S. (1992). Sense of self in recovery from severe mental illness. *British Journal of Medical Psychology, 65*, 131-145.

Dixon. L. B., Dickerson, F, Bellack, A.S., Bennett, M., Dickinson, D., Goldberg, R.W., Lehman, A., Tenhula, W.N., Calmes, C., Pasillas, R.M., Peer, J., and Kreyenbuhl, J. (2010). The 2009 Schizophrenia PORT Psychosocial Treatment Recommendations and Summary Statements. *Schizophrenia Bulletin, 36*, 48-70.

Fenton, W. S. (2000). Evolving perspectives on individual psychotherapy for schizophrenia. *Schizophrenia Bulletin, 26*, 47-72.

Fuchs, T. (2007). Psychotherapy of the lived space: a phenomenological and ecological concept. *American Journal of Psychotherapy, 61*, 423-439.

García Cabeza, I. (2008). Evolución de la psicoterapia en la esquizofrenia [In spanish]. *Revista de la Asociación Española de Neuropsiquiatría, 28*, 9-25.

García-Montes, J. M. and Pérez-Álvarez, M. (2001). ACT como tratamiento de síntomas psicóticos. El caso de las alucinaciones auditivas [In spanish] *Análisis y Modificación de Conducta, 27*, 455-472.

García-Montes, J. M. and Pérez-Álvarez, M. (2010). Exposition in existential terms of a case of "negative schizophrenia" approached by means of acceptance and commitment therapy. *Journal of Existential Psychology and Psychotherapy, 1*, 1-18.

Gergen, K. (2010). The acculturated brain. *Theory and Psychology, 20*, 795-816.

Green, H. (1974). *Nunca te prometí un jardín de rosas* [In spanish] Barcelona: Barral Editores.

Haddock, G. and Spaulding, W. (2011). Psychological treatment of psychosis. En D. R. Weinberger y P. J. Harrison, eds. *Schizophrenia* (3ª edición, pp. 666-686). Oxford: Wiley-Blackwell.

Harrow, M. and Jobe, T. H. (2007). Factors involved in outcome and recovery in schizophrenia patients not on antipsychotic medications: a 15-year multifollow-up study. *Journal of Nervous and Mental Disease, 195*, 406-414.

Healy, D. (1989). Neuroleptics and psychic indifference: a review. *Journal of the Royal Society of Medicine, 82*, 615-619.

Hingley, S. M. (2006/2008). Encontrar un sentido a la psicosis. Contribuciones de la teoría y la práctica psicodinámicas [In spanish] En J. O. Johannessen, B. V. Martindale, y J. Culberg, eds., *Evolución de las psicosis* (pp. 363-386). Barcelona: Herder.

Kean, C. (2009). Silencing the self: schizophrenia as a self-disturbance. *Schizophrenia Bulletin, 35*, 1034-1036.

Keshavan, M. S., Nasrallah, H. A. and Tandon, R. (2011). Schizophrenia, "just the facts" 6. Moving ahead with the schizophrenia concept: from the elephant to the mouse. *Schizophrenia Research, 127*, 3-13.

Lemos Giráldez, Vallina Fernández, O., Fernádez Iglesias, P., Fonseca Pedrero, E. and Paino, M. (2010. Bases clínicas para un nuevo modelo de atención a las psicosis [In spanish] *Clínica y Salud, 21*, 299-318.

Lyseker, P. H. and J. T. Lysaker (2002). Narrative structure in psychosis: Schizophrenia and disruptions in the dialogical self. *Theory and Psychology, 12*, 207-220.

Lysaker, P. H. and Lysaker, J. T. (2008) *Schizophrenia and the Fate of the Self.* Oxford University Press.

Lysaker, P. H. and Lysaker, J. T. (2011). Psychotherapy and recovery from schizophrenia: A model of treatment as informed by a Dialogical Model of the self experience in psychosis. *Journal of Contemporary Psychotherapy, 41*, 125-133.

Lysaker, P. H, Taylor, A., Miller, A., Beattie, N., Strasburger, A. and Davis, L. W. (2006). The Scale to Assess Narrative Development: Associations with other measures of self and readiness for recovery in schizophrenia spectrum disorders. *Journal of Nervous and Mental Disease, 194*, 233-225.

May, R. (2005). Dar sentido a la experiencia psicótica y trabajar por la recuperación [In spanish] En J. F. M. Gleson y P. D. McGorry, eds., *Intervenciones psicológicas en la psicosis temprana. Un manual de tratamiento* (pp. 425-452). Bilbao: DDB.

McGorry, P. (2002/2009). Psicoterapia y recuperación en la psicosis temprana: un reto esencial en la clínica y la investigación [In spanish] En B. V. Martindale, A.Bateman, M. Crowe y F. Margison, eds., *Las psicosis. Los tratamientos psicológicos y su eficacia* (pp. 465—505). Barcelona: Herder.

McGorry, P., Killackey, E. and Yung, A. (2008). Early intervention in psychosis: concepts, evidence and future directions. *World Psychiatry, 7*, 148-156.

Mizrahi, R., Bagby, R. M., Zipursky, R. B. and Kapur, S. (2005). How antipsychotics work: the patients's perspective. *Progress in Neuro-Psychopharmacology and Biological Psychiatry, 29*, 859-864.

Morgan, C. and Hutchinson, G. (2010). The sociodevelopmental origins of pschosis. En C. Morgan y D. Bhugra, eds., *Principles of social psychiatry* (pp. 193-214). Oxford: Wiley-Blackwell.

Morrison, A, P. (2001). Cognitive therapy for auditory hallucinations as an alternative to antipsychotic medication: a case series. *Clinical Psychology and Psychotherapy, 8*, 136-147.

Mosher, L. R. (1999). Soteria and other alternatives to acute psychiatric hospitalization. A personal and professional review. *Journal of Nervous and Mental Disease, 187*,142-149.

Nicolosi, G. and Ruivenkamp, G. (2011). The epigenetic turn. Some notes about the epistemological change of perspective in biosciences. *Medicine, Health Care and Philosophy*, DOI: 10.1007/s11019-011-9342-z.

Nelson, B. y Sass, L. A. (2009). Medusas' stare: a case study of working with self-disturbance in the early phase of schizophrenia. *Clinical Case Studies, 8*, 489-504.

Nelson, B., Sass, L. A., Thompson, A., Yung, A. R., Francey, S. M., Amminger, G. P. and McGorry, P. D. (2009). Does disturbance of self underlie social cognition deficits in schizophrenia and other psychotic disorders? *Early Intervention in Psychiatry, 3*, 83-93.

Nelson, B., Yung, A., Bechdolf, A. and McGorry, P. D. (2008). The phenomenological critique and self-disturbance: implications for ultra-high-risk ("prodromal") research. *Schizophrenia Bulletin, 34*, 381-392.

Pérez-Álvarez, M. (2011). The magnetism of neuroimaging: fashion, myth and ideology of the brain. *Papeles del Psicólogo, 32*, 98-112.

Pérez Álvarez, M. and García Montes, J. M. (2007). The Charcot Effect: The invention of mental disorders. *Journal of Constructivist Psychology, 20*, 309-336.

Pérez Álvarez, M. García Montes, J. M. and Sass, L. (2010). La hora de la fenomenología en la esquizofrenia [In spanish] *Clínica y Salud, 21*, 221-233.

Pérez-Álvarez, M., García-Montes, J. M., Perona-Garcelán, S. and Vallina-Fernández, O. (2008). Changing relationship with voices: new therapeutic perspectives for treating hallucinations. *Clinical Psychology and Psychotherapy, 15*, 75-85.

Pérez-Álvarez, M., García-Montes, J. M., Vallina-Fernández, O., Perona-Garcelán, S. and Cuevas-Yust, C. (2011). New life for psychotherapy in the light of phenomenology. *Clinical Psychology and Psychotherapy, 18*, 187-201.

Ricoeur, P. (1996). *El sí mismo como otro* [In spanish] México: Siglo XXI.

Riggay, P. (2001). Restoring psychiatric disability: learning from first person recovery narratives. *Psychiatric Rehabilitation Journal, 24*, 335-343.

Roe, D. and Lysaker, P. H. (2012). The importance of personal narratives in recovery from psychosis. In J Geekie, P. Randal, D. Lampshire and J. Read, eds. *Experiencing psychosis. Personal and professional perspectives* (pp. 5-14). London: Rotledge.

Romme, M., Escher, S., Dillon, J., Cortens, D. and Morris, M. (2009). *Living with voices. 50 stories of recovery*. Ross-on-Wye, UK: PCCS Books.

Sass, L A. (1988). Humanism, hermeneutics, and the concept of human subject. En S. B. Messer, L. A. Sass and R. L. Woolfolk (Eds.), *Hermeneutics and psychological theory* (pp. 222-271). New Brunswick: Rutgers University Press.

Sass, L. (2007). 'Schizophrenic person' or 'person with schizophrenia'? *Theory and Psychology, 17*, 395-420.

Sass, L. y Parnas, J. (2003). Schizophrenia, consciousness, and the self. *Schizophrenia Bulletin, 29*, 427-444.

Searles, H.F. (1959). The effort to drive the other person crazy -an element in the aetiology and psychotherapy of schizophrenia. *British Journal of Medical Psychology, 32*, 1-18.

Sechehaye, M. A. (2003). *La realización simbólica y Diario de una esquizofrénica* [In spanish]. México: FCE.

Seikkula, J., Aaltonen, J., Alakare, B., Haarakangas, K, Kernen, J. y Lehtinen, K. (2006). Five-year experience of first-episode nonaffective psychosis in open-dialogue approach: Treatment principles, follow-up outcomes, and two case studies. *Psychotherapy Research, 16*, 214-228.

Seikkula, J. y Olson, M. E. (2003). The Open Dialogue Approach to acute psychosis: its poetics and micropolitics. *Familiy Process, 42*, 403-418.

Stanghellini, G., and Lysaker, P.H. (2007). The psychotherapy of schizophrenia through the lens of phenomenology: Intersubjectivity and the search for the recovery of first- and second-person awareness. *American Journal of Psychotherapy, 61*, 163–179.

Tai, S. and Turkington, D. (2009). The evolution of cognitive behavior therapy for schizophrenia: current practice and recent developments. *Schizophrenia Bulletin, 35*, 865-873.

Tandon, R., Nasrallah, H. A. and Keshavan, M. S. (2010). Schizophrenia, "just the facts" 5. Treatment and prevention Past, present, and future. *Schizophrenia Research, 122*, 1-23.

Veiga-Martínez, C., Pérez-Álvarez, M. and García-Montes, J. M. (2008). Acceptance and Commitment Therapy Applied to Treatment of Auditory Hallucinations. *Clinical Case Studies, 7*, 118-135.

Whitaker, R. (2004). The case against antipsychotic drugs: a 50-year record of doing more harm than good. *Medical Hypotheses, 62*, 5-13.

Zahavi, D. (2006). *Subjectivity and Selfhood: Investigating the First-Person Perspective.* Cambridge, MA: MIT Press.

Zhang, T.-Y. and Meaney, M. J. (2010). Epigenetics and the environmental regulation of the genome and its function. *Annual Review of Psychology, 61*, 439–466.

In: Psychotherapy
Editors: A. J. Lancaster and O. Sharpe
ISBN 978-1-61942-611-5

Chapter 2

DYADIC DEVELOPMENTAL PSYCHOTHERAPY: AN EVIDENCE-BASED, EFFECTIVE, AND EMPIRICALLY VALIDATED TREATMENT

Arthur Becker-Weidman*
Center for Family Development, Williamsville, New York, US

ABSTRACT

This chapter will describe Dyadic Developmental Psychotherapy, its primary components, and the differential use of those components in the different stages of treatment.

The empirical research and other materials demonstrating the efficacy and evidence-base of this approach will be summarized. The use of this treatment with families who have children who have experienced complex trauma will be described. This approach was originally developed for use with adopted and foster children and has now been demonstrated as valuable as a general treatment model.

The use of this model in residential treatment settings will also be described. Case examples and excerpts from treatment sessions will be used to illustrate the differential use of components in different phases of treatment and other aspects of this treatment.

INTRODUCTION

This chapter describes Dyadic Developmental Psychotherapy, its primary components, and the differential use of those components in different phases of treatment. The empirical research demonstrating the efficacy and evidence-base of this approach is summarized. Dyadic Developmental Psychotherapy was developed originally as an approach to treat adopted and foster children who have experienced complex trauma (Hughes, 2007). It is now been demonstrated to be a valuable as a general treatment model. Dyadic Developmental Psychotherapy is a family therapy grounded in attachment theory (Becker-Weidman, 2010;

*E-mail: AWeidman@Concentric.net

Becker-Weidman, 2011; Hughes, 2007). The treatment has been used in a variety of settings including inpatient, residential treatment centers, group homes, foster care homes, clinic settings, outpatient settings, and in private practices.

Dr. Hughes developed this model over several years, beginning in the late 1980's. Dyadic Developmental Psychotherapy continues to evolve as research, described below, and clinical practice have led the way toward a richer and deeper understanding of the factors that help families and children. As the creator of this model, Dr. Hughes has written several texts that describe this model (Hughes, 2004; Hughes, 2006; Hughes, 2007). These texts present Dyadic Developmental Psychotherapy as a model for treatment that is firmly grounded in shared experiences and the healing power of emotions within the therapeutic setting. The model has now been extended and can also be described as Attachment Focused Family Therapy because of its broad applicability to a variety of settings and for a variety of clients. Dyadic Developmental Psychotherapy can be thought of as the application of this approach to families where disorders of attachment and trauma are central difficulties.

This chapter is intended to provide reader with an overview of the practice of Dyadic Developmental Psychotherapy. By explicating the primary principles, components, and phases of treatment, this chapter will help ensure continued integrity to this model of treatment as taught at the Center For Family Development and at other training insitututes. Integrity in the application of the model facilitates reliability of delivery across a spectrum of practitioners and facilitates the highest quality research.

After absorbing the material in this chapter the reader should have a clearer understanding of the practice of Dyadic Developmental Psychotherapy, and how one can practically use it. Advanced clinicians will find this useful to develop a more focused understanding of the work. Therapists, parents, residential treatment staff, social workers, psychologists, child welfare workers, and many others should also find this chapter useful. It will provide them with a deeper understanding of the practice of Dyadic Developmental Psychotherapy. The practice of Dyadic Developmental Psychotherapy is both art and science. The use of self is central to this approach, and one should be able to implement Dyadic Developmental Psychotherapy in a manner consistent with individual personality, history, and pattern of attachment; that is the art.

Dyadic Developmental Psychotherapy

The principles of Dyadic Developmental Psychotherapy include the following:

First, the maintenance of a contingent, collaborative, sensitive, reflective, and emotionally empathic relationship between the therapist and client is a primary principle of treatment. The therapist is responsible for creating and maintaining positive concordant intersubjective experiences (Stern, 1985; Trevarthen 2001) with the client and for helping caregivers create these experiences with their children. Intersubjectivity is a comprehensive emotional, reflective, and behavioral experience of the other. It is the discovery within the relationship of the other. It emerges from shared emotions (attunement), joint attention and awareness, and shared complimentary intentions. Creating and maintaining an alliance is the vital first phase of treatment. The creation and maintenance of an alliance is necessary for the creation of a secure base, which allows for exploration, which is necessary for integration and ultimately, healing.

Second, the caregivers' and therapist's state of mind with respect to attachment should be organized and largely resolved before beginning treatment with the child. The therapist's and the caregiver's state of mind with respect to attachment has been found to be very important for treatment success (Tyrell et. al., 1999; Dozier, et al. 2001).

Third, PACE and PLACE describe the basic stance of the therapist and caregiver. PACE describes the therapist's responsibility for creating a healing pace of treatment by being playful, accepting, curious, and empathic. PACE allows the therapist to generate and regulate the emerging emotional experiences that are explored in treatment. PLACE refers to the caregiver's responsibility for creating a healing place or environment by being playful, loving, accepting, curious, and empathic.

Fourth, interactive repair is another important principle of treatment. Inevitable conflicts, misunderstanding, and mistakes that occur in all relationships are directly addressed and repaired. This process facilitates emotional regulation. It is the responsibility of the adult to initiate and model this process.

Fifth, "resistance" is treated with PACE. Resistance is viewed as reflecting fear, shame, and the child's past negative experiences with caregivers. "Resistance" is not a pejorative and should not be interpreted as negative. Resistance is viewed as an expression of fear and may reflect that the therapist has gone too far, or too fast, for the client. Resistance may be viewed as an adaptive strategy for managing upsetting and disturbing affect. The response to resistance will then be interactive repair or more follow and less lead of the follow-lead-follow component, which is described below.

Sixth, the therapist continually assesses (Becker-Weidman, 2010a) the caregiver's readiness to be a sensitive, responsive, insightful, reflective, and committed attachment figure for the child. If the therapist has concerns about the child's emotional and psychological safety, the therapist will continue to work with the caregiver without the child to help the caregiver resolve whatever barriers exist for the caregiver's creating this secure base and sense of safety for the child. Parents and other caregivers are central to Dyadic Developmental Psychotherapy. Caregivers are the keystone for how treatment proceeds and its outcome. In many respects the best predictor of outcome is not "how disturbed" is the child, rather it is the caregivers (Becker-Weidman, 2010, Becker-Weidman, 2010a):

- State of mind with respect to attachment
- Reflective function and reflective abilities
- Commitment
- Insightfulness
- Sensitivity

Evidence-Based, Empirically Validated, Effective Treatment

Dyadic Developmental Psychotherapy is a fusion of several evidence-based and empirically validated principles and methods (Becker-Weidman; 2010; Becker-Weidman, 2011, Becker-Weidman and Hughes, 2008). Dyadic Developmental Psychotherapy is an effective, evidence-based (Craven and Lee, 2006) and empirically validated treatment. Craven and Lee (2006) determined that Dyadic Developmental Psychotherapy is a supported and acceptable treatment (category 3 in a six level system). However, their review was only based on results from a partial preliminary presentation of two ongoing follow-up studies, subsequently completed and published in 2006 (Becker-Weidman, 2006a; Becker-Weidman, 2006b). The first study (Becker-Weidman, 2006a) compared the results of Dyadic Developmental Psychotherapy with other forms of treatment, "usual care", one year after treatment ended. A second study (Becker-Weidman, 2006b) extended these results to four years after treatment ended. Based on the Craven and Lee classifications (Saunders *et al.* 2004), inclusion of those studies would have resulted in Dyadic Developmental Psychotherapy being classified as an evidence-based category 2, "Supported and probably efficacious". Since the development of Dyadic Developmental Psychotherapy, there have been two empirical studies demonstrating the effectiveness of Dyadic Developmental Psychotherapy published by this author (Becker-Weidman, 2006a, Becker-Weidman, 2006b). These two studies each had a sample size of 64.

The first study (Becker-Weidman, 2006a) compared two groups of children who met the criteria for Reactive Attachment Disorder and Complex Trauma (Cook, et. al., 2003; Cook, et. al., 2005). The experimental group received Dyadic Developmental Psychotherapy at The Center for Family Development, while the control group received other standardized treatments by other qualified professionals at other clinics. The two groups were matched and were not significantly different on a variety of variables including age, gender, length of time in placement or adoption, and their pre-treatment scores on the Child Behavior Checklist (CBCL) (Ackenbach, 1991) and various other demographic variables. Both groups of children had scores in the clinical range on the CBCL before treatment. One year after treatment ended, the children in the experimental group (Dyadic Developmental Psychotherapy treatment) had post-test scores on all scales of the CBCL that were in the normal range and that were statistically significantly different (lower) than their pre-test scores. The children in the control group had post-test scores that remained in the clinical range and there were not statistically significantly different from their pre-test scores.

The second study (Becker-Weidman, 2006b) followed these same families for four years after treatment ended. This study found that the children who had received Dyadic Developmental Psychotherapy continued to have CBCL scores in the normal range, remaining statistically significantly lower than their pre-test CBCL scores. Children in the experimental group, who actually continued to receive other treatment from other providers at other clinics, not only had CBCL scores that remained in the clinical range, but on four of the CBCL scales their scores were statistically significantly worse: Anxious/Depressed, Attention Problems, Rule-Breaking Behavior, and Aggressive Behavior. Tables 1 and 2 summarize the results of the two empirical studies cited above.

Dyadic Developmental Psychotherapy is an affect-focused family therapy based on Attachment Theory (Bowlby 1980, 1988; Holmes, 1993) and draws on the best of several previously established, evidence-based approaches, methods, and techniques that have a strong evidence base. Dyadic Developmental Psychotherapy uses a variety of principles, interventions, and methods with well researched and empirically supported foundations. For example, Dyadic Developmental Psychotherapy is consistent with the basic principles of effective treatment for complex trauma (Cook et al., 2003, 2005). Cook, et. al., identify six core components of complex trauma interventions: 'safety, self-regulation, self-reflective information processing, traumatic experience integration, relational engagement, and positive affect enhancement' (Cook et al, 2005 p. 395). Dyadic Developmental Psychotherapy emphasizes each of these six core components, specific components, methods, and principles of Dyadic Developmental Psychotherapy that have good empirical support and are shared with other treatment approaches (Orlinsky, Grawe, and Parks, 1994).

Table 1. Statistical Analysis of Treatment Group

	Pre-test		Post-test				2ND post-test		
Measure	Mean	SD	Mean	SD	t-value	p-value	Mean	SD	t-test prob
CBCL *syndrome scale scores*									
Withdrawn	65	11.8	54	6.0	4.897	<.0001	56	6	.008
Anxious/depressed	62	10.5	58	8.1	2.665	.006	58	5	.006
Social problems	67	9.7	59	5.5	4.376	<.0001	56	5	.001
Thought problems	68	9.5	65	3.9	6.133	<.0001	60	8	.02
Attention problems	72	12.5	57	6.1	5.836	<.0001	57	6	<.0002
Rule-breaking behavior	69	6.9	53	3.8	12.181	<.0001	52	3	<.0001
Aggressive behavior	71	9.1	55	4.5	10.576	<.0001	54	4	<.0001

Table 2. Statistical Analysis of Control Group

	Pre-test		Post-test				2ND post-test		
Measure	Mean	SD	Mean	SD	t-value	p-value	Mean	SD	t-test prob
CBCL *syndrome scale scores*									
Withdrawn	65	10.5	63	9.45	1.427	.16	71	49	.18
Anxious/depressed	62	10.6	60	10.3	1.060	.30	70	10	.03*
Social problems	64	11.1	65	11.25	-0.854	.40	65	2	.5
Thought problems	63	8.6	62	8.1	0.984	.33	67	8	.8
Attention problems	68	11.9	66	10.8	0.927	.36	77	9	.02*
Rule-breaking behavior	67	7.4	66	9/6	1.8691	.07	81	4	.02*
Aggressive behavior	70	10.2	68	9.4	0.919	.37	81	4	.02*

* Statistically significant

Other elements of Dyadic Developmental Psychotherapy that have been found to have a strong evidence-base in the psychotherapy outcome research literature include the following elements.

First, affect arousal has been found to be important for positive outcomes in psychotherapy (Beutler et al., 2004). Affect arousal (achieved by the Dyadic Developmental components of follow-lead-follow, affective/reflective dialogue, and PACE, among other components, is managed within the context of the co-regulation of affect and interactive repair) is a significant theme in Dyadic Developmental Psychotherapy.

Second, explaining how the past may be continuing to affect present behavior, emotions, and meanings has been found to be an effective mode of treatment in 63% of studies reported (Orlinsky et al., 1994).

Third, forming and maintaining a therapeutic alliance is a core principle of Dyadic Developmental Psychotherapy. The therapeutic alliance has been shown to be vital to successful treatment outcome (Norcross 2001; Lambert and Ogles 2004). The use of PACE is expected to help facilitate this. There is a significant positive association between outcome and the therapeutic bond (Lambert and Ogles, p. 308). In looking at the therapist's contribution to the therapeutic alliance, a significant positive association with outcome was also found. "The therapist's contribution was positively associated with outcome 67% of the time and never negatively implicated" (Lambert and Ogles, p. 321). "The strongest evidence linking process to outcome concerns the therapeutic bond or alliance" (Lambert and Ogles, p. 360).

Fourth, acceptance is a significant component of Dyadic Developmental Psychotherapy and is a significant element in the "PACE" attitude. Affirmation (acceptance, non-possessive warmth, or unconditional positive regard) was found to be a significant factor in positive therapeutic outcome. Acceptance involves an entirely nonjudgmental stance directed towards the thoughts, feelings, intentions, etc., that characterize the child's 'inner life'. Described differently, the creation of concordant intersubjective experiences or the level of empathic understanding and personal rapport has a substantial history of having been shown to be important factors in positive outcome. There is now, "general acceptance of empathy as a factor in outcome, which has been clearly confirmed again in a current meta-analysis" (Orlinsky *et al.* 2004, p. 350).

Fifth, Dyadic Developmental Psychotherapy has both cognitive and experiential dimensions. Both these dimensions have a large body of empirical support. "The existing research is now more than sufficient to warrant a possible valuation of experiential therapy in four important areas: depression, anxiety disorders, trauma, and marital problems," (Elliott *et al.* 2004, p. 527).

Sixth, relationship factors are important for successful treatment outcome (Lambert and Ogles 2004). The development of a secure base from which exploration can occur requires the development and maintenance of an alliance. It is these common factors across therapies that account for a significant portion of treatment outcome. "A therapeutic relationship that is characterized by trust, warmth, understanding, acceptance, kindness, and human wisdom" (Lambert and Ogles 2004, p. 180), is described as a broad set of factors that are common across therapies and associated with client improvement. These are the very same factors that form the core attitude of Dyadic Developmental Psychotherapy; PACE.

Overall such factors as empathy, the capacity for reflection, intersubjective sharing of experience, the therapeutic alliance, furthering reflection, deepening emotional processing, enhancing adaptive skills, developing and maintaining the therapeutic bond, therapist affirmation, communication attunement, and the bond of relatedness between therapist and patient are all important factors in psychotherapy outcome and are all important components of Dyadic Developmental Psychotherapy.

Attachment-Facilitating Parenting: Central for Treatment Success

In this chapter I use the term parents in the broad sense to mean care-givers: parents, relatives caring for a child, and child care workers in residential treatment centers, for example. This principles, components, and methods of Dyadic Developmental Psychotherapy are used in the same manner by all these primary caregivers. Whether the primary attachment figure is a birth-parent, adoptive-parent, foster-parent, kinship placement, or residential treatment center staff member, the primry attachment figure can use this approach to facilitate healing.

Parents are the keystone of good treatment outcomes. The proper preparation of caregivers to engage in treatment and create a healing PLACE (an acronym described below, standing for Playful, Loving, Accepting, Curious, and Empathic) is a necessary and essential component of the treatment process. This section provides a brief overview of this necessary and essential component. A much more detailed account of parenting and parent training consistent with Dyadic Developmental Psychotherapy can be found in the book, Attachment Parenting (Becker-Weidman and Shell, 2010) and in several other publications (Becker-Weidman, 2010; Becker-Weidman, 2011; Becker-Weidman, 2006c; Hughes, 2007; Hughes, 2009; Ring 2011)

Helping caregivers see below surface behavior and catch a glimpse of the underlying emotions and perceptions driving that behavior are the first step in helping parents change the lens through which they view their child. The parent's assumptions and understandings about the child's motives, intentions, and purposes directly determine how the parent views the child and the experience, and this directly affects how the parent feels about the child and the experience. For example, a child is found in her room with her brother's juice box and other food items in the closet, behind some boxes. If the parent's understanding of this situation is that the child "stole" the items and was hiding, and being sneaky, the parent will feel one way toward the child, probably annoyed and frustrated. If this has been the umpteenth time the parent told the child not to steal her brother's juice boxes and hide food in her closet, and each time the child agrees with the parent not to do that, the parent may now be feeling quite upset with the child. On the other hand, if the parent understands the child's behavior as being driven by a different set of motives and intentions, the parent will feel quite differently. For example, if the parent goes deeper and recalls that the child has grown up in settings in which there was inconsistent caregiving, a lack of any reliable source of food, and no one to help the child, then the parent may view the child's behavior as reflecting that experience and being driven by fear of going hungry and a belief that the only one she can count on is herself. In this instance, the parent may have much more empathy for the girl and respond accordingly. By helping parents see below the surface and understand the forces driving behaviors, the therapist can help parents feel differently and then act differently, more therapeutically, toward their child.

"All behavior is adaptive" and "Kind Attributions" are two important principles for the therapist to communicate to the caregivers. All behavior is adaptive refers to the notion that one develops in response to people, situations, relationships, and experiences that shape how a person feels and acts. Behaviors develop that are adaptive to the situation in which those behaviors originally formed. In many respects "symptoms" can be viewed as behaviors that were adaptive and that evolved in response to a specific set of circumstances, but these same behaviors are now "symptoms" because they are now occur in new situations in which the behaviors are no longer adaptive. The new situations are inhibited from having an effect on these old behaviors if the old experiences evoked the stress response system on a chronic basis. In these instances it is the "survival brain" and not the" learning brain" that is primarily active. The survival brain does not function to incorporate new information, experiences, or emotions. This is vital for caregivers to understand, so that they can focus on creating a healing PLACE at home with a deep sense of safety: emotional, psychological, and physical.

The principle of *kind attributions* is related to the principle of *all behavior is adaptive and has meaning*. This principle is that when in doubt attribute benign motivations or intentions to the client. Helping a parent have kind attributions regarding their child's intentions is more likely to lead to the creation of positive concordant intersubjective experiences and the creation of safety and security, which is most conducive to the functioning of the learning brain. This same principle applies to the therapist's understanding and relationship with the parents. While the behavior may not be laudable, most often the deeper intention is more positive. There are several other important elements of attachment facilitating parenting that are grounded in Dyadic Developmental Psychotherapy that the therapist will want to communicate to the parents. Parents can certainly learn these various elements by reading books or articles, and therapists can "train" parents using psycho-educational models. However, early in treatment, and this is when the material is imparted, it is useful to remember that the therapist's focus is on building and maintaining a secure base. At times just telling the caregivers what to do and why can be effective. Often, even within that first session, the parents feel enough safety and comfort that direct instruction is appreciated and effective. However, frequently there are times when the therapist will find it therapeutic to evoke the material and principles from the parents by exploring with the parents what is their thinking, their feeling states, their experiences as parents, and how they understand their child. Using PACE and follow-lead-follow, the therapist can explore all of these areas and help parents come to a deeper understanding of themselves and of their child.

Phases of Treatment

This section briefly summarizes the phases of Dyadic Developmental Psychotherapy. The phases occur in a recursive and repetitive manner, much like the phases of the moon. The phases overlap and occur in a cyclical manner and so should not be considered discrete or rigidly defined. The value of considering these phases is that the various components of Dyadic Developmental Psychotherapy are used differently in the different phases of treatment (Becker-Weidman, 2010; Becker-Weidman, 2011). Like a continual spiral, development and treatment continue ever deeper. As treatment proceeds, the therapist must continually work to maintain the alliance, explore to achieve integration and healing, and then ensure that the alliance remains strong enough to proceed. Exploration and integration can lead to a more secure alliance, which will allow for deeper exploration and further integration and healing. Healing often allows for a stronger alliance to develop, which will facilitate further integration.

While the general principles remain constant, each phase requires a different mix of the components of Dyadic Developmental Psychotherapy. It is the application of the various components of Dyadic Developmental Psychotherapy in a differential manner that is the art of this treatment. One phase may last several sessions, and many phases may be present in one session. Healing may begin in the very first session, for example the phases described here are defined in terms of attachment theory: developing and maintaining the alliance (secure base), exploration, integration, and healing. An alliance is necessary to create and maintain a secure base. A secure base is necessary to begin exploration. Exploration leads to integration. Integration is the basis for healing.

Developing the Alliance

Developing the alliance is a critical phase of treatment. Without an alliance, there can be no exploration, integration, and healing. Children and parents or carers with unresolved traumas and hurts will have a more difficult time forming an alliance with the therapist. In these instances, the therapist will have to pay particular attention to developing the alliance and relationship.

Creating a secure base in treatment becomes the therapist's primary task. There are four primary tasks in this phase:

- Forming a therapeutic alliance
- Developing a "treatment contract." Why are we here? Why are we meeting? What are we doing here?
- Forming initial theories of behavior: the meanings to be explored.
- Creating a secure base

While all components of Dyadic Developmental Psychotherapy may be used, a few stand out as more salient in this phase: PACE, the "follow" dimension of follow-lead-follow, intersubjectivity, and the co-regulation of affect. Creating a secure base and then maintaining that alliance is a necessary and essential precursor to beginning the Exploration phase. Therapist's use of self is also an important component in creating a secure base in treatment. The therapist must be emotionally engaged in the intersubjective experiences within treatment and this requires good self-awareness, reflective abilities, and insightfulness on the part of the therapist. In working with parents and careers, it is also important to help them appreciate the importance of the construct, "it's about connections, not compliance," (Becker-Weidman, 2010, Hughes and Becker-Weidman, 2010).

Maintaining the Alliance

Maintaining the Alliance is a phase that the therapist must attend to throughout treatment. At times it is in the forefront of the work, and at other times it recedes into the background. Focusing on this phase becomes particularly important when there has been some breach in the alliance or relationship and interactive repair becomes a prominent component used by the therapist or parent. The therapist's use of self also is an important component in this phase. When the therapist or parent has made a mistake it is vital to treatment that adult not allow the adult's shame to preclude the adult's acknowledging the mistake the adult has made and the breach that results. One of the therapist's primary responsibilities is to maintain a healing and therapeutic pace of treatment. As described elsewhere (Becker-Weidman, 2010), it is not mistakes that cause problems in treatment. It is the lack of acknowledgement and repair of those mistakes that creates problems in treatment.

Once the Alliance has been formed, the therapist acts to deepen, strengthen, and maintain the alliance. As with the other phases, this phase overlaps the other phases and the other phases cycle back to this phase. For example, Exploration that leads to Integration and Healing helps Maintain and strengthen the alliance.

The primary tasks of Maintaining the Alliance are:

- Deepening and strengthening the therapeutic alliance
- Managing emotional proximity
- Exploring initial theories of behavior: the meanings to be explored.
- Repairing relationship breaches.

Five components of Dyadic Developmental Psychotherapy are particularly salient during this phase of treatment: PACE, intersubjectivity, follow-lead-follow, interactive repair, and the co-regulation of affect. In this second phase of treatment the therapist will want to pay particular attention to using follow-lead-follow as the beginning approach into the exploration phase. How the client responds to the "lead" step of follow-lead-follow is a measure of how quickly and deeply the therapist can move into exploration and a measure of the strength and depth of the alliance. This phase of treatment takes on less importance as treatment progresses. The reason for this is that later in treatment the client has experienced the therapist's intentions as being helpful and exploration, integration, and healing have led to a more flexible and present-reality grounded internal working model. Later in treatment the therapist does not have to focus as much on maintaining the alliance because the alliance has greater emotional depth and strength. The client will have experienced the therapist's intentions to be helpful and the client will have experienced the positive results of difficult explorations.

Exploration

Exploration requires a secure base (an Alliance) and can occur within the very first meeting. Exploration requires a sense of safety (physical, emotional, and psychological) and security. There are four primary tasks during the Exploration phase. The goal is to explore history, memories, events, and experiences that continue to shape the client's relationships and that continue to affect behavior and functioning. Primary tasks in this phase are:

- Exploring how the past is alive in the present
- Exploration of internal working models
- Exploring the meanings of events and behavior.
- Developing the reflective function.

The primary components of Dyadic Developmental Psychotherapy that are especially important in this phase are: PACE, creating and maintaining intersubjectivity, developing the reflective function, insightfulness, follow-lead-follow, interactive repair, commitment, co-creation of meaning, and the co-regulation of affect. Of these, the co-creation of meaning and the co-regulation of affect are particularly important. PACE leads to concordant intersubjectivity. Concordant intersubjectivity, interactive repair, and the reflective function help co-regulate emotions. The affective/reflective dialogue and insightfulness, along with PACE, facilitate the co-creation of meaning.

INTEGRATION

Integration occurs in a cyclic manner. Exploration leads to Integration, which allows for deeper exploration and further Integration and Healing. Integration includes neurological integration, emotional integration, and psychological integration. Its hallmark is the capacity to see shades of gray instead of absolutes. Integration is seen when a client is able to hold disparate feelings at the same time. Integration occurs repeatedly in treatment and over time. In many regards it is a developmental process in which experiences, memories, events, relationships, emotions, and one's autobiographical narrative are reworked in a flexible manner. Many mental health difficulties can be viewed as representing a lack of integration. For example, the flash-backs associated with Post Traumatic Stress Disorder and Complex Trauma are a function of the lack of integration of episodic and implicit memories. Many of the cognitive difficulties associated with Complex Trauma are a function of problematic neurological integration.

Integration requires that past events, situations, and experiences be reviewed and revisited (exploration) so that the internal working modelscan be made explicit, subject to exploration, and new meanings thereby created. It is the new meanings that represent a new integration of emotions and cognitions. It is most useful to think of integration as a process or spiral. In this view, developmental tasks run vertically, and integration is an ascending spiral that returns to each element in a deeper and deeper fashion. In this way the person achieves greater levels of integration over time (Becker-Weidman, 2010).

The primary task of Integration is the developmental of a coherent autobiographical narrative. Creating a coherent autobiographical narrative involves two elements: the integration of trauma and reduction of splitting off of implicit from episodic memories, and an enhanced reflective function. Within this phase the Dyadic Developmental Psychotherapy components that are most relevant are: PACE, the affective/reflective dialogue, and co-creation of meaning. During this phase, which may constitute the bulk of treatment toward the middle and end of treatment, a review of the client's life story and a reflection on the client's current state and how the past may still be active in the present make up a large proportion of treatment. Exploration and Integration occur in tandem and reinforce each other. Exploration leads to Integration and Integration allows for deeper Exploration.

HEALING

Healing occurs throughout treatment. Healing is not so much a separate phase as it is, in part, an outgrowth of Integration. Integration is a healing process. However, it is important to note that the development and maintenance of an alliance can be healing in and of itself. The development of an emotionally meaningful relationship is healing and can remedy some of the effects of early, chronic, maltreatment that has occurred within a care-giving relationship. The outcomes of healing include the development of a more complex, nuanced, and integrated autobiographical narrative, and a better developed reflective function. A few of the components of Dyadic Developmental Psychotherapy that may be more salient during Healing include the following: Co-creation of new meanings, Insightfulness and reflection, affective/reflective dialogue, and PACE.

As treatment is drawing to a close, there is increased time spent reflecting on the treatment experiences and a celebration of how life is different. This is not to say that the therapist doesn't note and comment on positive experiences in each and every session. That is often an important element of each session; the reflection on what good has occurred. This reflection on positive changes and a celebration of the long and difficult journey is an important element of beginning to end treatment and integration of the experience. This process helps frame the treatment experience and find its place in the family narrative. During this process, all the components of Dyadic Developmental Psychotherapy will be evident.

COMPONENTS OF DYADIC DEVELOPMENTAL PSYCHOTHERAPY

These components include:

1. Therapist use of self
2. Process focused: It's about connections not compliance
3. PLACE and PACE (Playful, Loving, Accepting, Curious, Empathy and Playful, Accepting, Curious, Empathy)
4. Intersubjectivity
5. Reflective Capacity
6. Affective/Reflective dialogue
7. Commitment
8. Insightfulness
9. Coherent Narrative
10. Co-regulation of emotions
11. Co-creation of meaning
12. Follow-lead-follow
13. Interactive repair
14. Nonverbal-verbal dialogue

A few of the basic principles of Dyadic Developmental Psychotherapy may be summarized in the following four paragraphs.

1. Both the caregivers' and therapist's own attachment strategies are organized and resolved before the onset of the child's treatment. Previous research (Tyrell *et al.* 1999; Dozier *et al.* 2001) has shown the importance of the caregivers' and therapist's state of mind with respect to attachment for good treatment outcomes.
2. The therapist and caregiver provide the intersubjective experiences for the child that were seldom present in situations of abuse and neglect. These intersubjective experiences are characterized by shared emotion (affect), attunement, shared awareness and attention, and complementary intentions. Intersubjective experiences are the primary means by which the infant and young child learn about self, other, and the world (Trevarthen 2001). Complex trauma will significantly disrupt the development of concordant intersubjectivity and increase the risk that the child will be unable to create a coherent meaning for many events, particularly traumatic ones. The therapist must provide concordant intersubjective experiences for the parent that help create a secure base within which the parent, child, and therapist can co-create new and more therapeutic meanings for experiences. Whenever possible, the child's primary caregiver (biological, adoptive, or foster parent or primary caregiver in a residential setting) is an active participant in the session. The therapist must provide to the caregiver support and guidance in communicating thoughts, emotions, and intentions to the child in a therapeutic and concordant positive intersubjective manner. The primary caregiver serves as the primary source of safety, security, and comfort while the child explores events, experiences, and emotions that may generate fear and shame. The caregiver's presence allows the therapist to facilitate the successful exploration and resolution of behavior problems in the home by modeling for the parent PACE (Playful, Accepting, Curious, Empathic, described more fully below) as an effective means of achieving conflict resolution and increasing emotional and behavioral regulation within the home. The therapist will generally only see a child, usually a teenager, as an individual client when a primary attachment figure is not available. In these instances, the treatment will proceed at a markedly slower pace since the child is essentially emotionally alone the rest of the week in the process of integrating the therapeutic themes. The lack of a primary attachment figure is a severe impediment to creating the security and safety necessary for exploration and integration.
3. Use of PACE and PLACE. These acronyms describe the "attitude" of the therapist and caregiver. PACE refers to the therapist setting a healing pace of treatment by being playful, accepting, curious and empathic. Through PACE, the therapist is able to both generate and regulate, through empathy (and playfulness when appropriate), the emerging emotion that is associated with the events being explored. Positive concordant intersubjective experiences are largely created with PACE. The therapist is also able to facilitate an open, reflective attitude to reorganize the experience of these events through the therapist's accepting and curious stance. PLACE refers to the parent creating a healing environment by being playful, loving, accepting, curious and empathic. All interventions are utilized within the context of PACE/PLACE along with the other principles presented in this chapter. Any technique may lead to

dysregulation if these basic principles, which are needed to generate general safety, are ignored. These ideas are described in more detail in Becker-Weidman, (2010), Becker-Weidman, (2011), Becker-Weidman and Shell (2010), Becker-Weidman and Shell (2010), and Hughes (2006, 2007, 2009).

4. The inevitable misattunements and conflicts that arise in relationships are directly addressed and repaired through the ongoing qualities of the relationship using PACE; interactive repair. The creation of concordant intersubjectivity facilitates the co-creation of meaning and the co-regulation of emotions. The need for interactive repair is especially important as the themes being explored are often characterized by shame and fear. Repair helps with both affect and behavioral regulation. Repair directly addresses the child's convictions, based on past negative experiences of neglect and abuse, that the child must face stressful events alone or that any conflict will lead to abandonment. The attachment figures are responsible for the initiation of repair, not the child. These same principles apply to the therapist-caregiver relationship. Inevitable misattunements between therapist and parent are directly addressed and repaired thought the relationship. It is the therapist's responsibility to initiate the repair, not the parent.

Therapist Use of Self

A carpenter uses levels, saws, nails, and hammers. The Dyadic Developmental Psychotherapist uses self. Use of self by the therapist is at the core of how Dyadic Developmental Psychotherapy is implemented. Use of self involves the creation and maintenance of concordant intersubjective experiences; the sharing of one's experiences of the other in a therapeutic manner. This use of self is always focused on helping the client achieve greater self-knowledge, more flexible modes of relating, and more authentic emotional experiences that reflect the nature and quality of the current relationship. All the other components of Dyadic Developmental Psychotherapy are enacted through the therapist's use of self. PACE is largely a function of the therapist's use of self in a therapeutic manner. The therapeutic use of self requires a well-developed reflective function and secure state of mind with respect to attachment. As the therapist creates concordant intersubjective experiences, the therapist monitors the effect on the other and the other's emotional experience. The goal is to create emotionally meaningful experiences that facilitate the integration of memories and emotions that were dissociated (split off) as the result of early relational trauma. The therapist must constantly monitor the other's affective state to keep the interactions emotionally meaningful and not dysregulating (Becker-Weidman, Ehrmann, LeBow, 2012). The therapist's use of self involves keeping up an affective/reflective dialogue among family members. By reflecting on and monitoring the immediately occurring experiences, the therapist keeps a balance between the affective and the reflective elements of the dialogue. The therapeutic use of self as described here is what allows for the creation of a new and coherent autobiographical narrative, the co-regulation of emotions, and the co-creation of new meanings. Much of this occurs on a non-verbal level through the use of tone of voice, volume, gestures, cadence, expressions, and modulation of voice: the verbal-non-verbal dialogue. In order to help the client explore potentially painful and disturbing memories, emotions, and experiences, the therapist consciously follows the client (through acceptance and curiosity), then leads the client deeper, and again follows at this deeper level. Finally, when inevitable misunderstandings arise, the therapist must be able to manage the experience of shame so that the therapist can accept responsibility for the therapist's mistake. By acknowledging one's errors, mistakes, and misjudgments, the first steps toward interactive repair can occur. In this manner the therapist models with the caregiver how the caregiver can respond to the child when there is a breach in that relationship.

To effectively and therapeutically use self, the therapist must have a relatively secure state of mind with respect to attachment, reasonably developed reflective abilities, good self-awareness, and be tolerant of ambiguity. A secure state of mind with respect to attachment has been found to be important in therapeutic work (Tyrell, et. al., 1999). A secure state of mind with respect to attachment allows the therapist to experience a range of emotions and to reflect on these emotions in a relatively unbiased manner. Self-knowledge involves being aware of personal biases and being able to reflect on internal states. The therapist must be aware of to what extent what experiences reflect the current interactions with the other and to what extent the experiences reflect personal past history being evoked by the current interactions. Finally, tolerance for ambiguity is an important element for use of self because being tolerant of ambiguity allows the therapist not to jump prematurely to conclusions regarding what the other is experiencing and the meaning the other ascribes to the experiences. This suspension of certainty allows the therapist to form various hypotheses regarding the meaning of experiences while keeping an open mind, so that the therapist's curiosity can emerge in an authentic and emotionally meaningful manner. Uncertainty promotes curiosity and questions with an emotional tone that reflect genuine interest in and acceptance of the other's thoughts, feelings, meanings, and experiences. Finally, ongoing consultation can be a significant aid in this work. Consultation can support the therapist in exploring the therapist's own experiences and use of self.

IT'S ABOUT CONNECTIONS NOT COMPLIANCE

Relationships (friendly, intimate, therapeutic, etc.) are built on connections or experiences that have emotional valance and value. The Dyadic Developmental Psychotherapy therapist focuses primarily on relationships and connections, not compliance. It is not that compliance is not important; it is. It is that the way to secure genuine and authentic compliance is through connections and relationships. This is an important concept for caregivers to integrate into their parenting. It is through connections that the child will internalize the parent's "voice" and develop impulse control, morals, values, and more positive social functioning. The story of Pinocchio, in some respects illustrates this. As long as Jiminy Cricket was on Pinocchio's shoulder, Pinocchio was well-behaved. But whenever Jiminy Cricket was away, that was when Pinocchio got into trouble; he'd not internalized "compliance." At the end of the story Pinocchio becomes a "real" boy when he goes off to save his father Gippetto. In other words, Pinocchio becomes a real boy when he cares about another.

PACE AND PLACE

PACE is the attitude of the therapist. It is the therapist's responsibility to maintain a healing pace of treatment. It is an acronym for being Playful, Accepting, Curious, and Empathic. PLACE is the attitude of the caregiver. It is the caregiver's responsibility to maintain a healing place. It is an acronym for being Playful, Loving, Accepting, Curious, and Empathic. It forms the core of how the therapist or parent begins to explore an event or issue. PACE is also the primary means of initiating "interactive repair" (described below) during the session. This is required whenever the child initiates a break in the relationship or the break is created by a misattuned initiative or response by the therapist or parent.

INTERSUBJECTIVITY

As previously described, intersubjectivity is shared affect, intention, and attention. Intersubjectivity can be concordant, when all three elements are in accord, or it can be discordant. When an interchange seems to be going awry, it is useful to consider which element of the intersubjective experience is discordant. Very often it will be that the intentions are discordant. An example may serve to illustrate this. In this example, the therapist is talking with a single parent, Steve, about his son, Eric, age thirteen. Steve appears to be rather critical and punitive, and the therapist wants to help Steve focus on what is driving Eric's behavior rather than on surface behavior. However, in this example, the interchange does not go well.

Steve: I just got Eric's five week report and it is awful. He's failing math and Science and is barely passing his other subjects. I told him if he doesn't do better, he'd be grounded until he does. I am so mad at him.

Therapist: OK, so you want him to get better grades. Why did he do so poorly? (Problem solving rather than looking deeper)

D: Because he doesn't study and missed a lot of homework.

T: I see, so you figure you can get him to study more and do his homework if he's grounded and has no TV or computer or games?

D: Exactly!

T: You've done this before, and it hasn't worked. Why do you think it will this time? (Problem solving. The therapist is now beginning to feel annoyed with Steve not getting what they've talked about before)

D: What else should I do? (Steve starts to become defensive; no surprise)

T: I think you have to understand that the way to get him to do well is by having a better relationship with him. "It's about connections not compliance," is what I say. (This problem solving intellectualized statement has a strong undertone of blame. Perhaps the therapist is feeling that he has to defend Eric. This is where the therapist could have moved the interchange into a concordant intersubjective experience.)

D: What, so I'm supposed to be his buddy and ignore his bad grades?

(And now, Steve and the therapist are on opposite sides of the fence and are arguing. They are not engaged with each other in a concordant manner.)

T: No. What I mean is the way to get good grades is to focus on having a relationship with him so that he wants to do well. Right now he feels you are forcing him to do well. (Here the therapist is beginning to act as Eric's advocate, defending him against his father).

D: So what's wrong with that?

T: What's wrong with that is that now you are both in a control battle with Eric's grades. Privileges being the ammunition, you each are shooting at each other. (And the therapist is in a control battle of sorts with the father).

It goes downhill from here. While what the therapist is saying may be on target, the interchange is not concordant on the dimensions of intention or emotion. The therapist appears to be set on "explaining" what Steve should do, and Steve appears to be set on defending his approach. They don't have joint shared intention. It is also likely that Steve may be feeling blamed by the therapist and that the therapist may be feeling annoyed that Steve just doesn't "get it." Maybe the therapist is thinking, "Eric is a good kid, if only Steve would see that." So the therapist begins to try to act as Eric's advocate and defender. This may then lead to an interpersonal conflict between the therapist and Steve when the conflict between caring about Eric and wanting to have him get good grades should be intrapersonal (within Steve).

The following example illustrates how focusing on the elements of intersubjectivity and what is discordant can lead to a more effective interchange.

Steve: I just got Eric's five week report and it is awful. He's failing math and ELA and is barely passing his other subjects. I told him if he doesn't do better he'd be grounded until he does. I am so mad at him.

Therapist: You sound upset. (The therapist moves to affect)

D: You bet I am. I know he can do better; he's just lazy!

(Now, the therapist could argue with Steve about whether or not Eric is lazy or if he just feels so bad about himself that he acts in a way to confirm his self-image, or maybe that Eric's past experiences have led him to feel nothing he does matters, so why try? However, instead the therapist will stay focused on Steve for now to deepen their concordant intersubjectivity and keep all three dimensions in sync.)

T: You sound disappointed or hurt, maybe that Eric isn't doing better.

D: I am disappointed. I know he can do better; he's a smart kid. He could have a great future if he applied himself. (Steve is now talking more softly, and he appears more somber).

T: You really love Eric and want him to do well, don't you?

D: Yes, I'm his Dad. I've been trying for four years now, and I just get so frustrated sometimes that nothing I do makes a difference. What am I going to do?

T: Let's figure it together, OK? I'm sure we can come up with something.

D: OK

T: You said Eric is a bright kid and could do so much better. What is your guess on why he doesn't? (The therapist has now created joint intention and attention: "we will figure this out together).

D: I just think he's lazy.

T: Education is really important to you, and you've said that he could go far with his brains, so what would make such a kid be lazy? (Here the therapist accepts Steve's view and tries to go deeper by asking a question, by being curious.).

D: Maybe he never had anyone teach him how to work?

T: You mean that maybe, because he was so neglected as a young child, he never learned to put forth effort and all those foster homes he was in never made him feel anything mattered or that he mattered?

D: I never thought about it that way, but yea, that makes sense, the poor kid. So what do I do now?

T: Well, let's figure out how to help him feel he's capable and see what you see in him.

D: Well, punishing him like I've been doing doesn't work. All it probably did, I now see, is confirm that he's a failure and that I'm mad at him. How do I make that up to him? (Because of the safety created by the therapist, Steve is able to explore what he's been doing and consider alternatives).

Within this concordant intersubjective experience, Steve and the therapist have achieved two things. First, they have deepened their relationship. The therapist understands Steve better, and Steve feels the therapist wants to help him by understanding him. The therapist has modeled with Steve what the therapist may want Steve to do with Eric. Second, they co-created a new meaning for Eric's poor grades that leads to a different and more effective set of behaviors.

Reflective Capacity

Reflective capacity refers to the capacity to simultaneously be in an experience and to be able to think about that experience. Peter Fonogy (Fonogy, et. al. 2002) describes this as mentalizing.

It means having a mental representation of self, other, and the relationship. This mental representation allows one to anticipate the other's potential actions, feelings, and thoughts and then act accordingly.

It is the basis for empathy, the capacity to see and feel with the other. Obviously the therapist must have a well-developed reflective function. One of the goals of treatment is to enhance and develop the caregiver's reflective capacity and to develop and enhance the child's reflective capacity. The reflective function is necessary for impulse control.

It provides that half second of pause, so one can consider a response within the context of what one believes the other's intention, feelings, and thoughts are.

Affective/Reflective Dialogue

An affective/reflective dialogue can be described as a conversation that contains emotional, reflective, and cognitive elements. It is a relaxed and meandering dialogue that has a story-telling quality to it. In many ways the affective/reflective dialogue describes the ebb and flow of a conversation in which there is an experience with emotional valance and then some reflection about the experience. There is emotional engagement in this dialogue. This relaxed and meandering dialogue often side-steps resistance since the client is an active participant in the dialogue and the resulting co-creation of meaning.

COMMITMENT

The therapist's commitment is to the family; to help the family become a "happier" place. To achieve this, the therapist may find that the therapist's primary commitment will have to be to the parents since they are the keystone for healing and a successful outcome.

Many therapists trained as child therapists find themselves in the awkward position of feeling, "If only the parents would get a grip, this child would be fine." What then often happens is that the therapist begins to feel and act as the child's advocate, speaking for the child and trying to convince the parents to be better parents. This path frequently leads to an impasse or to the family discontinuing treatment.

If the parents have difficulties that impair their ability to create a healing place, the therapist will have to use PACE and the affective/reflective dialogue to create a secure base that will allow the parents to explore what is interfering with their being the sort of parents they would like to be. The therapist use PACE to join with, accept, understand, and support the parents so that the parents can accept, understand, and support their child. "Whatever the therapist wishes the parents to be able to do with their child the therapist has to be able to do with the parents." This forms the bedrock of the therapist's stance in regard to the primary caregivers.

INSIGHTFULNESS

Insightfulness is related to the reflective function described above. To be insightful means to look within, "in" "sight." Insight involves the ability to look within and to more deeply understand one's self, one's motives and intentions, and how these have been shaped by past and current experiences, relationships, and events.

Insight allows the therapist to better understand what emotions are being activated by the therapist's past experiences and which emotions are being activated by the current experiences. Developing insightfulness among family members is one of the important tasks of the therapist practicing Dyadic Developmental Psychotherapy.

The therapist accomplishes this through the use of the affective/reflective dialogue, by the co-creation of meanings, by follow-lead-follow, by interactive repair, and by the verbal/non-verbal dialogue. The affective/reflective dialogue along with the verbal/non-verbal dialogue is one method by which insight is achieved. This dialogue with its emotional and reflective components is how the client achieves greater self-knowledge. When entered into, this dialogue is how new and more helpful meanings of experiences are co-created. This dialogue is led by the therapist in the follow-lead-follow format.

Interactive repair ensures that the inevitable mistakes that occur in this process are owned and accepted and then explored and repaired. It is within the safety of the secure base that the exploration necessary to achieve integration and healing can occur. This integration and healing occurs by exploring current experiences and their connections to past experiences. By exploring how the past is alive in the present, the therapist assists the client in achieving deeper insightfulness.

Coherent Narrative and the Co-Creation of Meaning

The creation of a coherent autobiographical narrative is one marker of mental health. A personal narrative changes over time, and it is this narrative that gives meaning to one's life and experiences. Those with a secure pattern of attachment are able to tell a coherent story about their life, regardless of how difficult that life may have been. A coherent autobiographical narrative reflects the integration of the left brain hemisphere function of containing explicit memories with right hemisphere where affect and implicit memories are located. Trauma interferes with this integration. Without this integration, one's sense of self with a past, present and future can become distorted, vague, and disconnected. Clients who have experienced complex trauma frequently have disjointed, split-off, and dissociated autobiographical narratives. The episodic and emotional elements of the trauma are split off and disconnected from each other. While the emotional sequelae of the trauma are clearly evident in the person's behavior, the person is not aware of this. Revisiting the trauma in detail and in a titrated manner so that the emotions are experienced in the safe and secure setting of the therapy session and in the family allows for the integration of emotional and episodic memories and the conscious awarenessof how these events and feelings are operating in the present. It is this insightfulness that provides an important healing dimension to treatment. Once dissociated elements are integrated into a coherent autobiographical narrative, the client is able to manage the underlying emotions and engage the reflective function to select an appropriate and self-advancing response.

Co-Regulation of Emotions

Children and adults with difficult histories often have not received the necessary experiences that would allow them to effectively regulate their own emotions. In most typical circumstances, a parent first regulates the infant's emotional world and so regulates the infant's emotional experiences. The "good enough" parent provides stimulation to activate the infant but is careful not to over-stimulate. The "good enough" parent sooths the upset infant and reduces distress. In this fashion, the parent regulates the infant and young child's level of arousal and emotional experiences. Over time the child begins to internalize this shared co-regulation of affect and becomes self-regulating. The sequence is first the parent regulates the child, then the child is able to achieve emotional regulation with the parent's help, and then the child can self-regulate.

Follow-Lead-Follow

Follow-Lead-Follow describes the ebb and flow of the dialogue within the Dyadic Developmental Psychotherapy session. This framework is designed to encourage client engagement and to increase the client's sense of safety, security, and personal control. The therapist begins by using the PACE framework, accepting what the client says. The therapist follows the client's flow of dialogue and emotion and stays in step with the client. The objective here is to, metaphorically, walk with and next to the client. This helps create a secure base by providing the client with acceptance and a concordant intersubjective experience. Client and therapist are sharing affect and are attending to the same thing. Intentions are conjoint and complimentary, so the therapist is interested in what the client is interested in at the moment. The client will feel valued because the therapist is focusing on what the client finds of interest. Once the dialogue has moved along to some degree, the therapist can then begin to lead the client into a related path that has a different trajectory. For example, the therapist may begin to note how this situation is similar to one that occurred in the past or comment on what the client may have been feeling. The therapist leads the discussion deeper. Once on this new trajectory, the therapist again follows the client and the cycle continues.

Interactive Repair

Interactive repair (Tronick 1989, Tronick 2005) describes how the therapist or parent responds to the inevitable breaches that occur in any relationship during the ebb and flow of experience. Interactive repair refers to the caregiver's (or therapist's) actions to repair the relationship and to emotionally reconnect with and reestablish an attuned relationship with the child (or parent) after there has been a breach in the relationship. Interactive repair is the process by which a caregiver repairs some misattunement in the relationship in a manner that reduces shame. Interactive repair leads to the development of greater capacity to experience negative emotions without resultant shame and dysregulation. Interactive repair requires a caregiver who is sensitive and collaborative. When the caregiver helps the child recover from a negative affective state, the amount of shame experienced is reduced. When the caregiver engages in interactive repair on a fairly consistent basis, the child develops an internal experience of self as effective, that the child's intentions are positive, and that distress is reparable. These same effects of interactive repair apply when it is the therapist who initiates interactive repair with a caregiver. This models for the caregiver how to engage in this most vital process.

The healing dimension of interactive repair is that it reduces shame. Interactive repair can help a child progress developmentally from a shame-based identity to the experience of healthy and appropriate guilt. The parent setting a limit may cause the break in the relationship, specifically in some element of shared intersubjectivity, usually a discontinuity in shared emotion or joint complementary intention. A breach in the relationship can also be caused by an adult misunderstanding the child or missing important emotional cues. The disruption in the relationship that occurs may lead to the child experiencing shame. The cycle of experiencing positive affect following negative experiences teaches the child that negative emotions can be tolerated and resolved and that the relationship can be repaired. Over time as the healthy parent reestablishes attunement, the child begins to experience the self as intrinsically good, although as one who occasionally does "bad" things. It is this movement from feeling that one is bad to feeling that one is good but does bad things that is at the core of the developmental step from shame to guilt.

Practice in Residential Treatment Settings

Dyadic Developmental Psychotherapy can be used effectively within residential treatment, group home, and other congregate care settings. Clearly all the elements discussed in this chapter can be used with children in foster care; the foster parents are the primary caregivers. In residential treatment settings, the child care staff function as either co-parents with the child's parents or as the primary caregiver. When practicing this approach in residential treatment settings, the therapist will involve the care staff with the child in treatment, to the extent that this is possible. The more closely the care staff function as primary caregivers the more effectively can the underlying trauma and attachment disburbances be resolved. All of the components and principles of treatment described in this chapter can be integrated into the mileu of the residential care facility. However, it is important to recognize that a program using an attachment model of care operates differently than one using a behavioral model of care. Specific trainig for the staff is necessary to impliment such a model of care. My experience training staff in residential program around the world is that with the proper training, these staff can become a very powerful therapeutic influence in the child's life and the resulting change can be dramatic. The use of Dyadic Developmental Psychotherpy in residential settings is described fully elsewhere (Blackwell and McGuill, 2011; Clark, 2011)

Summary

This chapter has provided the reader with an overview of Dyadic Developmental Psychotherapy. This treatment has a good empirical base supporting the efficacy of the approach. In addition, it is consistent with generally accepted standards of care (Becker-Weidman, Ehrmann, LeBow, 2012).

Dyadic Developmental Psychotherapy is a family therapy model of treatment, grounded in attachment theory. However, the general principles and components of this approach can be used in other treatment modalities as well, such as in couples treatment, individual therapy, and group therapy. In addition, the model can be used in outpatient settings, inpatient settings, residental treatment centers, and othe venues. The model draws on of a number of well researched and common factors in effective psychotherapy.

References

Ackenbach, T.M., *Manual for the Child Behavior Checklist/4-18 and 1991 profile*. Burlington, VT: University of Vermont Department of Psychiatry, 1991.

Becker-Weidman, A., "Treatment for Children with Trauma-Attachment Disorders: Dyadic Developmental Psychotherapy," *Child and Adolescent Social Work Journal*, 23 (2), 147-71, 2006a.

Becker-Weidman, A., "Dyadic Developmental Psychotherapy: A multi-year Follow-up," in, *New Developments In Child Abuse Research*, ed. Stanley M. Sturt, Ph.D. NY: Nova Science Publishers, 43-60, 2006b.

Becker-Weidman, A., "Principles of Attachment Parenting" DVD. Williamsville, NY: Center For Family Development, 2006c.

Becker-Weidman, A., (2010), Dyadic Developmental Psychotherapy: Essential Methods and Practices. Lanham, MD: Jason Aronson.

Becker-Weidman, A., (2011). The Dyadic Developmental Psychotherapy Casebook. Lanham, MD: Jason Aronson.

Becker-Weidman, A., "Assessing Caregiver Reflective Capacity, Commitment, Insightfulness, and Sensitivity," DVD, Burlington VT: Resourceful Recordings, 2010(a).

Becker-Weidman, A., Becker-Weidman, S., Green, B., Hunt, K., and Walker, J.,"By Parents: The Healing of Three Families." Pp. 235-287 in *Creating Capacity for Attachment: Dyadic Developmental Psychotherapy in the Treatment of Trauma-Attachment Disorders.* Edited by, Arthur Becker-Weidman and Deborah Shell. Oklahoma City, OK: Wood N Barnes, Third Printing, 2011.

Becker-Weidman, A., Ehrmann, L., LeBow, D., (Eds), (2012). The Attachment Therapy Companion: Key Practices for Treating Children and Families. NY: Norton.

Becker-Weidman, A., and Hughes, D., (2008) "Dyadic Developmental Psychotherapy: An evidence-based treatment for children with complex trauma and disorders of attachment," Child and Adolescent Social Work, 13, pp.329-337.

Becker-Weidman, A., and Shell, Deborah, *Attachment Parenting: Developing Connections and Healing Children*. NY: Jason Aronson, 2010.

Becker-Weidman, A., and Shell, Deborah (Eds.), *Creating Capacity for Attachment: Dyadic Developmental Psychotherapy in the Treatment of Trauma-Attachment Disorders.* Oklahoma City, OK: Wood N Barnes, 2005, third printing, 2011.

Beutler, L., Malik, M., Alimohamed, S. and Harwood, T. (2004) Therapist variables. In: *Bergin and Garfield's Handbook of Psychotherapy and Behavior Change* (ed. M. Lambert), pp. 227–306. Wiley, New York.

Blackwell, S., and McGuill, J., "Dyadic Developmental Psychotherapy in Residential Treatment," pp. 143-163 in in Becker-Weidman, A., and Shell, D., (Eds), *Creating Capacity for Attachment: Dyadic Developmental Psychotherapy in the treatment of Trauma-Attachment Disorders.* Oklahoma City, OK: Wood N Barnes, 2005, third printing, 2011.

Bowlby, J. *Attachment, separation, and loss*. NY: Basic Books. 1980.

Bowlby, J. *A secure base*. NY: Basic Books, 1988.

Clark, C., "Dyadic Developmental Psychotherapy in Impermanent Settings," Pp. 130-131 and 163-185 in Becker-Weidman, A., and Shell, D., (Eds), *Creating Capacity for Attachment: Dyadic Developmental Psychotherapy in the treatment of Trauma-Attachment Disorders.* Oklahoma City, OK: Wood N Barnes, 2005, third printing, 2011.

Cook, A., Blaustein, M., Spinazolla, J. and van der Kolk, B., "ComplexTrauma" in *Children and Adolescents. White Paper from the National Child Traumatic Stress Network Complex Trauma Task Force*. National Center for Child Traumatic Stress, Los Angeles, CA, 2003.

Cook, A., Spinazzola, J., Ford, J., Lanktree, C., Blaustein, M., Cloitre, M. et al., "Complex trauma in children and adolescents." *Psychiatric Annals*, 35,390–398, 2005.

Craven, P. and Lee, R. (2006) "Therapeutic interventions for foster children: a systematic research synthesis." *Research on Social Work Practice*, 16, 287–304.

Dozier, M., Stovall, K. C., Albus, K. E., and Bates, B. "Attachment for infants in foster care: The role of caregiver state of mind." *Child Development*, 70, 1467–77, 2001.

Elliott, R., Greenberg, L. and Lietaer, G. (2004) Research on experiential psychotherapies. In: *Bergin and Garfield's Handbook of Psychotherapy and Behavior Change* (ed. M. Lambert), pp. 493–539. Wiley, New York.

Fonagy, P., Gergely, G., Jurist, E. and Target, M. *Affect Regulation, Mentalization, and the Development of the Self.* Other Press, New York, 2002.

Holmes, J. *John Bowlby and attachment theory*. New York: Routledge, 1993.

Hughes,D. "An attachment-based treatment of maltreated children and young people." *Attachment and Human Development*, 6, 263–78, 2004.

Hughes, D. *Building the Bonds of Attachment*, 2nd ed., Jason Aronson, Lanham, MD, 2006.

Hughes, D., (2007), Attachment Focused Family Therapy. NY: Norton.

Hughes, D. Attachment-Focused Parenting, W.W. Norton: New York, 2009.

Hughes, D., (2011) The development of Dyadic Developmental Psychotherapy. In Becker-Weidman, A., and Shell, D., (Eds) Creating Capacity for Attachment, 3rd printing, Oklahoma City, OK., Wood 'N' Barnes, pp. vii – xvi.

Lambert, M. *Bergin and Garfield's handbook of psychotherapy and behavior change.* NY: Wiley, 2004.

Norcross, J.C. (2001) Purposes, processes and products of the task force on empirically supported therapy relationships. *Psychotherapy*, 38,345–356.

Orlinsky, D., Grawe, K. and Parks, B. (1994) Process and outcome in psychotherapy. In: *Handbook of Psychotherapy Research and Behavior Change* (eds A. Bergin and S. Garfield), pp. 270–376. Wiley, New York.

Orlinsky, D., Ronnestad, M. and Willutzki, U. (2004) Fifty years of psychotherapy process-outcome research: continuity and change. In: *Bergin and Garfield's Handbook of Psychotherapy and Behavior Change* (ed. M. Lambert), pp. 307–389. Wiley, New York.

Ring, M., "For Parents," Pp. 216-234 in Becker-Weidman, A., and Shell, D., (Eds), *Creating Capacity for Attachment: Dyadic Developmental Psychotherapy in the treatment of Trauma-Attachment Disorders*. Oklahoma City, OK: Wood N Barnes, 2005, third printing, 2011.

Saunders, B., Berliner, L. and Hanson, R. (2004) *Child physical and sexual abuse: guidelines for treatment.*http://academicdepartments.musc.edu/ncvc/resources_prof/OVC_guidelines 04-26-04.pdf (15 September 2011).

Stern, D. *The Interpersonal World of the Infant*. Basic Books, New York, 1985.

Trevarthen, C. "Intrinsic motives for companionship in understanding: their origin, development, and significance for infant mental health." *Infant Mental Health Journal*, 22,95–131, 2001.

Tronick, E. Z., "Emotions and Emotional Communication in Infants". *American Psychologist*, 44(2), 112-119, 1989.

Tronick, E.Z. "Why is connection with others so critical? The formation of dyadic states of consciousness: coherence governed selection and the co-creation of meaning out of messy meaning making." Pp. 293-315 in J. Nadel and D. Muir (eds). *Emotional development*. Oxford University Press, 2005.

Tyrell, C., Dozier, M., Teague, G.B. and Fallot, R. "Effective treatment relationships for persons with serious psychiatric disorders: the importance of attachment states of mind." *Journal of Consulting and Clinical Psychology*, 67,725–733 1999.

In: Psychotherapy
Editors: A. J. Lancaster, and O. Sharpe

ISBN 978-1-61942-611-5

Chapter 3

HOPE-FOCUSED COUPLE APPROACH: RESEARCH ON EFFICACY AND ANALYSIS OF WHY IT MIGHT BE EFFECTIVE

Everett L. Worthington, Jr.*[1], *Jennifer S. Ripley*[2], *Joshua N. Hook*[3], *Andrea J. Miller*[4], *Yin Lin*[1], *Caroline Lavelock*[1], *and Shannan Crawford*[2]
[1]Virginia Commonwealth University
[2]Regent University
[3]University of North Texas
[4]Georgia Southwestern State University

ABSTRACT

Hope-focused couple enrichment (HFCE) has been evaluated as one of four empirically supported couple enrichment interventions (Jakubowski et al., 2004). We first review the essence of the hope-focused approach. We then review outcome research on HFCE and its components. We present and discuss four possible reasons for the efficacy of the non-religiously accommodated hope-focused approach. These include (a) a focus on hope, (b) a simple strategy with diverse techniques, (c) a focus on repairing damaged emotional bonds through forgiveness, and (d) reliance on systematic research on the components of the method. We hope to interest researchers and clinicians in the hope-focused approach as well as improve couple therapists' counseling.

INTRODUCTION

Hope-focused couple enrichment (HFCE) has been evaluated to be one of four empirically supported approaches to couple enrichment (Jakubowski, Milne, Brunner, and Miller, 2004). The other three empirically supported couple enrichment approaches are the Premarital and Relationship Enhancement Program (PREP; Markman, Stanley, and Blumburg, 1994), Couple Communication (Butler and Wampler, 1999) and Relationship

Enhancement (Guerney, 1977). Over the years, these four programs have been investigated multiple times with demonstrated efficacy using many couples. Other approaches to couple enrichment may have been used frequently, but they have not met the criteria for an empirically supported treatment (i.e., effective in at least two randomized clinical trials conducted by two different research teams; Chambless and Hollon, 1998).

The hope-focused couple approach (HFCA) includes both couple therapy (HFCT) and couple enrichment (HFCE, Worthington, 2005). The most thorough exposition of the method is a book describing the Christian-accommodated approach (Worthington, 2005). We will describe the secular version in the current chapter—the version with the majority of research supporting it. Thus, practitioners who wish to use the secular version can merely ignore the Christian terminology in the book; whereas practitioners who wish to use the Christian-accommodated version can rely on the book. A recent meta-analysis of religiously/spiritually (R/S) accommodated treatments found that strictly R/S accommodated treatments—those that are the same secular version but framed for Christians or other spiritual approaches—are equally efficacious in terms of couple relationship outcomes in either the secular or accommodated versions (but tend to have better R/S outcomes in the R/S accommodated versions for similar R/S clients; see Worthington, Hook, Davis, and McDaniel, 2010). Several case studies describe how to apply the method (Ripley, Worthington, and Maclin, 2011; Turner and Ripley, 2007; Worthington, Mazzeo, and Canter, 2005).

Table 1. Acrostics in Frequently Used Interventions in the HFCA

STEPS (Communication)
S = Situation
T = Thoughts
E = Emotions
P = Plans and Actions
S = Statement of Value (e.g., "I value you more than I value winning this argument")
TANGO (Communication)
T = Tell What Happened
A = It Affected Me …
N = Nurture (Value Your Partner)
G = Get It? (Reflect)
O = Observe Your Effects
LOVE (Conflict Resolution)
L = Listen and Repeat
O = Observe Your Effects
V = Value Your Partner
E = Evaluate Both Partner's Interests
CLEAVE (Intimacy)
C = Change Actions to Positive
L = Loving Romance
E = Employ a Calendar to Create Time Together
A= Adjust Intimacy Elsewhere if Needed to Focus on the Relationship
V = Value Your Partner
E = Enjoy Yourselves Sexually

Worthington (2005) describes the theoretical frameworks of the HFCA that helps as (1) focusing on hope and (2) employing a strategic emphasis on rebuilding love, engaging in work (i.e., time and effort) on the relationship, and restoring faith, in each other, in the counselor, in therapy, and (if the couple is Christian) in God. Worthington also focuses on making change "sensible" (i.e., easily sensed) by using tangible objects or spatial manipulations in each interaction. This theory of change assures that misunderstandings that might arise from mere talk can be minimized by referring back to concrete objects of people's bodily movement (which, in most cases, are less easily forgotten). In addition, he describes over 150 specific interventions in the text. Many are easily remembered through using acrostics (see Table 1 for a list of the most frequently used acrostics).

Because HFCA has been judged to be efficacious (Jakubowski et al., 2004), in the present chapter, we focus our attention on (a) research supporting its efficacy and the efficacy of its various components and (b) the reasons that we believe it is efficacious. We discuss four characteristics of the HFCA that we believe provide the basis for its efficacy. First, the HFCA focuses on hope. Second, the HFCA teaches a simple strategy. Third, the HFCA aims to repair the emotional bond between partners. Fourth, the HFCA has been responsive to modification suggested by research.

Efficacy is established through carefully controlled clinical trials. Effectiveness is the scientific demonstration that a treatment produces consistent change when done in actual practice (McHugh and Barlow, 2010). Typically, demonstration of effectiveness requires large dissemination trials. However, HFCA has not yet been researched in a large dissemination trial. There is some evidence that therapists who do explicitly Christian-accommodated couple therapy do use the HFCA (Hook and Worthington, 2009). However, dissemination trials to demonstrate the effectiveness of the HFCA are needed.

Whereas dissemination trials have not been undertaken, efforts have been made to disseminate the methods (see www.hopecouples.com, www.people.vcu.edu/~eworth). These include therapist and participant manuals (Ripley, Quigley, Davis, and Worthington, 2009; Worthington, 1997; www.people.vcu.edu/~eworth), books (Worthington, 2005), and Web- and DVD-based training program (Ripley and Worthington, 2007; www.hopecouples.com).

We hope this discussion will interest and motivate practitioners. We also hope to interest researchers in studying and publishing on the efficacy and effectiveness of the HFCA.

RESEARCH ON THE HFCA TREATMENT PACKAGE

The HFCA has been investigated as a whole (Ripley et al., 2007; Worthington et al., 1997) and has been found to be efficacious in clinical trials for enrichment in secular form and for couple therapy in both secular and Christian-accommodated forms. The various components of the HFCA have been tested in their own clinical trials. The components have been of variable duration from 1 hour to 9 hours. We have created a schematic summary of the various components (see Figure 1). Broadly speaking, the HFCA has two major components: Handling Our Problems Effectively (HOPE) and Forgiveness and Reconciliations through Experiencing Empathy (FREE). HOPE can be further divided into four subcomponents: (a) interview assessment and feedback, (b) communication training, (c) conflict resolution training, and (d) intimacy training. FREE can be further divided into two subcomponents: interventions (a) to REACH Forgiveness and (b) to promote a Bridge to Reconciliation. To better investigate the efficacy of HFCA, a summary of the overall efficacy and research on components of HFCE are described below.

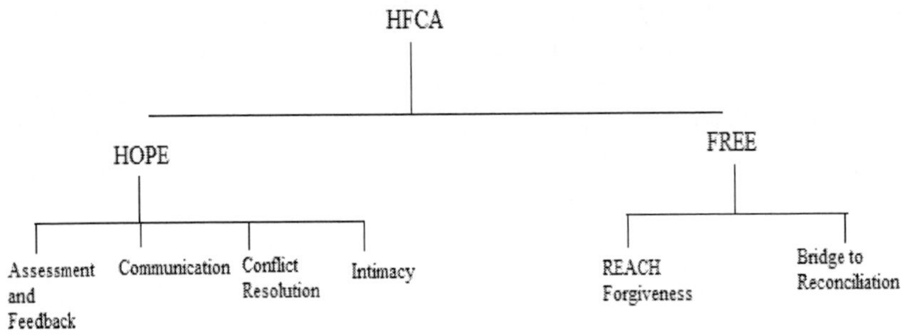

Figure 1. Schematic of the Components of the Hope-Focused Couple Approach.

Efficacy of HFCE

Worthington et al. (1997) studied 51 couples (16 married, 24 cohabiting, 11 engaged) using a 5.5-hour secular version of the HFCE relative to written assessment only. Couples were randomly assigned to conditions. All elements of the HFCE were used with assessment interviews and feedback taking 1.5 hours, and communication, conflict resolution, intimacy, and forgiveness training taking 4.0 hours. Effect sizes for dyadic adjustment were 0.95 (from pre-test to post-test) and 1.20 (from pre-test to follow-up). Effect sizes for commitment were 0.25 (from pre-test to post-test) and 0.20 (from pre-test to follow-up). To provide a perspective for meta-analyses of couple enrichment interventions, the mean effect size has ranged from 0.23 to 0.45 (Hawkins, Blanchard, Baldwin, and Fawcett, 2008; Hight, 2000; Jakubowski et al., 2004).

Components of HFCE

Assessment and Feedback

Worthington et al. (1995) randomly assigned 48 couples (26 married, 15 cohabiting, 7 engaged) to receive two hours of interview assessments and a written feedback report that was processed by the counselor and couple for one additional hour. The comparison was to a written assessment only, and the assessment plus feedback session was superior to written assessment alone in promoting couple adjustment and commitment. Ripley et al., (2002) conducted a small study of 14 community couples with a one-hour distance-based assessment and feedback consisting of paper questionnaires and written and telephone feedback only. There was significant movement in stage of change on intention to change, but not change in relationship measures.

Use of HFCE in Groups Versus with Individual Couples

Worthington, Buston, and Hammonds (1989) studied modality of delivery of some brief components of HOPE. Ten-minute informational videotapes on communication, conflictresolution, and intimacy were used to stimulate conversation in couples. Couples ($N =$ 36) were randomly assigned to a 2-hour discussion group of couples with tapes, a 2-hour discussion group of couple with no tapes, a one-hour meeting with tapes and a counselor, or neither tapes nor discussion (written assessment only). They found watching the brief informational tapes did not improve couple satisfaction. However, couples who participated in the discussion group reported higher levels of couple satisfaction than did couples who did not have the discussion group. We concluded that the delivery of the content of information was too weak to draw conclusions about the content.

Comparison of HOPE and FREE (or REACH)

Ripley and Worthington (2002) compared a 5-hour version of secular HOPE versus secular FREE versus written assessment only. The study involved 43 community-based couples cohabiting or married, ranging from 1 to 19 years. Treatment was in groups. HOPE resulted in changes in coded positive-to-negative ratio for communication relative to the written assessment control condition but did not change in forgiveness relative to controls. FREE did not produce changes in either communication or forgiveness relative to the written assessment control condition. The researchers concluded that the group format was not effective for forgiveness intervention with established community-based couples who often had substantive hurts to resolve. Future FREE interventions were conducted dyadically.

Burchard et al. (2003) studied 20 early married couples within their first five months of marriage at the outset of the study. The couples were randomly assigned to a 9-hour secular treatment of HOPE versus FREE versus written assessment only. Treatment was delivered by a couple consultant who met with the husband and wife pair in their first year of marriage. FREE and HOPE both produced positive changes in quality of life relative to written assessment only. Consistent with much research on the first year of marriage, the written assessment only couples experienced lower quality of life over the five months of the study. Treated couples reported higher quality of life over the study.

The Burchard et al. (2003) study was a pilot study for a larger study conducted by Worthington et al. (2003) that reported data of 150 couples. Worthington et al. (2003) found that FREE produced the most changes post-treatment and those changes were maintained at 3 months follow-up. HOPE produced post-treatment gains relative to initial assessment but about half of the gains were lost by follow-up. Both HOPE and FREE were superior to written assessment only. Worthington et al. (2011) reported the data of some new measures for the earlier study. This included assessments pre-treatment, post-treatment, and at 3 months, 6 months, and 1 year follow-up. Both HOPE and FREE were superior to written assessment only on all measures. HOPE was found equivalent to FREE on dyadic adjustment, commitment, and salivary cortisol. However, HOPE was superior to FREE on communication self-reports and coded positive and negative communication ratio (post-test, but not follow-up). Furthermore, FREE was superior to HOPE on forgiveness of a serious early-marriage transgression (post-test and follow-up).

Implications of Existing Research on HFCE

The HFCE method and its major components, HOPE and FREE, have been shown to be effective when couples meet with a counselor (Burchard et al., 2003; Worthington et al., 2003; Worthington et al., 2011; Worthington et al., 1997). All studies used a secular version of HFCE. Sufficient dosage is required to make an impact—at least 5 hours or more. HOPE, but not FREE, was effective in a psychoeducational group of couples (Ripley and Worthington, 2002), though social support in couple groups might be helpful in as few as 2 hours (Worthington et al., 1989). The interview assessment and feedback of results in 3 hours can itself make a positive impact (Worthington et al., 1995) but produce only intention to change in a 1 hour distance format (Ripley et al., 2002). Some evidence suggests that some of the gains of HOPE might fade somewhat, though still superior to control conditions, but the gains of FREE, once achieved, do not fade with time.

Efficacy of HFCT

Ripley et al. (2007) tested the full HFCA both in a secular form and a Christian-accommodated version among Christian couples using couple therapy (HFCT), not couple enrichment. The couple therapy was done by counselors meeting with individual couples. Ripley et al. found both the secular and Christian-accommodated versions equally effective relative to a waiting list (Leon et al., 2008). This intervention studied 87 couples at intake and 59 at 6-month follow-up integrated the HOPE and FREE interventions in a 10-hour format with participants randomly assigned to secular or Christ-accommodated versions. Effect sizes were moderate to large with overall relationship adjustment from pre to post-treatment at Cohen's d= .69 for within subjects design; decrease of negative affect in a videotaped conversation had an effect size of .93; increase of communication skills of .90, and increase of hope, or sense of self-efficacy in the relationship of 1.36.

Subsequently the HPCT approach conducted research (Ripley et al., 2010) that allowed for self-selection of religion-accommodative treatment with 75% of community-based couples who sought treatment at a couples clinic (at an explicitly Christian university) selecting to include something relevant to religion or spirituality in their treatment. This study integrated the HOPE and FREE manuals with 76 clinical couples and ranged from 8 to 14 hours of intervention, tailored to the couples needs. Effect size of treatment was moderate to large. There were large effect sizes (Cohen's d over .70) for the Revised Dyadic Adjustment Scale, Relationship Efficacy Scale, the "impact" stage of forgiving on the Gordon-Baucom forgiveness scale, IDCS behavioral codes of videotapes on negative affect, problem solving skills, conflict and communication skills. Moderate effect sizes (Cohen's d over .40) were found for the "moving on" stage of forgiving in the Gordon-Baucom forgiveness scale, Manifestations of God in the relationship scale; and IDCS behavioral coding of positive affect.

Research Support for the HFCA Theoretical Mechanisms of Change

Standards for determining whether a treatment is a bona fide evidence-based practice are not consensually agreed upon (David and Montgomery, 2011). Chambless et al. (1998) suggested guidelines for determining the empirically supported status of a treatment, which rely on randomized clinical trials. An empirically supported treatment is one that has been found superior to a control condition or equal to an established effective treatment when investigated by two or more independent research teams. As we mentioned previously, the HFCA has been designated as empirically supported (Jakubowski et al, 2004). However, recently David and Montgomery (2011) observed that stricter standards might be needed to determine the degree to which a treatment approaches the gold standard as an evidence-based bona fide treatment. They observed that it was possible for a treatment to be efficacious without being scientifically true. They offered the example of an early treatment for malaria. Malaria was thought to be caused by bad air. A preventative treatment that was somewhat effective was to shut the windows, which presumably would stop the bad air from circulating. Given that malaria was actually caused by a pathogen transmitted by the anopheles mosquito, closing the windows could be an effective preventative intervention. However, the scientific theory on which the treatment was based was incorrect.

David and Montgomery (2011) suggested that not only the treatment package be analyzed for efficacy but also the theory of change be analyzed for degree of evidential support. Evidence-based bona fide scientific treatments—the term for the highest level of evidence-based data—would be supported both in theory and efficacy of treatment package. Treatments with less support might be considered *intervention-driven* (i.e., they might have little support for the underlying theory but substantial support for the efficacy of the package as a whole), or *investigational* (i.e., substantial support for theory but insufficient support for the treatment package) treatments. We have taken the critique by David and Montgomery seriously. Worthington (2005) has suggested several theoretical change mechanisms. We will examine each of them and make a subjective evaluation of the degree of research support for each.

In Table 2, we have summarized the theoretical change mechanisms of the HFCA. First, hope was theorized to affect motivation to change and, through that, to affect couple adjustment and commitment—the two primary indices of the quality of a couple relationship. Research on hope is plentiful (with numerous studies summarized in a book by Snyder, 1994); this is considered supported with a high level of empirical support. Second, the strategy that is taught to couples—to love (i.e., to value the partner), to work (i.e., to exert effort and time at bettering the relationship), and to have faith in God (if religious), each other, therapy, and the therapist as change agents—permeates the literature on the therapeutic relationship. This affects motivation and effort put into each component and efficacy of the HFCA. But specifically, there is little established evidence directly investigating these mechanisms of change stated as such. On the other hand, one might adduce *much* evidence on the role of love in couple relationships (e.g., Graber, Laurenceau, Miga, Chango, and Coan, 2011), work as the impact of homework in couple counseling or dose-response relationships in psychotherapy (e.g., Dattilio, Kazantzis, Shinkfield, and Carr, 2011), and faith if we consider it to be demonstrated by the placebo effect of expectancy (Blow, Morrison, Tamaran, Wright, Shaafsma, and Nadaud, 2009). Third, making change sensible (i.e., using tangible objects and acts instead of mere discussion) is thought to affect willingness for partners to collaborate with each other and improve memory for in-session changes. Again there is little direct scientific evidence that supports these theoretical assumptions within the couple enrichment or couple therapy contexts.

Each subcomponent of HOPE and of FREE (see Table 2) is also thought to promote change by working through proximal variables to affect the two listed measures of marital quality (also see Table 2)—couple adjustment and commitment. Assessment and feedback is theorized to assure couples of their normalcy and to identify problems for which the feedback report makes direct suggestions for change. These theoretical mechanisms are hypothesized to affect couple adjustment. There is little direct scientific evidence to support that these change mechanisms are operating in couple enrichment or couple therapy.

Table 2. Mechanism Affecting Proximal and Distal Couple Variable for Each Component of the HFCE and Each Change Mechanism

HFCE Component or Proposed Theoretical Change Mechanism	Mechanism Affecting Proximal Variables	Most Directly Affected Distal Variable
Theoretical Change Mechanism		
Hope	Motivation to change	Couple adjustment Couple commitment
Love (Valuing the Partner)	Included in all subcomponents of HFCE	Couple adjustment Couple commitment
Work	Effort put into each component	Couple adjustment Couple commitment
Faith	Motivation to change	Couple adjustment Couple commitment
Making Change Sensible	Willingness to collaborate with the partner; memory of in-session changes	Couple adjustment Couple commitment
HOPE		
Assessment and Feedback	Assurance of normalcy; identification of problems that can be solved	Couple adjustment
Communication Training	Increase positive interactions; decrease negative interactions	Couple adjustment
Conflict Resolution Training	Decrease negative reactions; reduce number of problems	Couple adjustment
Intimacy Training	Promote emotional and sexual intimacy; strengthen emotional bond	Couple adjustment Couple commitment
FREE		
Forgiveness	Old conflicts resolved; negative affect reduced; sentiment override reduced; repair of damaged emotional bond	Couple adjustment Couple commitment
Reconciliation	Trust restored; emotional bond restored after trust violations	Couple commitment

Communication training and conflict resolutions training are theorized to affect the couple's ratio of positive to negative interactions (Gottman, 1993). There is much scientific support for this theoretical proposition (Markman et al., 2010). There is less, but still substantial, evidence that intimacy training to produce emotional and sexual intimacy is effective (e.g., Hickmon, Protinsky, and Singh, 1997).

Forgiveness training has been found to affect couple interactions and affective bond in substantial research (Fincham et al., 2005; 2006). Reconciliation training has substantial support within the literature on communication (Waldron and Kelly, 2008).

Overall, we conclude that the empirical support for the theoretical change mechanisms purported to be behind the efficacy of HFCA is strong but not conclusive. There is empirical evidence that creating an environment of hope, communication training, conflict resolution training, intimacy training, forgiveness training, and reconciliation training is effective in promoting change. However, direct evidence within couple enrichment or counseling contexts is needed to demonstrate that (a) teaching the couples faith, work, and love strategy, (b) using tangible manipulations to promote partner collaboration and memory for in-session change, and (c) establishing how assessment and feedback may affect change, are scientifically supported. In the following section, we describe theoretical change mechanisms of the HFCA in more detail.

Factors Hypothesized to Contribute to the Efficacy of the HFCA

Focus on Hope

Hope is essential to positive living and to counseling in general. In the HFCA, the therapist's or couple consultant's aim is to help the couple build hope. Many approaches to helping couples are educational and focus on building communication skills or problem solving. Some of the other empirically supported approaches to couples enrichment use skill-building models, which are certainly helpful to couples. However, we suggest that the change that is occurring is not simply due to learning communication skills. Instead, the skills are a means to (a) re-route negative marital relational patterns, (b) give the couple a safe space to bond with each other or at least not offend each other, and (c) provide hope that things can be different.

Although teaching skills, such as communication, conflict resolution, or forgiveness is often used in the HFCA, skill-training is not the overarching focus of therapy. We suggest that the higher-order focus on hope may be a reason for the efficacy of HFCA. Hope is essential for individual counseling (Frank, 1973), and we believe that it is essential for work with couples. Snyder (1994) has defined hope using two components. First, hope involves a willingness to change (i.e., willpower). Second, hope involves a sense that one knows how to bring about change (i.e., waypower). In addition, we believe that hope also helps people remain positive and courageous in the times that they do not see change occurring (i.e., waitpower; Marcel, 1962). Worthington (2005) has shown that each of the over 150 interventions used in the HFCA primarily promotes willpower, waypower, or waitpower.

We believe that hope is the essential component in couple counseling. In our experience, most people come to couple therapy without much hope in solving their problems. Many people do so because they believe that if they try couple therapy, they can divorce with less guilt. Couple therapy is extremely difficult when hope and motivation are low. If the couple therapist can inspire hope, the couple can often get back on track. Hope strengthens the emotional connection between the partners (Johnson, 2004), allows skills to be built

(Christensen and Jacobson, 1996), and permits couples to apply existing skills during times of need (de Shazer, 1988).

Furthermore, even couple therapists often lack hope. Individual psychotherapy is effective in approximately 80-85% of all instances (Howard, Kopta, Krause, and Orlinsky, 1986). According to a *Consumer Reports* survey on psychotherapy, patients reported that mental health professionals could effectively help relieve distress, but marriage counselors had the lowest success rate compared to other psychologists, psychiatrists, and social workers (Seligman, 1995). Only addictions had an equally low self-reported success rate. It is easy for couple therapists to become discouraged over low success rates. Most couple therapists believe in marriage, yet they are often unable to help couples solve their problems and regain a sense of emotional connection. We suggest that the path to marital change includes a couple therapist who retains hope for change throughout the process of couple therapy—even if there are periods in which change is non-existent or the couples appear to be getting worse.

Promote Hope through a Strategy of Building Love, Work, and Faith

Targeting Love

Enhancing love makes sense to couples. Partners, from Western cultures at least, usually say they got married because they love each other. They believe that they are having problems because their love has eroded. They believe that a renewed marriage means a renewed sense of love. The strategy of building love into their relationship—and referring specifically to it in that language throughout couple therapy—not only makes sense to couples, it inspires them to cooperate with the counselor. Teaching the couple to value one another and build love back into the relationship is infused in all subcomponents of the HFCA.

Requiring Work

Energy must be put into the relationship if it is going to improve. The couple is encouraged to work for their relationship. In the HFCA, the counselor challenges the couple to put in just one hard work-week of effort into their couple therapy (i.e., 40 hours). This is more time than most troubled couples ever put into their marriage during couple counseling. Most couples have unrealistic expectations of couple therapy. They believe that all their relationship problems that took years to develop should disappear in five to ten hourly sessions. The therapist challenges them to commit explicitly to 40 hours of work, which might include 10 hours in session and 30 hours out of session. If couples follow through on their commitment, clinical experience suggests that those couples often preserve their relationship. This has not yet been investigated empirically.

Work is essential to promote and maintain change in couples. When the relationship turns negative, almost all interactions are seen within a negative framework. Fincham, Hall, and Beach (2005) have labeled this negative framework *negative sentiment override*. Expectancies are negative, perceptions are negative, and memories are modified to be more negative. In other words, partners look through dark-colored glasses. A study by Carrere, Buelman, Gottman, Coan, and Ruckstuhl (2000) found that perceptual bias and selective attention were correlated positively with marital distress and longitudinally with higher rates of divorce. Couples characterized by negative sentiment override might work diligently in their weekly session. Yet, because of their negative mindset, they might undo much of the beneficial work during the 167 hours of the week that they are not in session. Effective therapy must show how negative sentiment override can be undone. We hypothesize that engagement in positive out-of-session exercises provides a structure that allows reinforcing interactions to occur.

In the HFCA, positive out-of-session exercises are provided in at least four ways: (a) HFCA provides easy-to-remember cues. These include focus on hope; the strategy of faith, work, and love; the acrostics to cue STEPS to good communication, and a TANGO of interaction, LOVE to resolve differences, CLEAVE to promote intimacy, five steps to REACH forgiveness and four planks in a bridge to reconciliation that FREE the partners. The acrostics are explained in Table 1 (for descriptions, see Worthington, 2005). (b) HFCA therapists engage the couple in memorable events within the session such as empty-chair exercises, using the space in the therapy room to represent intimacy, and teaching communication with physical movement using the STEPS or TANGO acrostics. (c) Therapy provides powerful positive bond-building emotional processes, such as empathizing with the spouse as he or she learns REACH or affirming the spouse during writing or recounting reasons the partners married. (d) Therapists elicit an overt commitment to work on the relationship for at least 40 hours and follow through on obstacles to that commitment.

Promoting Faith

In the secular version of the HFCA, faith means the belief in one's partner's willingness to restore their relationship. Couples in therapy have usually lost this faith. Having lost faith in each other, couples may place some of their faith in the counselor and his or her ability to help the couple improve the relationship. The counselor can help restore the couples' faith in their own abilities to improve their marriage.

Faith is a way that couples can restore their relationship to a covenant with healthy norms and rules of giving and receiving. Research has indicated that couples who focus on giving to the relationship without a sense of obligation for repayment have a stronger sense of security (Clark and Mills, 1993). Couples who are caught in the negative sentiment override with coinciding negative attributions and behaviors have lost their sense of faith, and they may focus instead on protecting themselves as individuals rather than investing in or taking risks for the marriage.

The HFCA counteracts this self-protective stance by building faith through a covenantal values system. Covenantal values are a system of beliefs that each partner will act in good faith and do all he or she can for the marriage and view the relationship as central to their lives. Weiss (1998) hypothesized that programs promoting a covenantal-type of system would produce enduring change because this value system promoted the development of the emotional bond and attachment. Thus, in addition to promoting love through work, the HFCA encourages couples to develop a covenant of faith that binds them together.

A Simple Strategy

The HFCA incorporates a strategic and practical approach to couples therapy and enrichment. The strategy is simple and powerful.

The HFCA Is Simple but Not Simplistic

Couples need to learn a simple yet personal approach if they are going to benefit from therapy or enrichment. Some of the approaches that couple therapists, and especially researchers, suggest can be complicated, difficult to understand, and overwhelming for therapists and couples. Researchers often develop complex models with many variables. Crucial connections between situational, individual, couple, and outcome variables are mediated or moderated by an array of variables. Couple therapists may be simultaneously responding to emotional interactions between partners, inferring couple dynamics, assessing personalities, making diagnoses, attending to the situation, and planning the next therapeutic maneuver.

Clients, too, can be overwhelmed. They may be managing feelings of embarrassment and shame at having to attend counseling, adjusting to an unfamiliar setting and the role as client, responding to an irate partner, trying to tell their stories and gain understanding from the therapist or counselor, and monitoring their own thoughts and feelings as well as those of partner and therapist. Even couple enrichment can tax couples' cognitive and emotional capacities.

Both therapists and clients need an approach that is simple yet not simplistic. Simple approaches can be more easily tailored to the couple by any level of therapist. When an experienced therapist enters a room with a couple, he or she may be considering about 50 options about how to help. The inexperienced therapist may be virtually paralyzed over what is important, thinking, *what should I be looking for? One theory says one thing. Another theory says something else*. The task of helping the couple seems almost impossible.

The HFCA Avoids too Much Information

In basic psychological science, researchers have investigated the usefulness of information in decision making. The results have been consistent. Information is helpful in making right decisions. But too much information (TMI) is devastating. For example, Iyengar and Lepper (2000) studied consumer behavior in over 700 consumers in a grocery store. They evaluated the effect of the number of choices available on buying a product after passing an advertisement booth. Either 6 or 24 choices of a single product were presented. When six choices were presented, about 30 percent of the consumers purchased the product. However, when 24 choices were available, only three percent of consumers purchased the product. TMI simply overwhelms. It prevents people from being decisive.

Providing too much verbally-based educational information affects memory and diverts attention from what one perceives. Consider verbal overshadowing. People remember faces, colors, or anything perceptual less accurately when they are allowed to create verbal or written cues to their memory than when they rely on their perception alone (Schooler and Engstler-Schooler, 1990). Therefore, more information can be worse, not better.

The Simple Strategy Format—Promoting Faith, Work, and Love-- Helps Beginning Counselors

The simplicity of this strategy is important, especially for beginning counselors. Like new sports players, beginning counselors need a simple strategy, or they can be overwhelmed by the amount and intensity of emotion in couple counseling. When the beginning counselor has a simple, powerful strategy in which he or she can be confident, the counselor works on the relationship with the focus of a laser instead of the scatter of a shot-gun blast. Clinical anecdotal evidence suggests that employing the simple strategy with couples is helpful, however, this has not been investigated empirically.

The Simple Strategy Format May Also Help the Expert Counselor

It is not just the beginning counselor who may be helped by a clear strategy. The strategy of promoting faith, work, and love actually can possibly benefit the expert counselor even more than the beginning counselor. Research on expert decision making has shown clearly that experts make decisions differently and more effectively than do people who are less expert.

Most studies of expert thinking have used chess problems (Ross, 2006). Novices tend to respond to the pieces in front of them. They try a limited number of moves. They do not often think ahead. As players gain experience, they then tend to think ahead in the many combinations. However, grandmasters, who are extremely expert, try *fewer,* yet more *effective* combinations than do those who masters. Why? Grandmasters have a storehouse of past experiences from which they draw. They compare the current board conditions to recognized patterns that have been repeated in their experiences many times. Their experiences may come from reading and working through other people's games as well as playing their own games.

In couple counseling, most expert counselors have similar templates against which they judge individual cases. The strategy of promoting faith, work, and love enriches the experienced therapists' template. The expert counselor can look at a case and see that the couple needs stronger faith, work, and love. But in this particular casc, they encourage the couple to stop dcvaluing each other. They can foresee potential obstacles several sessions down the road, and options for circumnavigating them. They have a sense of the amount of work necessary to turn the relationship around. This template of experience is enriched by the simple strategy of HFCA that can be tailored to each couple.

Assessment as the Foundation

The expertise of experienced counselors depends especially on being able to assess the differences among troubled couples. The HFCA is built on assessment. Assessment occurs at the initial session, or even prior to the session if the therapist can obtain written or online questionnaires. The first session is scheduled for at least 1.5 hours. The assessment session involves not only an interview but also a 10-minute videotaped discussion by the couple over a problem. The discussion allows the counselor to see how the partners communicate during conflict, and the couple to observe themselves.

Explicit up-front assessment helps provide a more objective way of detecting important difficulties. Each of the areas of a couple's relationship is considered in this assessment. Even the novice counselor can identify the major weaknesses of the couple. As the counselor gains experience, the interview can focus the counselor's attention quickly on the likely sources of the difficulties of the relationship.

The combination of written (or online) assessment, videotapes, and interview serves four purposes. First, it provides a confirmation for the counselor's judgment by providing multiple sources of assessment information. Second, more experienced counselors often already know what the issues are, thus the assessment provides concrete confirmation to the couple that these are indeed the issues of importance. Third, the assessment is a tool for intervention and not just a tool for diagnosis and treatment planning. An assessment report to the couple, which can usually be written in less than half an hour, is seen as "objective" information by the couple. The intervention suggested by the counselor will be justified with the couple's own response as the basis of suggested change. Fourth, assessment and feedback report persuades the client to fully engage in the therapeutic process. For instance, many men are more reluctant to attend couple counseling than their wives. However, those men who are analytical or business-oriented are typically more open to an objective assessment of the relationship than to rapport-building through relationship. So the reluctant partner may be persuaded to participate in an objective, analytical assessment phase of treatment. This is used as a foot-in-the-door technique. Compliance with subsequent therapeutic aims should be greatly increased by using assessment and feedback as a persuasion technique.

Diversity of Techniques

Worthington (2005) has suggested a variety of discrete techniques to help couples make change in their marriage. A framework for intervention with a focus on hope allows for eclectic incorporation of many techniques from other couple therapy and enrichment approaches. Many interventions involve concrete manipulations of space or materials with memorable experiences inside and outside of therapy. The hallmarks of individual psychotherapy are (a) change in people's perceptions and understandings of their internal experiences and (b) different actions based on the perception and understanding. However, Worthington (2005) has suggested that couple therapy is not as effective when it concentrates on changed *perspectives* as when it concentrates on changed mental, relational, and physical *structures*. This philosophy of intervention is informed by Minuchin's structural family therapy, solution-focused therapy, and integrative behavioral couple therapy.

Partners whose therapists primarily rely on talking to promote internal change often disagree about what happened even in session. When an intervention involves manipulating space or material—such as completing a questionnaire, creating a body "sculpture" to represent the relationship, or representing intimacy by moving their position in the room to show the emotional closeness they desire and currently feel—couples can more readily agree on what has happened in therapy and can therefore carry that agreement throughout the week. These types of interventions are also memorable, which helps create a better chance that couples will remember the principles from therapy when the need for them arises.

Repairing Damaged Emotional Bonds

Emphasis on Skill-Building and Skill-Changing

Worthington, Lerner, and Sharp (2005) surveyed the research on marriage and couple counseling between 1997 and 2005. They concluded that marriage and couple relationships have undergone a transition during these ten years. Before 1995, most couple problems were thought to be due to skill deficits. Areas of skill deficit included communication, sex, conflict-resolution, and intimacy. Most therapists helped couples improve their skills. In addition to developing skills, some therapists promoted insight about the dynamics between partners, of family systems, or couple interactions. Insight was thought to allow the couple to apply the skills that were necessary to bring ego control to their behavior, or to allow them the freedom to disrupt harmful patterned responses. Behavioral and cognitive-behavioral couple therapists were straightforward in their advocacy of skill-building.

The Focus Changed from Skill-Building and Skill-Changing to Forming, Maintaining, Strengthening and Repairing the Emotional Bond

After 1995, the focus of many couple therapies moved from skill-building to repairing the emotional bond (Worthington et al., 2005). The attachment relationship of the partners and the way that those elements affected the relationship between the couples became important. Fincham, Stanley, and Beach (2007) reviewed research on marriage and observed (similarly) that new topics—forgiveness, willingness to sacrifice—had been recent additions of intense scrutiny to the marriage and couple literature.

The Foundation of the HFCA Already Emphasized the Emotional Bond

Even before Worthington's (2005) formal reconceptualization of the HFCA, we conceptualized the HFCA to emphasize the change and the restoration of the emotional bond (see Ripley and Worthington, 2002). We described how hope, love, and faith could change the climate of the marriage, especially by promoting forgiveness. The recent formal reconceptionalization (Worthington, 2005) merely helps practitioners focus more clearly and explicitly on restoring the emotional bond.

Forgiveness and Reconciliation

Forgiveness and reconciliation have been important aspects of the HFCA from the beginning (see Worthington, 1989). Revised versions of the HFCA recommend focusing even more on forgiveness issues in counseling and embedding forgiveness and reconciliation in an attachment conceptualization. We believe lack of forgiveness manifests as a strained or broken attachment for most troubled couples. We postulate that lack of forgiveness for a large event or chronic small events leads to a lack of empathy, reduced motivation to use good marital skills, and negative reciprocity.

Healing the Emotional Bond

Healing ruptured bonds can be ameliorated by simple acceptance (Christenson and Jacobson, 1996). Sometimes *forbearance*—suppressing negative expression of emotion and behaviors arising from negative emotion—can prevent worsening of ruptures, because it should at least stop negative reciprocity. Partners also formulate narratives about the partner's and their own role in the causes of and responsibilities for a misunderstanding, and generous attributions for offenses should help couples overcome offenses (Fincham et al., 2005). However, forgiveness may be an important way of healing past ruptures in the emotional bond that may be more effective than acceptance, forbearance, and using generous attributions. *Acceptance* focuses on moving on with one's life. It does not restore the emotional bond as much as it stops paying attention to the negativity. It then reduces or eliminates negative affect. The same is true with forbearance. Forbearance effortfully suppresses negative responses, but, unlike acceptance, emotional turmoil often lingers. Even telling different stories about what happened, which changes attributions, often does not eliminate negativity. It often merely spreads out the blame. On the other hand, forgiveness not only reduces negativity over transgressions through decisions, but it also can build positive emotions back into the relationship (Fincham, 2000).

In couple therapy, forgiveness is often an important avenue to reconciliation. Freedman (1998) and Worthington and Drinkard (2000) differentiated forgiveness and reconciliation. Reconciliation is an interpersonal process of restoring trust through mutually trustworthy behaviors. Forgiveness is an individual's internal change that modifies negative behavioral intentions, motives, and emotions to more positive ones. Worthington (2003; see also 2006) defines two types of forgiveness. *Decisional forgiveness* involves deciding to control one's behavior or an act of will. That decision might be made quickly; however, emotional unforgiveness (i.e., resentment, bitterness, and anger) can still be experienced even if one decides to forgive. *Emotional forgiveness* involves replacing negative unforgiving emotions with positive other-oriented emotions such as empathy, sympathy, compassion, and love for the partner. Emotional forgiveness would be a change in the heart. Emotional forgiveness usually takes longer to experience than does making a decision to forgive, though some partners may withhold decisional forgiveness until emotional forgiveness has been achieved. Emotional forgiveness may be facilitated by decisional forgiveness in a "act as if" kind of behavioral strategy motivated by cognitive decisions. Furthermore, emotional forgiveness does not have to stop with just eliminating negative emotions. Positive emotions can continue to be generated even beyond the full replacement of the negative emotions, making the relationship even stronger than before the transgression. Both decisional and emotional forgiveness may strengthen a couple's emotional bond. In sum, a focus on forgiveness and reconciliation can promote a positive emotional bond.

Responsive to Research

For years, the HFCA has relied on scientific study of what was happening in therapy rather than merely on theory or clinical experiences. Outcome studies have documented the efficacy of the approach (Jakubowski et al., 2004). Furthermore, unlike many other approaches, Worthington and his colleagues have systematically observed and analyzed components of the HFCA to see which parts work best. Just as keeping current with research literature can be difficult, understanding revisions in emphases in HFCA requires a commitment on the part of the clinician. Yet those researching HFCA are committed to refining the approach to make it as helpful as possible to the couples who receive it. There is a sense of responsibility among the researchers toward those couples and clinicians who participate in HFCA. This commitment to studying empirically the components of the HFCA has demonstrated that (1) several of the aspects of the HFCA were indeed effective, and (2) several components (such as merely providing information; Worthington, Buston, and Hammonds, 1989) or relying on groups to direct themselves without thoughtful direction by leaders (Hammonds and Worthington, 1985) were not as helpful.

CONCLUSION

HFCA has been found to be efficacious in helping couples change (Jakubowski et al., 2004). In the present chapter, we have considered the strength of empirical evidence supporting both the treatment package and the theory of change underneath the treatment package. In both cases, there is substantial evidence. The evidence could, of course, be stronger and there are some holes in the evidence base. We advanced potential reasons that such efficacious changes occur. We hope that our speculation not only interests people in the HFCA, but will also affect the way therapists conduct their own couple counseling. We hope that therapists will analyze their approach in light of these principles. Do they promote hope? Do they teach a simple strategy? Do techniques supplement talk therapy with concrete change? We hope that therapists will sustain or initiate a commitment to studying their own practice with empirical measures and method instead of relying on clinical experience, which is valuable but can be at times misleading.

ACKNOWLEDGMENT

This research was supported in part by the John Templeton Foundation (grant #520) and a grant by the American Association of Christian Counselors both to the first author.

REFERENCES

Blow, A. J., Morrison, N. C., Tamaren, K., Wright, K., Schaafsma, M., and Nadaud, A. (2009). Change processes in couple therapy: An intensive case analysis of one couple using a common factors lens. *Journal of Marital and Family Therapy, 35*(3), 350-368. doi: 10.1111/j.1752-0606.2009.00122.x.

Butler, M. H., and Wampler, K. S. (1999). A meta-analytic update of research on the Couple Communication Program. *The American Journal of Family Therapy, 27*, 223-227.

Carrere, S., Buehlman, K. T., Gottman, J. M., Coan, J. A., and Ruckstuhl, L. (2000). Predictive marital stability and divorce in newlywed couples. *Journal of Family Psychology, 14,* 42-58.

Chambless, D. L., and Hollon, S. D. (1998). Defining empirically supported therapies. *Journal of Consulting and Clinical Psychology, 66*, 7-18.

Chambless, D. L., Sanderson, W. C., Shoham, V., Bennett Johnson, S., Pope, K. S., Crits-Chrostoph, P., et al. (1998). An update on clinically validated therapies. *The Clinical Psychologist, 49*, 5-18.

Christensen, A., and Jacobson, N. S. (1996). *Integrative couple therapy: Promoting acceptance and change*. New York: W. W. Norton and Company.

Clark, M. S., and Mills, J. (1993). The difference between communal and exchange relationships: What it is and is not. *Personality and Social Psychology Bulletin, 19*, 684-691.

Dattilio, F. M., Kazantzis, N., Shinkfield, G., and Carr, A. G. (2011). A survey of homework use, experience of barriers to homework, and attitudes about the barriers to homework among couples and family therapists. *Journal of Marital and Family Therapy, 37*(2), 121-136. doi: 10.1111/j.1752-0606.2011.00223.x.

Fincham, F.D. (2000). The kiss of the porcupines: From attributing responsibility to forgiving. *Personal Relationships, 7,* 1-23.

Fincham, F. D., Beach, S., Lambert, N., Stillman, T., and Braithwaite, S. (2008). Spiritual behaviors and relationship satisfaction: A critical analysis of the role of prayer. *Journal of Social and Clinical Psychology*, *27*, 362-388. doi:10.1521/jscp.2008.27.4.362.

Fincham, F. D., Hall, J. H., and Beach, S. R. H. (2005). "'Til lack of forgiveness doth us part": Forgiveness and marriage. In Everett L. Worthington, Jr. (Ed.), *Handbook of forgiveness* (pp. 207-225). New York: Brunner-Routledge.

Fincham, F.D., Hall, J., and Beach, S.R.H. (2006). Forgiveness in marriage: Current status and future directions. *Family Relations, 55,* 415-427, doi:10.1111/j.1741-3729.2006.00411.x.

Fincham, F. D., Stanley, S. M., and Beach, S. R. H. (2007). Transformative processes in marriage: An analysis of emerging trends. *Journal of Marriage and the Family, 69*, 275-292.

Frank, J. D. (1973). *Persuasion and healing: A comparative study of psychotherapy.* Oxford: John Hopkins University Press.

Freedman, S. (1998). Forgiveness and reconciliation: The importance of understanding how they differ. *Counseling and Values, 42*, 200-216.

Gottman, J. M. (1993). A theory of marital dissolution and stability.*Journal of Family Psychology, 7*, 57-75.

Graber, E. C., Laurenceau, J.-P., Miga, E., Chango, J., and Coan, J. (2011). Conflict and love: Predicting newlywed marital outcomes from two interaction contexts. *Journal of Family Psychology*, in press, posted Jul 11, 2011 doi: 10.1037/a0024507.

Guerney, B. G., Jr. (1977). *Relationship enhancement: Skill training programs for therapy, problem prevention, and enrichment.* San Francisco: Jossey-Bass.

Hammonds, T. M., and Worthington, E. L., Jr. (1985). The effect of facilitator utterances on participant responses in a brief ACME-type marriage enrichment group. *American Journal of Family Therapy, 13,* 59-69.

Hawkins, A. J., Blanchard, V. L., Baldwin, S. A., and Fawcett, E. B. (2008). Does marriage and relationship education work? A meta-analytic study. *Journal of Consulting and Clinical Psychology, 76*(5), 723-734.

Hickmon, W. R., Protinsky, H. O., and Singh, K. (1997). Increasing marital intimacy: Lessons from marital enrichment. *Contemporary Family Therapy: An International Journal*, 19, 581-589. doi:10.1023/ A:1026191223476.

Hook, J. N., and Worthington, E. L., Jr. (2009). Christian couple counseling by professional, pastoral, and lay counselors from a Protestant perspective: A nationwide survey. *American Journal of Family Therapy, 37,* 169-183.

Howard, K. I., Kopta, S. M., Krause, M. S., and Orlinsky, D. E. (1986). The dose-effect relationship in psychotherapy. *American Psychologist, 41*, 159-164.

Iyengar, S. S., and Lepper, M. R. (2000). When choice is demotivating: Can one desire too much of a good thing? *Journal of Personality and Social Psychology, 79*, 995-1006.

Jakubowski, S. F., Milne, E. P., Brunner, H., and Miller, R. B. (2004). A review of empirically supported marital enrichment programs. *Family Relations, 53*, 528-536.

Johnson, S. M. (2004). Attachment theory: A guide for healing couple relationships. In S. W. Rholes and J. A. Simpson (Eds.), *Adult attachment: Theory, research, and clinical implications* (pp. 367-387). New York: Guilford Publications.

Leon, C. R. (2009). Factors associated with forgiveness in intimate relationships and the impact of Hope-Focused Marriage Therapy. *Dissertation Abstracts International: Section B: The Sciences and Engineering*, 7141.

Leon, C., Ripley, J.S., Davis, W., Mazzio, L., and Smith, A. (2008, February). Forgiveness in intimate relationships: The impact of hope focused couples therapy. American Psychological Association Division 36 midwinter conference on religion and spirituality, Columbia, MD.

Marcel, G. (1962). *Homo viator: An introduction to the metaphysics of hope.* New York: Harper and Row.

Markman, H., Stanley, S., and Blumberg, S. L. (1994). *Fighting for your marriage.* San Francisco: Jossey-Bass.

Markman, H.J., Rhoades, G.K., Stanley, S.M., Ragan, E.P., Witton, S.W. (2010). The premarital communication roots of marital distress and divorce: The first five years of marriage. *Journal of Family Psychology, 24*, 289-298.

McHugh, R. K., and Barlow, D. H. (2010). The dissemination and implementation of evidence-based psychological treatments: A review of current efforts. *American Psychologist, 65*(2), 73-84.

Ripley, J.S., Borden, C.R., Albach, K., Barlow, L.L., Kemper, S.D., Valdez, S.,Babcock, J., Smith, C. and Page, M. (2002). Providing personalized feedback for marriage enrichment through distance formats: A pilot project. *Marriage and Family: A Christian Journal,* 5, 215-228.

Ripley, J. S., Leon, C., Davis, E., Smith, A.,and Worthington, E. L., Jr. (2008, August). *Hope-focused couples therapy clinical trial: Does religion matter?* Paper presented at the meeting of the American Psychological Association, Boston.

Ripley, J. S., Leon, C., Davis, W., and Worthington, E.L., Jr. (2009). *Hope-focused couples therapy manual.* [Hope project publication, 2009 edition]. Available from www.hopecouples.com.

Ripley, J. S., Maclin, V. L., Pearce, E., Tomasulo, A., Smith, A., Rainwater, S., et al. (2010, August). *Religious accommodative couples therapy: Process and outcome research.* Presented at the 118th Annual American Psychological Association National Conference, San Diego.

Ripley, J. S., and Worthington, E. L., Jr. (1998). What the journals reveal about Christian marital counseling: An inadequate (but emerging) scientific base. *Marriage and Family: A Christian Journal, 1*, 375-396.

Ripley, J. S., and Worthington, E. L., Jr. (2002). Comparison of hope-focused communication and empathy-based forgiveness group interventions to promote marital enrichment. *Journal of Counseling and Development, 80,* 452-463.

Ripley, J. S. and Worthington, E. L., Jr. (2007) *Hope Focused Marriage Counseling DVD Training*. Produced by Center for Teaching and Learning, Regent University.

Ripley, J. S., Worthington, E. L., Jr., and Maclin, V. (2011). Hope-focused couples approach to couple enrichment and counseling. In David K. Carson and Montserrat Casado-Kehoe (Eds.), *Case studies in couples therapy: Theory-based case studyapproaches* (pp. 369-381). New York: Routledge.

Ross, P. E. (2006, August). The expert mind. *Scientific American,* 64-71.

Schooler, J. W., and Engstler-Schooler, T. Y. (1990). Verbal overshadowing of visual memories: Some things are better left unsaid. *Cognitive Psychology, 22*, 36-71.

Seligman, M. E. P. (1995). The effectiveness of psychotherapy: The Consumer Reports study. *American Psychologist, 50*, 965-974.

Snyder, C. R. (1994). *The psychology of hope*. New York: Free Press.

Turner, P., and Ripley, J. S. (2007). Applying hope-focused marriage therapy to conflict resolution in marriage: Case study. *Journal of Psychology and Christianity, 26*(1), 65-67.

Waldron, V. R., and Kelley, D. L. (2008). *Communicating forgiveness*. Thousand Oaks, CA: Sage Publications.

Weiss, R. S. (1998). A taxonomy of relationships. *Journal of Social and Personal Relationships, 15*, 671-683.

Worthington, E.L., Jr. (1989). *Marriage counseling: A Christian approach to counseling couples*. Downers Grove, IL: InterVarsity Press.

Worthington, E. L., Jr. (1997). *Handling Our Problems Effectively (HOPE) and Forgiveness and Reconciliation through Experiencing Empathy (FREE): Two manuals for a clinical trial of early marriage enrichment using components of Hope-focused Marriage Enrichment*. Unpublished therapist and participant manuals, Virginia Commonwealth University, Richmond.

Worthington, E. L., Jr. (2003). *Forgiving and reconciling: Bridges to wholeness and hope*. Downers Grove, IL: InterVarsity Press.

Worthington, E. L., Jr. (2005). *Hope-focused marriage counseling: A guide to brief therapy*. Downers Grove, IL: InterVarsity Press.

Worthington, E. L., Jr. (2006). *Forgiveness and reconciliation: Theory and application*. New York: Brunner-Routledge.

Worthington, E. L., Jr., Berry, J. W., Canter, D. E., Sharp, C. B., Scherer, M., and Yarhouse, M. (2003, October). *Forgiveness and communication in marital enrichment and with parentss*. Paper presented at the Scientific Findings on Forgiveness conference, Atlanta.

Worthington, E. L., Jr., Berry, J. W., Miller, A. J., Sharp, C. B., Canter, D. E., Hook, J. N., Davis, D. E., Scherer, M., Campana, K. L., Wade, N. G., Yarhouse, M., Ripley, J. S. (2011). *Forgiveness-reconciliation and communication-conflict-resolution interventions versus retested controls in early married couples*. Unpublished manuscript under editorial review.

Worthington, E. L., Jr., Buston, B. G., and Hammonds, T. M. (1989). A component analysis of marriage enrichment: Information and treatmentmodality. *Journal for Counseling and Development, 67*, 555-560.

Worthington, E. L., Jr., and Drinkard, D.T. (2000). Promoting reconciliation through psychoeducational and therapeutic interventions. *Journal of Marital and Family Therapy, 26*, 93-101.

Worthington, E. L., Jr., Hight, T. L., Ripley, J. S., Perrone, K. M., Kurusu, T. A., and Jones, D. R. (1997). Strategic hope-focused relationship-enrichment counseling with individual couples. *Journal of Counseling Psychology, 44*, 381-389.

Worthington, E. L., Jr., Hook, J. N., Davis, D. E., and McDaniel, M. A. (2010). Religion and spirituality. *Journal of Clinical Psychology: In Session, 67*(2), 204-214.

Worthington, E. L., Jr., Lerner, A., and Sharp, C. (2005). Repairing the emotional bond versus skills training for marital intervention. *Journal of Psychology and Christianity, 24*, 259-262.

Worthington, E.L., Jr., Mazzeo, S.E., and Canter, D.E. (2005). Forgiveness-promoting approach: Helping clients REACH forgiveness through using a longer model that teaches reconciliation. In Len Sperry and Edward P. Shafranske (Eds.), *Spiritually-oriented psychotherapy* (pp. 235-257). Washington, D.C.: American Psychological Association.

Worthington, E. L., Jr., McCullough, M. E., Shortz, J. L., Mindes, E. J., Sandage, S. J., and Chartrand, J. M. (1995). Can marital assessment and feedback improve marriages? Assessment as a brief marital enrichment procedure. *Journal of Counseling Psychology, 42,* 466-475.

In: Psychotherapy
Editors: A. J. Lancaster, and O. Sharpe

ISBN 978-1-61942-611-5

Chapter 4

GRACEFUL SURRENDER: EMBODIED RELATIONAL TRANCEWORK

Asaf Rolef Ben-Shahar[1], and Grace MacDonald•
[1]The Israeli Centre for Mind-body Medicine, Ramat Hasharon, Israel

ABSTRACT

After over nine years of Jungian analysis, Grace was shocked to discover repressed memories of sexual abusesurfacing shortly after commencing psychotherapy. The focus on body, the use of hypnosis, and a relational positioning are believed to have contributed to this emergent biography, which illuminated for Grace many of her dissociative and sexualizing tendencies.

Co-written by psychotherapist and client (a psychotherapist herself), this chapter illustrates some clinical applications of relational-embodied hypnosis. Through exploring transferential and generative aspects of trance, the paper further introduces relational facets of hypnotic work, while explaining issues of touch, intimacy, regression, and influence.

Moreover, this case material presents a psychotherapeutic dialogue with surrender: surrender to the edge of love, to the charge of erotic transference, and to an intersubjective third, which threatens to touch and change both parties deeper than they intended to.

•* Asaf is an Israeli relational psychotherapist incorporating body-psychotherapy and trancework within his work. He lectures on body-psychotherapy in a variety of clinical and academic settings in Israel and Europe. He teaches body-psychotherapy at the Israeli Centre for Mind-Body Medicine and at The Centre for Relational Coaching and Psychotherapy, both in Israel.

• Grace MacDonald is the pseudonym chosen by the client, who has co-written this paper. Grace is a relational psychotherapist.Grace MacDonald is the pseudonym chosen by the client, who has co-written this paper. Grace is a relational psychotherapist.

1. Gliding through the Dark

At the height of our work together, when stories of familial physical and sexual abuse began to surface from a deeply repressed past, Grace sang to me:

> River of dreams take me with you tonight
> Islands of wonder that gleam and glow
> Under the stars
> As we glide through the dark
> To the heart of the night
> Hayley Westenra[1], River of Dreams

Aside from the obvious erotic side, Grace was expressing her deep desire to be known, to have a container, a womb, and had done so through her powerful angelic voice. As she sang, she was not a client singing to her psychotherapist. She sang as a lover would sing to her sweetheart; as a young daughter would sing admiringly to her father; as a heart would sing to nature when it celebrates its aliveness. We spoke of river Styx, which separated earth from the underworld. Grace recognized that life was awakening in her (also sexually) and she was called, for the first time in her life, to take an active stance: does she choose life? Can she let go of control? I remember closing my eyes and listening to her powerful voice, to the seductive words intertwine with Vivaldi's music, wondering what kind of father I would grow to be when my "real" daughter became a teenager.

This intense engagement characterized our therapeutic work from the beginning. On the one hand our relationship was deeply transferential and regressive. Grace kept sexualizing the therapeutic situation, deflected painful material, and expressed endless craving for a loving father. On the other hand, we shared a deeply loving equality, a creative, intelligent, and generative work. Grace dared me to open to the real, reciprocal engagement, where the centrality of the therapeutic relationship was not only transferential but also present to the *real*subjects we both were. The tension between the strong transferential pull (primary intersubjectivity) and our post-oedipal dance (the secondary intersubjectivity) created a fascinating, affect-laden and never boring journey.

Surrendering to relational flow[2] in psychotherapy has a quality of dreaming together, of opening to a space that is both in-time and transcendent of time, dreamlike and real at the same time (Bromberg, 1996). It is, as any hypnotherapist would recognize, a trance state.

When Grace started psychotherapy with me she was already an experienced psychotherapist and an experienced client. While on one hand she was reserved and softly spoken, she also readily surrendered into wider-mind (relational-trance). Our relationship had soon become a symbiotic shared self[3], accompanied by a strong eroticized paternal transference, which had later gathered novel, I-thou qualities. Our shared understanding of transference dynamics allowed us to take risks in noticing the multiplicity of dyads that have emerged. In a diary entry, Grace wrote:

---

[1] (Westenra, 2003).River of Dreams was written to the music of Vivaldi's Winter.

[2] Called by different names in different settings. Gilligan (1996), for example, speaks of *relational self*, Ogden (1999), of the *analytic third*, and Tronick (2004), of*dyadic states of consciousness*.

[3] Alsodescribed as primary intersubjectivity (Trevarthen, 1974) or regression into primary process (Nash, 1991, 2008).

> Did he know what unconscious demands I was bringing with me? Not only was I looking for a new therapist, I wanted the perfect partner, the caring father, the soul mate, the person who would be able to somatically respond to my inability to vocalize my internal struggle.

This "potential space" of transferential trance gave birth, quite from the beginning, to an emergent third entity in the room with which we continuously dialogued. Indeed, like Winnicott's transitional space (DoronandMendlovic, 1999; Winnicott, 1971), we seemed to have softly danced the edge between Grace's play area and my own.

A few weeks into the beginning of psychotherapy, Grace sat in her chair, and I was suddenly overwhelmed by visual stimulation. I usually find it difficult to visualize, so this was a truly magical experience for me. The room became filled with color and Grace's gaze was like a lighthouse. Only one corner of the room wasn't touched by her light, and Grace averted her eyes whenever she approached that spot. I became curious to know what was there, but when I looked my stomach churned. There was something lurking in that corner which existed at the juxtaposition between inner and outer reality. I found myself "sucked into" that space, and asked Grace to join me and look there, at the secret corner of the room. Following is Grace's recollection of this session:

> I was sat in the chair and Asaf was sitting opposite me. He encouraged me to stare at the top far corner of the room. It was a sunny day and the light was dancing there making little intricate patterns on the wall. I seem to remember him telling me I could close my eyes if I wanted to but that might have been my imagination because I did want to and so I did. Something strange is happening, I'm not sure I understand what but I am feeling heavy and lazy so I just drift further into… I'm not sure where I am. It's darker I can't see the sun making patterns on the wall any more and I… I feel very little. Asaf asks me where I am… I'm in my cot… 'Of course you are' he replies. Yes, of course I am I'm only two and I am crying… I don't want to be there. Suddenly I am Flinching… I desperately turn away pressing myself further back into the surface beneath me as I try to move away from the blows to my head. Images flash through my mind: a book, a hair brush, a shoe… did my big sister really hit me with all those things? Yes she did!
>
> As I come back into the room I am shaking inside. I have found an unpalatable truth. I did not see it coming and yet in some ways perhaps I did. Looking back on the session I had thought that Asaf had hypnotized me with an eye fixation induction yet when I asked him recently about this event he replied that my eyes had kept wandering to the corner of the room so he had merely encouraged me to allow my bodymind to lead the way.
>
> Following the session I wrote in my reflective journal 'the space of the therapeutic relationship holds both a promise of rescue and a threat to my precarious autonomy*too close* and *too far away.*'

When client and therapist both manage to surrender to the developing intersubjective field, they partake in a wider-mind (Bateson, 1979), which Tronick (2004; Tronick et al., 1998) called "dyadic state of consciousness" and is termed here *Relational Trance*.

A significant part of the intersubjective field takes place somatically. By learning to pay close attention to somatic countertransference[4] and by bringing it appropriately into the therapeutic dialogue with the client we might be able to learn about our clients through our own bodies.

---

[4] For example, Michael Soth (2005) discusses the therapeutic use of somatic countertransference.

2. Meeting through Grace

It is impossible to ignore Grace's physical presence. With her raven-black hair, her huge green eyes and fair skin she looks beautiful and mysterious, like a castle so vast you will never manage to explore all of its chambers. Grace met me at a workshop, where I presented my work in integrating relational psychotherapy with body and trance. At the end of the workshop she asked to work with me.

Grace had previously completed eight years of Jungian analysis with a renowned male analyst and a further year with a woman therapist. In our first session, Grace sat in her chair and looked naked and ashamed. She spoke of her sexual difficulties and fears and I felt breathless and wanted the earth to swallow me; I felt so little.

Shortly after the commencement of therapy, I asked Grace to write a concise autobiography. Her story told of an idyllic childhood in a loving family, with a later disastrous marriage to a depressive, dependent and emotionally abusive man that had turned her life sour. Reading her story I felt a great sense of unease and a strong physical nausea and stomachache. This nausea, which I had shared with Grace, accompanied me well into therapy. Only when the lost narratives started to emerge did my nausea disappear. Fairbairn understood repression as a special case of dissociation. While dissociation involved keeping the mental contents unconscious, repression involved keeping the mental structures unconscious (Wollnik, 2005).

The relational-self becomes an auxiliary organization for (potentially) loosening rigid habitual patterns in the two subjectivities from which it emerged. The self that is co-created by the therapeutic dyad may manifest a different attachment style to that of the two subjectivities. It therefore allows the therapist and client to process somatic, affective, and biographical material through their partaking in the intersubjective field. The intersubjective field provides a playground which is not only between reality and fantasy, internal and external (Winnicott, 1971), but also concurrently manifesting different attachment styles. As such, this is a fertile ground for loosening habitual patterns of relating, although it poses a threat to the therapist's *unmoved* positioning.

And, I must admit, the work with Grace terrified me. It challenged my own disorganization and my habitual ways of dealing with terror and chaos through creating internal repetitive order. Witnessing Grace making more life-affirming organizations, I could not but question myown rigidities. The emotional involvement with Grace, the dipping into enmeshed dynamics and dipping out into differentiation, these were very confusing indeed and, quite from the start, Grace featured regularly in my supervision and personal therapy sessions.

The most frightening places for me as a therapist are not found in the traumas or terror, the transferential inflammations of hate or love. Rather, they are the times where my own shame is touched. Kilborne (1998) stated that "there can be no regression without shame. Neither can there be trauma without shame" (p.227). Grace needed me to enable her utmost regression without shame[5]. To do so, I was reluctantly forced to face my own self-hate and bodily shame in a way I have not been able to previously.

Neither of us planned to meet each other's story so deeply. "The *Thou* meets me through grace," wrote Buber (1958) - "It is not found by seeking" (p. 11). Grace wrote: "Of course

[5] As Ferenczi (1932) recommended.

I had no idea at that time myself about these unconscious desires. I arrived in your room as a head separated from a body, thinking lots, feeling as little as possible - at that point terrified and I can see now, looking back, excited."

3. Grace's Story

Her father and mother were first cousins, and so Grace came into the world, the youngest of five, as a product of sin; at least, this is how her religious environment and family saw it. Grace reiterated how loving her mother and father were to each other, but the family did not look kindly at this bond. "I inwardly struggled with this knowledge as I questioned my own existence," wrote Grace, "but I had one saving grace: my singing voice."

Grace met me when she was 50-years-old. A psychodynamic psychotherapist, she was coherent and eloquent, resourceful and artistic. She narrated the story of her first marriage, which she then viewed as the starting point of her difficulties. She married young, and her first husband was sexually demanding. Grace was sexually naive, gentle, and frightened and what Mark wanted was an aggressive thrust. His disposition towards depression kicked in soon enough into their marriage, and Grace ended up caring for four children: her two daughters, her son, and Mark. Unstable and paranoid, he sought a mother in Grace as well as a wild animal in bed. Mark humiliated and crashed Grace's confidence and sense of worth, having affairs, and culminating in episodes of actively seeking the wild animal – engaging in bestiality. When one day Mark thought that someone saw him in his act, his paranoia escalated, followed by severe depressive episodes, suicide attempts, and emotional abuse of his children and his wife. Grace, forever wearing the rose-tinted-glasses, brought cakes and drinks to the psychiatric hospital to have family picnics. Overburdened with guilt, terror, and the need to support her children and keep working, Grace stayed in this relationship for many years, daring to leave the scene only when she found Ross, her current husband: a good man.

In my mind, the severity of this first relationship, and even more so Grace's responses to it, did not fit her idyllically described childhood. As soon as safe connection was established between us, and without prompting of any kind, Grace began to regularly regress in therapy. I was faced with a toddler, a young girl, a seductive teenager, a young woman. And as Grace changed I felt that I was changing too: the young father, the older father, the brother, the first husband, the second husband, and more. These spontaneous regressions were not an expression of fully-blown dissociative alters. Instead, these felt like abandoned aspects of Grace showing up in the room, telling their story, wanting to be heard. It was as if Grace was waiting for a good-enough relationship that would holdfast to her safety, allowing her to remember, repeat, and work through those traumas. It seems to me that the main criterion for this good-enoughness was surrender. Unintentionally, we surrendered, and suffered together, and healed together.

The first to emerge were memories of hitting. Her sister, six years older than her, would repeatedly and violently hit her with sharp objects while Grace was a baby in her cot. Grace recalled being tipped out of her cot. Fighting over what little attention the parents did give their children, Grace got slightly more in the first three years of her life. She was, after all, a baby. And April resented her for that and hit her. The parents did not take great notice. To protect her, Grace was locked in the attic. Grace elaborates:

> When you think of that baby experience of being tipped out of my cot and then being 'banished' upstairs out of harms way, albeit for my own good, there is good reason for an avoidant attachment? Add to this the fact that my parents whilst loving and caring were mostly wrapped up in each other and their involvement around church activities it's not surprising that I am somewhat uncomfortable being close to others; I find it difficult to trust them completely, difficult to allow myself to depend on them. I am nervous when anyone gets too close, and often, others want me to be more intimate than I feel comfortable being.

Even this physical hitting should not be seen as the beginning. By then, the psychosomatic organization of self-negating was already well at place: Grace and her siblings were perceived as dirty, even if this was not explicitly spoken. Their history merely repeated those early relational organizations, following the biblical predicament: "The fathers have eaten sour grapes, and the children's teeth are set on edge" (Jeremiah 31:29).

Then memories of sexual abuse started to come up in the sessions. These were not prompted. We sat together and when Grace started to drift I would make some subtle physical contact, take her hand or put my feet near hers, as if to ground us to the here-and-now of our relationship, and encourage Grace to allow herself to follow the rhythms of the trance. I, too, was following my own resonant trance, coming along with her. The memories emerged clear, with both visual images and somatic memories – alive in her and in my countertransference, with a narrative that became clear and was later substantiated and echoed by two of her sisters: Grace remembered her uncle's repeated sexual abuse. Here's Grace:

> Get away… suddenly out of nowhere the most disgusting taste in my mouth… I know what that is… it's horrible… I'm going to be sick… I jumped up like a thing possessed... I wanted to scrape every last bit of that stuff in my mouth out of the way… I struggle to hold back the tears as this inner body memory from three years of age makes itself known… for a moment I am back there... I even struggle to look Asaf in the eye… he is after all a man.
>
> For years afterwards if we went to visit I would hide behind a big armchair when we heard my uncle's footsteps in the alleyway. Everyone else thought it was a funny game I played.

This caught her by surprise as nothing like this had come up in nine years of previous therapy with excellent psychotherapists, where Grace could sense a presence wishing to emerge, yet none did. Here, these themes come up spontaneously, effortlessly, and very quickly into therapy. How come? Notwithstanding the contribution of her previous psychotherapeutic experiences to the *ripening* of Grace's readiness, it was probably the combination of working with touch and trance and even more so, doing it within a *relational* context that provided Grace with a safe enough container to do this important work.

Grace recalled a rape at five-years-old by a brother of a kindergarten friend, and she traced back the mechanisms of dissociation and repression that were put into place. Suddenly, the marriage to Mark, her defense mechanisms, her tendency for dissociation and her *Pollyanna* attitude all made sense, but they required the deconstruction of her self-told narrative of ideal childhood. The relational dyad provided sufficient safety to deconstruct Grace's powerfully internalized relational organizations.

4. Dreaming Together

Grace's dreams were a central axis of our work together. As she becomes aware of the repressed scenes of childhood abuse, her dreams changed. Not only was Grace bringing dreams to sessions, she also dreamt during the sessions. These powerful moments were not defensive acts (Alexander, 1976), but rather therapeutic opportunities to *work live* (e.g. Geffner, 2004). My therapeutic interventions simply facilitated holding open *the door into the flux of unknown and non-habitual organization* slightly longer. In practice, it meant noticing when a trance developed through nonverbal observation and attuning to my resonance. I then pointed such a trance out (verbally or nonverbally), and invited Grace to stay with it. Together, we were both called to surrender to the pulsating flow of dreaming. Grace writes:

> Something is definitely waking up in me… it's both scary and intriguing… I am remembering more details of events in my childhood. My dreams have increased and I find my mind drifting whenever I try to relax. I think about Freud's (1914) assertion that all therapy is remembering, repeating, and working through. This certainly seems to be the essence of our shared journey.

Relational-embodied trancework allows for a joining in with the dream in a way that brings the dream alive in the session. When the therapist surrenders into the dyadic-self, thoughts, images, feelings and memories that surface could be better understood as meaningful for the therapeutic process and not merely as intrapsychic events. Somatic countertransference becomes the simultaneous subtitles for the muted narrative of the client. Within a therapeutic relationship, each fragment of experience, however irrelevant it may seem, may be understood as belonging to the subject as well as to the intersubjective, relational self.

Tracking down the whereabouts of the client can therefore be achieved through paying close attention to the therapist's own body, all the while noticing the client's nonverbal communication. Lewis, Amini, and Lannon (2000) termed this phenomenon *limbic resonance*, acknowledging the wordless harmony we see reverberating between minds (and bodies).

In essence, we attune ourselves to our somatic countertransference – the resonance which is at the basis of all living organisms (Beck, 2006; Capra, 2002; Rolef Ben-Shahar, 2008). We turn the scrutiny of curiosity to ourselves, inasmuch as we are part of a wider-mind, examining the new somatic organization[6] of *us* in which we partake, in order to learn about the client.

A landscape that was usually pitch-black is slowly illuminated by an emergent lighthouse. The more deeply-established the relationship, the lighter it can become. This type of work is possibly parallel to the description of shamans who "travel along the strings" (Keeney, 2005, p.197). Bradford Keeney (ibid) further argued that shamans "not only move their awareness from one place to another; they also shift the locus of identity to that of the other" (p.197). Relational trancework may follow a similar processes; it means that the therapist receives a slight opening into the dream.

[6] Hasegawa and Jamieson(2002) noted that systems may be understood and analysed on different levels of organization (p.104). Dyadic states of consciousness represent a utilization of different organizational order to learn about, and intervene with, a part of that system (you, me).

As Grace regressed and uncomfortable information surfaced, she sought the presence of her absent parents to protect her, and selected me as her *surrogate father* (Tosone, 1997). The traumas Grace experienced as a child: the repeating physical harm inflicted by her sister, the sexual abuseby her uncle at two-years-old, the rape at five-years-old, these were all made worse by the lack of awareness and support from her parents. Preoccupied with paying penance for their horrible sin, her parents' children were both a celebration of their love and at the same time proof of their deviation from social and religious taboo. The two lovers, the two cousins who were meant to be with one another, were always found at church, taking little interest at the suffering of their little Grace.

One day Grace arrived to the session stirred-up and troubled by a chain of dreams. In one of these dreams, I was telling her a story. When Grace told me of her dreams I felt myself becoming part of them. Letting go into my own biography, I was partly listening to Grace and partly cruising through the places my own life-stories. A precious memory came back to me, one of the fondest episodes from my own childhood. There was a time when I was three or four during which I had become terrified of thieves. It coincided with the birth of my sister and the loss of the *only-child* status. Mom was no longer mine alone, and I turned to dad. Each night I would run to my parents' bed, waking up my father and whispering: "there is a thief in the flat." Instead of dismissing my displaced anxiety or reassuring me patronizingly, my dad would wake up every night, take the flashlight out from the drawer and walk with me around the house, showing me that there was no thief there; that I was safe. I was then allowed into my parents' bed, and dad would hold me by his side. This ritual lasted for weeks, if not months. There, in the session with Grace, I relived this feeling and found myself positioned as the father. Perhaps I too was asking to be taken by the river of dreams. There was Grace, my daughter, late at night in bed. And I watched her, a little girl not older than three, superimposed on a face of a mature woman. Below is Grace's recollection of this session:

> In the next session I recited the dreams to Asaf. I needed his reassurance and help to understand them. Rather than making an attempt to analyze the dream, he simply helped me explore various aspects of them. In some ways it was as if he encouraged me to talk as one part in the dream to another part to discover lost aspects of myself and to integrate the emotions accompanying them; I think we both sensed something horrible inside is stirring, but I am still not sure what and Asaf is not pushing to find out…If there is anything there it will reveal itself in due course no doubt. What I wanted to know was if the metaphorical story he told me in the dream was really one he would have told me? His answer was to hold me close while he whispered his own version of the story and I swear it was almost word for word... How did he remember it so accurately or did I just hear what I wanted to hear? I drifted into a pleasant trance…daddy was holding me and I was falling asleep as he read me a bedtime story. After the turmoil of the previous week I didn't want to come back to reality. No matter which; it had the desired effect and I finished the session calm and grounded.

Knowing what story to tell Grace was no psychic act, a father knows his daughter well, and at that moment of shared transferential trance I *was* her father. While Freud (1912) recommended that the analyst "must turn his own unconscious like a receptive organtowards the transmitting unconscious of the patient" (p.115), Ogden (1996) emphasized this as a reciprocal task of attending the "jointly (but asymmetrically) created unconscious construction of 'the analytic third'" (p.891)[7]. Relational embodied trancework further advocates the somatic attunement to the three bodies present: the body of the therapist, the body of the client, and the *sensed* body of the dyad. This Attunement, as Peebles (2008) noted, helps in making sense of physical sensations, images, thought, and emotions. "Attunement is not hypervigilance," She continues (ibid), "It is openness to what is there, without judgment or premature conclusions" (p. 655).

That night, Grace's dreams were not symbolic but a surfacing of a lost narrative. Grace dreamt that night a memory; the story of rape she had experienced at the age of five.

Grace's dream exemplified contained processing of traumatic material that was previously inaccessible. I believe that these were made possible also because of the shared participation in the transferential trances. I was not observing Grace's transference and interpreting it (although we did that too), but allowed our shared stories to intertwine, got lost in them – and came back.

5. Dissociation and Trancework

> Therapeutic regression offers a powerfully transformative analytic experience, a new way of reexperiencing, reliving, and restoring longed-for, long-lacking, traumatic, and inadequate primal bonding because of an early environmental-maternal failure. Therapeutic regression postulates a return to the point where psychological growth has halted and enables a living breakthrough.
>
> Ofra Eshel[8]

Research has shown (d'Ardenne, 2009) that when trauma is accompanied by grief or loss, solely behavioral approaches are inappropriate. When faced with the real drama of being human, we need more than a recipe for cure: we require another human presence to heal.

Grace dealt with strong feelings through dissociation. Dissociative responses to trauma are a common coping mechanism, separating the narrative from the intense emotional, and possibly physical pain[9]. Grace frequently used her analytic experience to camouflage her dissociation with insight. She would tell of horrendous experiences in a manner that divorced feelings from narrative, body from story.

Working with dissociative experiences has been described as the royal road to unavailable and split of experiences (Davies andFrawley, 1991; Geffner, 2004). When therapists themselves open to this material, they demonstrate to the clients that they are willing to enter the flux of pain and survive: "Dwelling in it – without losing our bearings and without drowning in the psychic deconstruction," as Borgogno(2004, p.12) wrote. This process is similar to Jessica Benjamin's (2006) poetic notion of surviving the crash. When dissociative experiences are accessed in the shared-dyadic space, there is an opportunity for change in our internalized past (Alexander, 1954; Alexander and French, 1946). Perhaps this is the source of Ferenczi's(1932) optimism that all psychic processes are reversible.

[7] Aron(1991) also acknowledged the patient's tuning in to the analyst's attitudes and feelings (p.251).

[8] (Eshel, 2005, pp.719-720).

[9] There is extensive literature on the subject. For example see Bokanowski, 2004; Bremner et al., 1992; Cardeñaand Spiegel, 1993; Holmes, Oakley, Stuart, andBrewin, 2006; Kluft, 1985; Koopman, Classen, and Spiegel, 1994; Liotti, 2004; Marmar et al., 1994; McQueen, Kennedy, Sinason, andMaxted, 2008; Peebles, 2008; Putman, 1985; Rhoades Jr., 2006a, b; Seltzer, 2005; Sinason, 2008; Spiegel, 2003.

Processing traumas within the analytic-third may release us from the repetition-compulsion that early developmental traumas often carry with them (McFarlane and van der Kolk, 1996), contributing to what Kluft(1991) termed "Sitting ducks syndrome." Unless worked through, victims of abuse tend not only to repeat their traumas but also attract retraumatisation (Rolef Ben-Shahar, 2009).

Part of the therapeutic process between Grace and me was an exchange: we began with my (inadvertent) willingness to feel on her behalf. These part-digested traumas, the heartaches, the rage and terror; what Grace could not allow herself to feel I found myself feeling in the sessions with her and I let her know it. My role in the dyadic self was oftentimes to feel and name the unspeakable: *I am angry, I am terrified, I feel excited*. The relational-self, to the degree that it was an attachment-organization, was able to contain more than either of us could separately. Grace wrote:

> In some ways my returning memories helped to make sense of the dysfunctional course of my adult life. Just as in my previous therapies my first marriage came under the spotlight. I could recount many traumatic incidents almost without showing any emotion. I remember Asaf's typical response was to express his current reactions to what I had just said or done; 'Right now, I'm feeling angry as you're telling me about this'. His comments really had an impact, making me stop and think. Should I be feeling angry?

It was therefore not *I* who bore witness to the unspoken stories of Grace, it was *us*. When the narrative was uttered – it was uttered by the two of us. I frequently spoke the affect, and Grace unveiled the story. And when she was able to hold the two together, to speak and feel, a true transformation took place. She was first able to own her terror, then her anger, then her sexuality, her love, her hate. Frequently, I was the first safe object of these feelings. Later, they began expressing in her life too.

Grace started investing more in making her partnership equal, asserting herself and discovering the possible areas for her to explore sexually, and those that were still unsafe. At work, Grace left her institutional work and increased her private practice, and is a very busy and sought after psychotherapist. Perhaps more than all that, life flows through her now. It was not only I who met her through Grace; more importantly, it was her own meeting with herself.The re-entry into life goes through the river Styx. There, at the edge, when the depressive movement of mourning had been acknowledged, the lost childhood (and fantasies) grieved for, a boat awaits us. It is we who are the boatman, as were called to take those aspects of ourselves who sacrificed everything for love and grieve over their failure. Those sacrifices did not make us lovable; they did not deliver their promise. When we can compassionately choose life in face of the death of our old relational organizations, it means we can breathe into our trauma, and then it "loses its grip" on us (Hendricks, 1995).

6. Permission to Flow: Ventures to a Wider Mind

> Behind the wall we erect to protect ourselves from the history of our childhood still stands the neglected child we once were, the child that was once abandoned and betrayed. It waits for us to summon the courage to hear its voice. It wants to be protected and understood, and it wants us to be free from its isolation, loneliness, and speechlessness. But this child that

> has waited so long for our attention not only has needs to be fulfilled. It also has a gift for us, a gift that we desperately need if we truly want to live, a gift that cannot be purchased and that the child in us alone can bestow. It is the gift of truth, which can free us from the prison of destructive opinions and conventional lies. Ultimately, it is the gift of security, which our rediscovered integrity will give us. The child only waits for us to be ready to approach it, and then, together, we will tear down the walls.
>
> Alice Miller[10]

Two years into therapy, Grace arrived deeply unsettled to the session. The day before she witnessed an accident by two reckless bikers, and after assessing that it was not safe for her there, Grace decided to leave the scene. She felt guilty and remorseful. Is it always bad to leave the scene?

It was the first time Grace had left the scene. She had remained in her familial scene, loyal and loving, without questioning her own interest. She stayed by the side of her abusive dysfunctional husband, out of sense of duty, shame, and desire to give her children a family.

Even though I loved Grace from very early on, it was only when she *left the scene* that I started to trust her. The walls of silence were only then truly broken. Her tendency to lean towards the positive transference and idealize me had since been balanced by her assertive, challenging, and sometimes critical voice.

The way we sensed our connection has changed. Alongside the transference-countertransference dynamics, which were changing all the time, we discovered joy in meeting as people. Our positioning against one another shifted, and as it coincided with our planned ending, our resistance to the relational-self decreased, we both embraced the opportunity to spend time with each other and grow despite (perhaps also because of) the threat of heartbreak. I found Mindell's(1982) description of working with the *dreambody* very close to my experience of the last eighteen months of therapy with Grace: "Understanding the dreambody requires a feeling for the field in which the body exists, or, formulated less classically, understanding the body requires experiencing the field of which the body is a part" (p.17).

Trevarthen's(1974) differentiation between primary and secondary intersubjectivity is central to this paper's argument. I postulate that the analytic third is a trance process, having both regressive aspects (transferential dynamics) (McLaughlin, 1991; Nash, 1991, 2008) and progressive aspects (newness) (Mitchell andAron, 1999). Every intersubjective meeting includes both elements, and the therapeutic process therefore aims at changing the balance between the two. The *relational-self* is seen here as our primary way of attaining self-regulation and reorganization. Trance poses a greater threat to our habitual organization (Pulver, 1963) and as such it amplifies our flight into collective, relational self.

This amplification was traditionally seen as accentuating the *transference neurosis*(Freud, 1921, 1925; Mitchell, 2005; Pulver, 1963), and contaminating the therapeutic relationship with untraceable influences. While this regressive and potentially premature development of transference neurosis can occur in hypnotic therapies, it may be understood as existing alongside the potential for deeply engaging, progressive and novel intersubjective field. Navigating within the transferential matrix and the levels of intersubjectivity is not, and will hopefully never be, a precise science.

---

[10] (Miller, 1993, p.3).

If transference and countertransference are indeed like the weather, as Mitchell (2005) posed, continually changing but forever with us, then perhaps it is time to reconsider the inclusion of trance in psychotherapy. Indeed, tranceintroduces strong impactful affect into the therapeutic relationship and therefore needs to be closely monitored (as well as supported by good training and ongoing supervision and therapy), but it also offers unique opportunities for deepening human contact and for therapeutic growth and change.

The relational field between Grace and me was present from start. The quality of this analytic-third has changed and matured, not unlike the two subjectivities from which it emerged. We have both allowed the river of dreams to open us to the possibility of meeting one another. We have both grown and emerged from our shared-self happier and healthier, more able to relate, and slightly less shamed.ollowing is Grace's summary of our joint work, and this paper.

> In the sense that a therapist helps his client discover their own value as a person, psychotherapy is erotic, and as I discovered through my therapeutic journey with Asaf, it works best when the therapist and client learn to discern subtle and deep dynamics in the relationship. We have touched upon one of the most difficult and risky aspects of psychotherapy: these dynamics are risky because transference-countertransference dynamics is about love, sexual and romantic love. As I discovered in our work together these should not be something to be feared or avoided. Worked with sensitively and with awareness, I discovered life-affirming, playful, and nourishing connection.
>
> The willingness to surrender into connection was what characterized our work together, and this meant I had to put the trauma of the past into adult language, so as to 'break the spell,' of the past. It's a bit like how in the fairy tale of *Rumpelstiltskin* the queen was able to free herself from her dilemma by discovering Rumpelstiltskin's true name. I learned how profound, difficult, and beautiful this healing journey can be, and have felt blessed to make this journey within the true healing dyad of attentive listening and holding.
>
> When the therapist is able to promote an open discussion of issues related to erotic dynamics in psychotherapy, and has the courage to risk responding directly from his unconscious, allowing a true meeting of selves, while still maintaining the analytic frame, there is the possibility of a truly transformative therapeutic experience.
>
> The most delicious aspect of romance isn't the physical sexuality, but the sense of discovery of self which comes through reflected admiration. It's incredible that someone else admires, or enjoys, or celebrates aspects of your personality which you had taken for granted or perhaps even devalued. This kind of love profoundly reorganizes the sense of self, expands it, and establishes a stronger and more positive self-representation.
>
> I truly believe that I could not have completed this therapeutic journey without both of us, not just me, surrendering to relational flow.

REFERENCES

Alexander, F. (1954).Some quantitative aspects of psychoanalytic technique. *Journal of the American Psychoanalytic Association, 2*, 687-702.

Alexander, F., and French, T. M. (1946). *Psychoanalytic therapy*.New York: Ronald Press.

Alexander, R. P. (1976). On Patient's Sleep During the Psychoanalytic Session. *Contemporary Psychoanalysis, 12*, 277-291.

Aron, L. (1991). The patient's experience of the analyst's subjectivity. In S. A. Mitchell and L. Aron (Eds.), *Relational Psychoanalysis: The Emergence of a Tradition* (pp. 243-268). New York: The Analytic Press. 1999.

Bateson, G. (1979). *Mind and Nature: A Necessary Unity*. Cresskill, NJ: Hampton Press, 2002.

Beck, W. (2006).Countertransference in Groups. *Group Analysis, 39*(1), 100-107.

Benjamin, J. (2006). Crash: What We Do When We Cannot Touch: Commentary on Paper by MeiraLikierman. *Psychoanalytic Dialogues, 16*, 377 - 385.

Bokanowski, T. (2004). Splitting, fragmenting, and mental agony: the clinical thinking of Sandor Ferenczi. *International Forum of Psychoanalysis, 13*(1), 20 - 25.

Borgogno, F. (2004). Why Ferenczi today? The contribution of Sandor Ferenczi to the understanding and healing of psychic suffering. *International Forum of Psychoanalysis, 13*(1), 5 - 13.

Bremner, J. D., Southwick, S., Brett, E., Fontana, A., Rosenheck, R., andCharney, D. S. (1992). Dissociation and posttraumatic stress disorder in Vietnam combat veterans. *American Journal of Psychiatry, 149*, 328-332.

Bromberg, P. M. (1996). Standing in spaces: The multiplicity of self and the psychoanalytic relationship. *Contemporary Psychoanalysis, 32*, 500-535.

Buber, M. (1958).*I and Thou* (R. G. Smith, Trans.).New York: Scribner.

Capra, F. (2002). *The Hidden Connections*.London: Flamingo.

Cardeña, E., and Spiegel, D. (1993).Dissociative reactions to the San Francisco Bay Area earthquake of 1989. *American Journal of Psychiatry, 150*, 474-478.

d'Ardenne, P. (2009).The aftermath of trauma. *Sexual and Relationship Therapy, 24*(1), 1 - 3.

Davies, J. M., andFrawley, M. G. (1991).Dissociative processes and transference-countertransference paradigms in the psychoanalytically oriented treatment of adult survivors of childhood sexual abuse. In S. A. Mitchell and L. Aron (Eds.), *Relational Psychoanalysis* (pp. 269-304). Hilsdale, NJ: The Analytic Press, 1999.

Doron, A., andMendlovic, S. (1999). Hypnosis and Winnicott's Transitional Phase. *Contemporary Hypnosis, 16*(1), 36-39.

Eshel, O. (2005). A Bond of Love, Emotional Risk, and Daring. *Psychoanalytic Dialogues, 15*, 717-725.

Ferenczi, S. (1932).*The Clinical Diary of Sándor Ferenczi*. Cambridge: HarvardUniversity Press, 1988.

Freud, S. (1912). Recommendations to physicians practising psycho-analysis. In J. Strachey (Ed.), *The Standard Edition of the Complete Psychological Works of Sigmund Freud* (Vol. 12, pp. 109-120). London: Hogarth Press.

Freud, S. (1914). Remembering, repeating and working-through (further recommendations on the technique of psycho-analysis II) In J. Strachey (Ed.), *The Standard Edition of the Complete Psychological Works of Sigmund Freud* (Vol. 12, pp. 145-156). London: Hogarth Press, 1958.

Freud, S. (1921). Group psychology and the analysis of the ego. In J. Strachey (Ed.), *The Standard Edition of the Complete Psychological Works of Sigmund Freud* (Vol. 18, pp. 65-143). London: Hogarth Press, 1955.

Freud, S. (1925). An autobiographical study. In J. Strachey (Ed.), *The Standard Edition of the Complete Psychological Works of Sigmund Freud* (Vol. 20, pp. 1-74). London: Hogarth Press, 1959.

Geffner, A. H. (2004). "To Sleep, Perchance to Dream" ... on the Couch: The Interpersonal Nature of Dreams and Other Dissociative Processes - A Case Illustration. *Psychoanalytic Dialogues, 14*(1), 139 - 162.

Gilligan, S. G. (1996). The relational self: An expanding of love beyond desire. In S. G. Gilligan (Ed.), *The Legacy of Milton H. Erickson: Selected papers of Stephen Gilligan* (pp. 254-281). Phoenix: Zeig, Tucker andTheisen, 2002.

Hasegawa, H., and Jamieson, G. A. (2002). Conceptual Issues in Hypnosis Research: Explanations, Definitions and the State/Non-State Debate. *Contemporary Hypnosis, 19*(3), 103-117.

Hendricks, G. (1995). *Conscious Breathing: Breathwork for Health, Stress Release, and Personal Mastery*. New York: Bantam Books.

Holmes, E. A., Oakley, D. A., Stuart, A. D. P., andBrewin, C. R. (2006). Investigating Peri-Traumatic Dissociation Using Hypnosis During a Traumatic Film. *Journal of Trauma and Dissociation, 7*(4), 91 - 113.

Keeney, B. (2005). *Bushman Shaman: Awakening the Spirit through Ecstatic Dance*. Rochester, Vermont: Destiny Books.

Kilborne, B. (1998). Ferenczi, Regression and Shame. *International Forum of Psychoanalysis, 7*(4), 225 - 229.

Kluft, R. P. (1985). The Natural History of Multiple Personality Disorder.In R. P. Kluft (Ed.), *Childhood antecedents of multiple personality* (pp. 197-238). Washington, DC: American Psychiatric Press.

Kluft, R. P. (1991). Multiple personality disorder. In A. Tasman and S. Goldfinger (Eds.), *Review of Psychiatry* (pp. 375-384). Washington, DC: American Psychiatric Press.

Koopman, C., Classen, C., and Spiegel, D. (1994). Predictors of posttraumatic stress symptoms among survivors of the Oakland/Berkeley, Calif., firestorm. *American Journal of Psychiatry, 151*, 888-894.

Lewis, T., Amini, F., andLannon, R. (2000). *A General Theory of Love*.New York: Random House.

Liotti, G. (2004). Trauma, dissociation, and disorganized attachment: Three strands of a single braid. *Psychotherapy: Theory Research, Practice, Training, 11*(4), 472-486.

Marmar, C. R., Weiss, D. S., Schlenger, W. E., Fairbank, J. A., Jordan, B. K., Kulka, R. A., et al. (1994). Peritraumatic dissociation and posttraumatic stress in male Vietnam theater veterans. *American Journal of Psychiatry, 151*, 902-907.

McFarlane, A. C., and van der Kolk, B. A. (1996).Trauma and Its Challenge to Society. In B. A. Van der Kolk, A. C. McFarlane and L. Weisæth (Eds.), *Traumatic Stress: The Effects of Overwhelming Experience on Mind, Body, and Society* (pp. 24-46). New York: Guilford Press.

McLaughlin, J. T. (1991). Clinical and theoretical aspects of enactment.*Journal of the American Psychoanalytic Association, 39*, 595-614.

McQueen, D., Kennedy, R., Sinason, V., andMaxted, F. (Eds.).(2008). *Psychoanalytic Psychotherapy after Child Abuse*.London: Karnac Books.

Miller, A. (1993). *Breaking Down the Wall of Silence*.New York: Meridian.

Mindell, A. (1982). *Dreambody*.Henley-on-Thames: RoutledgeandKegan Paul.

Mitchell, S. A. (2005). *Influence and Autonomy in Psychoanalysis*. Hillsdale, N.J: The Analytic Press.

Mitchell, S. A., andAron, L. (1999).Preface. In S. Mitchell and L. Aron (Eds.), *Relational Psychoanalysis: The Emergence of a Tradition* (pp. ix-xx). New York: The Analytic Press.

Nash, M. R. (1991). Hypnosis as a special case of psychological regression. In S. J. Lynn and J. W. Rhue (Eds.), *Theories of Hypnosis: Current Models and Perspectives* (pp. 171-196). London: The Guilford Press.

Nash, M. R. (2008). A psychoanalytic theory of hypnosis: a clinically informed approach. In M. R. Nash and A. J. Barnier (Eds.), *TheOxford Handbook of Hypnosis: Theory, Research and Practice* (pp. 201-222). Oxford: OxfordUniversity Press.

Ogden, T. H. (1996). Reconsidering three aspects of psychoanalytic technique. *International Journal of Psychoanalysis, 77*(883-899).

Ogden, T. H. (1999). Afterword: The analytic third, overview. In S. A. Mitchell and L. Aron (Eds.), *Relational Psychoanalysis: The Emergence of a Tradition* (pp. 487-492). New York: The Analytic Press.

Peebles, M. J. (2008). Trauma-related disorders and dissociation. In M. R. Nash and A. J. Barnier (Eds.), *TheOxford Handbook of Hypnosis: Theory, Research and Practice* (pp. 647-679). Oxford: OxfordUniversity Press.

Pulver, S. E. (1963). Delusions Following Hypnosis.*International Journal of Clinical and Experimental Hypnosis, 11*(1), 11 - 22.

Putman, F. W. (1985). Dissociation as a response to extreme trauma.In R. P. Kluft (Ed.), *Childhood antecedents of multiple personality* (pp. 65-97).Washington, DC: American Psychiatric Press.

Rhoades Jr., G. F. (2006a). Cross-Cultural Aspects of Trauma and Dissociation.*Journal of Trauma Practice, 4*(1), 21 - 33.

Rhoades Jr., G. F. (2006b). Trauma and Dissociation in Paradise (Hawaii).*Journal of Trauma Practice, 4*(1), 133-145.

Rolef Ben-Shahar, A. (2008). Resonance: The gift of connection. *Self and Society, A Journal of Humanistic Psychology in Britain, 36*(1), 45-48.

Rolef Ben-Shahar, A. (2009). Trees in shades of grey: Trauma, attachment and dissociation in the personal, clinical and socio–political settings. *Attachment: New Directions in Psychotherapy and Relational Psychoanalysis, 3*(2), 121-143.

Seltzer, W. J. (2005). Pre-cognitive therapy: A way to integrate neuroscience and psychotherapy. *Journal of Systemic Therapies, 24*(3), 32-48.

Sinason, V. (2008). From social conditioning to mind control. In A. Sachs and G. Galton (Eds.), *Forensic Aspects of Dissociative Identity Disorder* (pp. 167-184). London: Karnac Books.

Soth, M. (2005).Embodied countertransference.In N. Totton (Ed.), *New Dimensions in Body-Psychotherapy* (pp. 40-55). Maidenhead: Open University Press.

Spiegel, D. (2003). Hypnosis and Traumatic Dissociation: Therapeutic Opportunities. *Journal of Trauma and Dissociation, 4*(3), 73-90.

Tosone, C. (1997). Sandor Ferenczi: Forerunner of modern short-term psychotherapy. *Journal of Analytic Social Work, 4*(3), 23 - 41.

Trevarthen, C. (1974). Conversations with a 2-month-old. *New Scientist, 2*, 230-235.

Tronick, E. Z. (2004). Why is connection with other so critical? The formation of dyadic states of consciousness and the expansion of individual's states of consciousness: coherence governed selection and the co-creation of meaning out of messy meaning making. In J. Nadeland D. Muir (Eds.), *Emotional Development - Recent Research Advances* (pp. 293-316). Oxford: OxfordUniversity Press.

Tronick, E. Z., Bruschweiler-Stern, N., Harrison, A. M., Lyons-Ruth, K., Morgan, A. C., Nahum, J. P., et al. (1998).Dyadically expanded states of consciousness and the process of therapeutic change. *Infant Mental Health Journal, 19*(3), 277-353.

Westenra, H. (2003). Pure: Decca Records / Universal Music New Zealand.

Winnicott, D. W. (1971). *Playing and reality*.London: Routledge.

Wollnik, S. (2005).Dissociation and repression in trauma. In J. S. Scharffand D. E. Scharff (Eds.), *The Legacy of Fairbairn and Sutherland* (pp. 121 - 128). Hove: Routledge.

In: Psychotherapy
Editors: A. J. Lancaster, and O. Sharpe

ISBN 978-1-61942-611-5

Chapter 5

Effects of Perceived Parental Bonding on Therapeutic Attachment Avoidance and Patients' Attitude toward Psychotherapy

András Láng
Institute of Psychology, University of Pécs, Hungary

Abstract

Attachment theory originating from the work of John Bowlby and Mary Ainsworth has been an influential paradigm in psychoanalysis, developmental and general psychology over the last 50 years bridging the gap between academic and clinical psychology. Representing a lifelong developmental perspective and having a relational emphasis attachment theory has become a very fruitful ground for practice and research of psychotherapy as well. Early infant-caregiver relations are pivotal for attachment theory and are the source of transference in the process of psychotherapy. Although there are studies proving the effect of early childhood memories on transference and therapeutic relationship in general, the effect of perceived parental bonding on the therapeutic relationship has not been investigated yet in a systematic attachment perspective. Moreover, the possible effect of perceived parental bonding on patients' attitude toward psychotherapy has been ignored.

In the study presented, psychotherapy patients (n=97) completed Parental Bonding Instrument, Attachment Avoidance in Therapy Scale and three items on attitude toward their psychotherapy in progress. Results show that a model consisting of six parental bonding scales, duration of psychotherapy and therapeutic attachment avoidance predicts 28 per cent of variance for attitude toward psychotherapy. Paternal care and therapeutic attachment avoidance proved to be significant predictors. Moreover, hierarchical linear modeling shows that paternal care and duration of psychotherapy have an indirect effect on patients' attitude mediated by attachment avoidance. The possible interpretations of this specific paternal contribution to experiencing psychotherapy relationship and attitude toward psychotherapy are discussed.

Introduction

Bowlby formulated attachment theory not only to understand infant-caregiver relation in a developmental, cognitive and ethological perspective, but also to reframe therapeutic work (Bowlby 1977). Clinical propagation of attachment theory always laid at the heart of Bowlby (Ainsworth and Bowlby 1991). Proposing certain stability in patterns of interpersonal relating, attachment theory is an ideal theoretical framework for investigating effects of early childhood experiences on adult functioning. Such an important functioning in adult patients is relating to the therapist. Early childhood factors influencing adult relationships – including that with a psychoanalyst – were described by Freud circa 100 years ago (Freud and Breuer 1985). In this chapter connections between psychoanalytic conceptualization of the therapeutic relationship and attachment are presented, along with a study aimed at observing the effects of perceived parental bonding on patient-therapist attachment and patients' attitude toward psychotherapy.

Patient-Therapist Relationship in Psychoanalysis – from Transference to Intersubjectivity

This part of the chapter does not intend to fully summarize 100 years of psychoanalytic history considering patient-therapist relation as title could imply. The aims of this part are twofold: (1) to give a working definition of transference, and to present how early childhood experiences get transferred from parents to therapist; (2) to emphasize the relational shift in psychoanalysis, and to present how modes of early relating are transferred to psychotherapy relationship.

International Dictionary of Psychoanalysis defines transference as a term denoting “a shift onto another person – usually the psychoanalyst – of feelings, desires, and modes of relating formerly organized or experienced in connection with persons in the subject’s past whom the subject was highly invested in” (Denis 2005, p. 1776). The idea is praised by Luborsky and colleagues (1985) as the grandest clinical hypothesis of Freud. Another highly important approach describes transference as a mode of patients’ remembering the events, which unconsciously cause psychological pain (Ursano, Sonnenberg and Lazar 2004). Importance of transference lays not only in its role in understanding relationship and inner world of the patient, but in transference being the principle of an effective technique in treatment. In psychodynamic approach transference enables patients’ problems to reanimate “here and now” in therapy, thereby delivering a chance to deeply explore the problem. Representing the essence of dynamic psychotherapies, short-term dynamic psychotherapy utilizes transference interpretation as heart of its work. In this method therapeutic work is done in two triangles: the triangle of conflict and the triangle of persons (Davanloo 2005). Work in the triangle of persons concentrates on revealing the connection between past and present relationships and transference. In short-term dynamic therapies the work of the therapist has been shifted from being an object of projection to a more active role.

This shift toward a more active role of analyst occurred already as soon as the work of Sándor Ferenczi, one of the prominent representatives of the Budapest School of Psychoanalysis. Unlike Freud he encouraged analysands to become a participant in the encounter created by the therapeutic dyad (Haynal 1993). Already present in the notion of corrective emotional experience (Alexander 1935) or the analyst becoming a real person for the alanysand in Lacanian psychoanalysis as a stage of relationship development after the transference interval (Fink 2000), the real advent of relational psychoanalysis was in the 1970s. The intersubjective approach of Kohutian self psychology deeply pervades both technique and epistemology. Kohut (1971, 1977) emphasized serving the narcissistic needs of the patient and thereby enabling transformational internalization which makes split parts of the self integrated. During this process therapist becomes a selfobject for the patient, lending his own self functions to the patient with fragmented self. Continuing with Kohutian tradition Stolorow and Atwood (1996) emphasize the intersubjective nature of the self. Accordingly, organization of the self always takes place in the encounter of two subjects, i.e. in the intersubjective space. They introduce the notion of selfobject transference, which contains patient's need for growth-motivating approval, the wish for the therapist to become a selfobject for him. According to Greenspan (1989) patient and therapist build a self-corrective relationship, which he calls reparative motherhood from the perspective of the therapist. Relation is always adjusted to the developmental level of the patient, emphasizing therefore attunement, optimal distance regulation and lending his self by the therapist as influential curative factors.

It is easily seen as common to all ideas above that therapist/analyst is not considered as neutral any more. Relation becomes formed not only by patients' transference, but a mutual process of co-construction by patient and therapist. Early influence is not ignored, but the role of therapist has shifted from being the passive receiver of transference to a therapist, who actively takes part in the establishment of the relationship. This relational shift is present in John Bowlby's (1977) ideas about psychotherapy as well. In the next part attachment-informed approach to therapeutic relation is introduced.

Transference and Relationship from Attachment Perspective – Theory, Practice and Research

As early as in the mid 1970s Bowlby (1977) proposed an attachment theory based reinterpretation of the therapeutic relationship and process. Accordingly five tasks of therapist were suggested:

a) To provide a secure base for the patient as a starting point for exploration. The existence of this secure base enables the patient to explore inner and outer, past and present environment, even if it would be unbearable alone.
b) To accompany the patient on these explorative journeys.
c) To encourage the patient to thoroughly observe and analyze the therapeutic relationship.
d) To support the patient in exploring the attachment history of actual perceptions and expectations.
e) To encourage the patient to evaluate his modes of relating, whether they are in accordance with present and future plans. This evaluation – and resulting possible reframing – guarantees the patient to be able to think and act in relative freedom.

Tasks c) and d) together can be considered as a reformulation of transference work, while on the other hand tasks a) and b) point to a more active role of the therapist in co-constructing therapeutic work together with the patient. According to the importance of security in his theory, Bowlby (1977) emphasized feelings of security or insecurity in transference contrasted with Freud's focus on childhood wishes – most of them sexual in nature. The transference of early attachment experiences to the therapeutic relationship is highly plausible considering the evidence for stability in attachment patterns. Fonagy and Target (2003) name five explanatory models for the continuity of interpersonal experiences, i.e. attachment patterns. (1) The most simple model suggests continuity in social environment, e.g. quality of caregiving as cause of stability. (2) The representations of interpersonal relationships as self-sustaining organizations governing perception, cognition and motivations also lead to continuity. (3) Thirdly a biological model is suggested: stability of attachment patterns are produced by continuity in organization of the nervous system and in gene expression. (4) The fourth model emphasizes regulation. Different attachment patterns as regarded as optimal modes of regulation in the given caregiving environment. These modes of relational regulation also mediate affective processes, thereby leading to stable modes of self-regulation. (5) As last mentalization as a mediator responsible for stability is suggested. As for empirical evidence, Scharfe and Bartholomew (1994) proved moderate to high stability of adult attachment patterns in an 8 month follow-up study of 114 young adults. Waters, Merrick, Treboux, Crowell and Albersheim (2000) found in a 20 years follow-up study, that 72 per cent of the persons in young adulthood received the same (insecure vs. secure) attachment category as at 12 months of age in Ainsworth's Strange Situation. Children experiencing a negative life event (e.g. loss of parent, divorce of parents, abuse) based on maternal report changed attachment category more frequently than children whose mothers did not report negative life events (44 vs. 22 per cents respectively). These results show that internal working models of attachment, i.e. representations guiding attachment behavior work in a self-sustaining manner. By guiding not only output, but the processing of input as well (how interpersonal encounters are perceived) they remain stable to a great extent. Yet they remain open to new, pervasive experiences such as negative life events or experience of a therapeutic relationship. This openness enables therapists to work with and transform attachment representations.

Wallin (2007) suggests different techniques and modes of relating for therapists to successfully transform prevailing attachment representations and behavioral patterns of their patients. Dismissing patients (Adult Attachment Interview analogue of avoidant attachment) lack emotional depth and devalue interpersonal relations as a result of their experiences with rejecting, cold caregivers in childhood. This obstacle can be best prevented if therapist is empathically attuned, monitors and discloses his countertransference feelings. But this is not enough, it can even scare away patients. Therapist must utter authentic feelings as well to give an example for the patient and to establish real relationship. In the case of preoccupied patients (Adult Attachment Interview analogue of anxious attachment) aim of the therapy should be to make it unnecessary for patients to visualize themselves with overflowing affects and anxiety as they did with unpredictable childhood caregivers. This is best achieved by letting denied ambitions and strengths come to the surface. Besides promoting autonomy, setting boundaries with empathy should soothe chaotic affects – mostly rage. Finally patients with unresolved trauma or loss should be assisted to integrate and verbalize dissociated experiences. This can be achieved through the establishment of a secure relationship with elimination of projective identification and other primitive defense mechanisms.

In the narrative approach of Holmes (1999) work with life narratives is in focus. Therapy is a process of deconstruction of an existing and mutual construction of a new life history. According to Barclay and Smith (1992) autobiographical memories can serve self- and interpersonal regulation. The same applies for attachment patterns as well. Avoidant attachment is a pattern generated by affect deactivation, while anxious attachment by affect hyperactivation as seen previously (e.g. Wallin 2007). These modes of regulation are present in patients' ability to create narratives. In case of a dismissing patient with idealizing, poor and unemotional narrative task of the therapist is to construct a narrative together with the patient congruent with his feelings. Holmes (1999) calls this story-making. Opposite has to be done in case of a preoccupied patient. Story-breaking means the deconstruction of patient's overflowing narrative with inadequate emotional outbursts. Naturally this deconstruction is followed by the co-construction of a new narrative.

Above a short summary was given considering the theory and practice of transference work from an attachment perspective. Next in this part of the chapter, former studies investigating effects of recalled childhood experiences on psychotherapy relationship are presented. In a study using a sample of 76 female clients Mallinckrodt, Coble and Gant (1995) showed that recalled parental bonding – especially bond with father – and clients' ratings of working alliance were moderately correlated. The same moderate correlation was found between recalled parental bonding and adult attachment measured as a social competency. Multiple regression analyses indicated that recalled parental bonds accounted for more variance in ratings of working alliance than social competencies (self-efficacy and adult attachment). In another study by Brent Mallinckrodt (1991) 102 client-counselor dyads were surveyed. Results indicated a moderate association between paternal care and counselor rated working alliance. No connection between client rated working alliance and recalled parental bonding was found. As described in the theoretical part above relation between patient and therapist as attachment cannot be equated with transference alone. Attachment to therapist contains both of the two other components of a therapeutic bond – working alliance and real relationship (Gelso and Carter 1994). This is evidenced by a study including therapeutic attachment as a measured variable (Woodhouse, Schlosser, Crook, Ligiéro and Gelso 2003). Results of this study showed that while secure attachment is correlated with frequency of negative transference, it is independent from frequency of positive transference. This shows that security of the therapeutic attachment is not simply a direct consequence of positive transference feelings and modes of relating (relative independence from frequency of positive transference). The other half of the results (correlation with negative transference) points out that patient-therapist attachment is crucial for negative transference to show.

Although studies presented above suggest a connection between childhood experiences or recollections of these memories – especially paternal care – and the therapeutic relationship, a methodologically systematic attachment approach (measuring therapeutic relationship from attachment perspective) in the field or a study investigating the effects of childhood memories on patients' attitude toward therapy are still wanting. The study presented in this chapter is aimed at making good for this absence.

Goal of the Study, Hypothetical Model

To investigate the effect of perceived parental bonding and patients' therapeutic attachment avoidance on attitude toward psychotherapy a hierarchical model was proposed and tested. In this model (Figure 1.) memories of childhood experience with parents were expected to affect attitude toward psychotherapy via the therapeutic relationship, namely via therapeutic attachment avoidance.

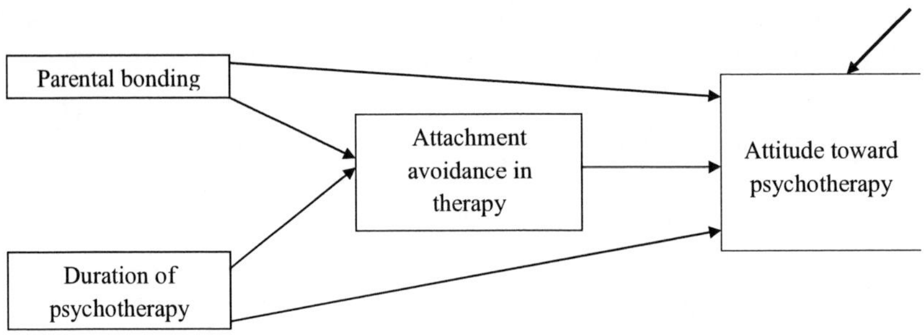

Figure 1. Effects of perceived parental bonding, duration of psychotherapy and attachment avoidance in therapy on attitude toward psychotherapy (hypothetical model).

It means that memories of parental bonding were expected to become a part of patients' perception of their relationship with the therapist – as proposed by the concept of transference, and to influence attitude toward psychotherapy through therapeutic attachment avoidance.

Method

Participants

Terms of intake for the study consisted of two conditions. First, participants must have participated in a psychotherapy running for more than three months, but not in the phase of termination. The fulfillment of this latter condition – being not in the phase of termination – depended on therapists' decision. Method or technique of psychotherapy was not predetermined, since patients' attachment to therapist is to be formed in every kind of psychotherapy irrespective of being an issue in therapy or not. Second, participants must have been older than 18 years of age. A total of 97 patients (out of 112 recruited) completed the questionnaire booklet fully. Incomplete respondents were omitted from the sample. 72.2 per cent of the patients were female (n=70). The average age of the patients in the sample was 35.26 years (SD = 10.55 years), the average duration of the psychotherapy 64.04 weeks (SD = 80.07 weeks). 78.4 per cent of the patients had high-school graduation or higher level of education(n=76).

Procedure

Participants received measures in an open envelop. Scales were completed either individually by patients in their homes, or in the case of inpatients during their free time in hospital. Participants returned the completed booklet in closed envelops dropping them into closed boxes. Therapists returned the questionnaire in person. Both therapists and patients gave their informed consent on participation. Neither patients nor therapists received any reward for participation.

Measures

Data on demographic and psychotherapy variables were collected from patients and therapists respectively. Matching of data was based on a code derived from name and date of birth. Codes allowed for patients to remain anonymous.

Attachment Avoidance in Therapy Scale (AATS). The AATS is an instrument developed by author and colleagues (Láng, Péley, Barlay and Bernáth 2011) to measure patients' attachment to therapist in terms of attachment avoidance. AATS measures three subscales of attachment avoidance, the score of which can be summed into a single indicator of attachment avoidance in general. In this study the 12-items measure was used as a unidimensional instrument. Previous psychometric work proved the instrument to have good internal reliability (Láng et al. 2011; Cronbach's alpha = .79 for general attachment avoidance in therapy).

Attitude toward psychotherapy. Attitude toward psychotherapy was measured by evaluation of three statements concerning patients' psychotherapy in progress on a 7-point Likert-scale ranging from 'totally disagree' to 'totally agree'. The first statement referred to the usefulness of psychotherapy, the second to the pleasantness of psychotherapy sessions, and the third to hope in recovery with help of psychotherapy. These components of attitude are all important indices of a successful psychotherapy session or positive psychotherapy outcome. Points obtained for the three statements were summed up into a single measure (Cronbach's alpha = .63) referring to an overall attitude toward psychotherapy.

Parnetal Bonding Instrument (H-PBI). The Hungarian version of Parental Bonding Instrument (Parker, Tupling and Brown 1979; Hungarian version Tóth and Gervai 1999) was used to measure patients' recollection of childhood memories in terms of parental bonding. Items describing different possible parental behaviors are evaluated according to how much the given behavior was characteristic of mother and father. H-PBI measures three aspects of parental behavior: (1) love and care, (2) control, and (3) overprotection.

Statistical Analyses

The hypothesized model was tested with hierarchical regression analysis. Enter method regression analyses were run on PC with SPSS 17.0 for Windows software.

RESULTS

The hypothesized model was tested with consecutive analyses of regression with enter method. Descriptive statistics for measures are presented in Table 1.

Table 1. Descriptive statistics for scales used in the study

Scales	M	Mdn	SD	Range
Attitude toward psychotherapy	19.39	20.00	1.86	11-21
Attachment avoidance in therapy	27.84	26.00	10.86	13-72
Maternal love and care	21.99	23.00	8.36	2-36
Paternal love and care	18.72	18.00	9.82	0-35
Maternal control	8.57	8.00	4.55	0-18
Paternal control	8.11	7.00	5.03	0-18
Maternal overprotection	11.26	11.00	5.56	0-21
Paternal overprotection	7.82	7.00	4.75	0-19

First, the effect of the six scales of parental bonding (love-care, control and overprotection both for mother and father), duration of therapy and therapeutic attachment avoidance on attitude toward therapy was tested. A significant model ($F_{(8)}$=4.22; p< .001) accounted for 28 per cent of variance in attitude toward psychotherapy. Therapeutic attachment avoidance and paternal love-care were significant predictors of attitude (Table 2.).

Table 2. Coefficients for attitude toward psychotherapy as dependent variable

Model	Unstandardized Coefficients		Standardized Coefficients	t	p
	B	Std. Error	Beta		
(Constant)	20.631	1.057		19.519	.000
Paternal love and care	.048	.024	.255	2.058	.043
Maternal love and care	-.006	.025	-.028	-.249	.804
Paternal overprotection	-.014	.051	-.037	-.281	.780
Maternal overprotection	-.017	.046	-.052	-.377	.707
Paternal control	.049	.057	.132	.863	.390
Maternal control	-.027	.065	-.066	-.419	.676
Duration of therapy	.002	.002	.084	.804	.424
Attachment avoidance in therapy	-.072	.017	-.417	-4.112	.000

Second, the effect of parental bonding (see six scales described above) and duration of therapy on therapeutic attachment avoidance was tested. A significant model ($F_{(7)}$=3.2; p< .01) accounted for 20 per cent of variance in therapeutic attachment avoidance. Duration of therapy and paternal love-care were significant predictors of attachment avoidance in therapy (Table 3).

Table 3. Coefficients for attachment avoidance in therapy as dependent variable

Model	Unstandardized Coefficients		Standardized Coefficients	t	p
	B	Std. Error	Beta		
(Constant)	38.246	5.006		7.641	.000
Paternal love and care	-.326	.139	-.295	-2.344	.021
Maternal love and care	-.120	.150	-.093	-.804	.423
Paternal overprotection	.396	.309	.173	1.281	.204
Maternal overprotection	-.412	.278	-.211	-1.479	.143
Paternal control	-.177	.345	-.082	-.512	.610
Maternal control	.477	.390	.200	1.223	.225
Duration of therapy	-.043	.014	-.320	-3.093	.003

Based on above analyses testing of the hypothesized model (Figure 1.) resulted in the model presented in Figure 2.

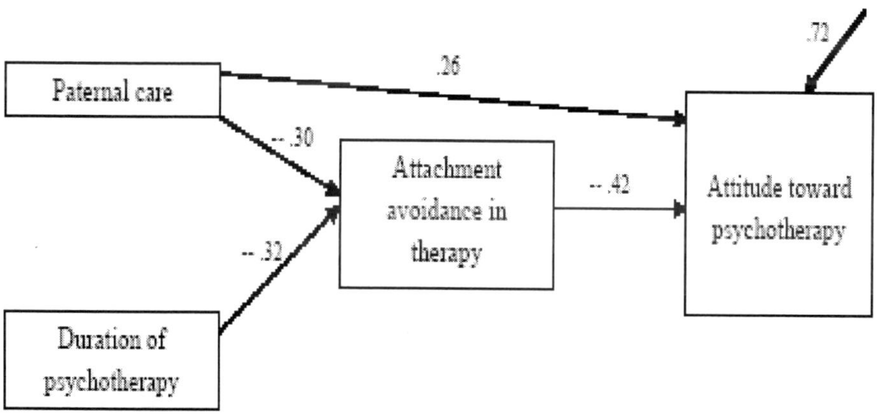

Figure 2. Effects of perceived parental bonding, duration of psychotherapy and attachment avoidance in therapy on attitude toward psychotherapy (pathway model).

CONCLUSION

Considering the whole model explaining 28 per cent of variance in attitude toward psychotherapy, this result is in accordance with the findings of Asay and Lambert (1999) who report 30 per cent of variance in psychotherapy change is due to variations in psychotherapy relationship. Formulating psychotherapy relationship as attachment proved to be a proper choice.

Some parts of above results are easily put into concordance with former theoretical statements and research findings. Immediate effects on attitude toward psychotherapy include attachment avoidance in therapy (reciprocal relation) and paternal love (direct relation). It means that lower attachment avoidance and a father perceived more loving lead to a more positive view of therapy. Effects mediated through therapeutic attachment avoidance include paternal love and duration of therapy. It means that longer therapy and recollections of a more caring father lead to less avoidance in patient-therapist attachment (i.e. a more secure attachment). First, immediate effects are discussed.

According to results, lower attachment avoidance leads to more positive attitude toward psychotherapy. Scoring low in therapeutic attachment avoidance can be equated with perceiving the relationship as more secure. Given the relation between insecure patterns of attachment and psychopathology (Dozier, Stovall-McClough and Albus 2008) psychiatric patients in this research are at a high chance of not having experienced secure relations yet. Though, with optimal relating and techniques presented above psychotherapists are able to transform former relational experiences creating a secure bond. In some attachment-informed methodological writings of Stern (1998) and Lyons-Ruth (1998) exactly the opportunity and process of learning such new relational modes are highlighted. Being-with-the-other interactional representation – instead of representations of self and significant others – becomes the focus of therapeutic change. Infant research has pointed out that interactional and affective regulation is not internalized but is the product of mutual infant-mother co-regulation from the very beginning of life. This idea is emphasized and used for understanding process of and change in psychotherapy by Beebe and Lachman (2002) and the Boston Change Process Study Group (e.g. Modell 1998). According to authors of the Boston Change Process Study Group change in psychotherapy occurs in implicit relational knowledge. Implicit relational knowledge is procedural in nature and therefore is qualitatively distinct both from verbal conscious knowledge and dynamic unconscious (Lyons-Ruth 1998). In the intersection of the implicit relational knowledge of patient and therapist an intersubjective space is created, where change promoting events are to be experienced. Stern (1998) calls the short time intervals including these events 'now moments'. They carry the potential for change. If a 'now moment' is recognized both by patient and therapist along the journey toward the goal of psychotherapy, it becomes a 'moment of meeting'. This short interval of sharing and connecting is followed by withdrawal and being alone in presence of the other. This is the time for experiences to integrate and for implicit relational knowledge to transform. A series of these 'moments of meeting' are generalized into a representation of 'feeling secure, being understood etc. with the therapist'. This creates freedom from anxiety (i.e. pleasantness) in psychotherapy sessions. These representations and pleasant relational experience are not restricted to the psychotherapy session, but create new possibilities for real life relationships to change. Hence, psychotherapy is found more effective, and if psychological problems are assumed to be of relational nature new hope for recovery emerges. The study presented above is ignorant of the causes of change in therapeutic attachment avoidance. It is proposed that no matter what happens in psychotherapy (insight through interpretation, learning, reframing, sharing through nonverbal work etc.) experiencing a new mode of relating has curative effects.

More positive attitude toward psychotherapy is also predicted by patients' childhood memories of a more loving father. For a long period in the history of developmental psychology paternal love and care were ambiguously judged for their importance in childhood development. For today it is unquestionable that fathers play an important role in the life of their children. Moreover, they have a unique contribution to happiness, life-satisfaction and level of distress in their adult children (Amato 1994). Several studies showed (Barrera and Garrison-Jones 1992; Cole and McPherson 1993) that perceived level of paternal support and care affects whether depressive symptoms are present or not in adolescents, while no such relation could have been proved for maternal care yet. Adolescents having a father perceived as more supporting reported less depressive symptoms. Simply put, paternal love seems to be a protective factor against depression. Depression is not only a mental disease, but certain patterns of feelings and cognitions are also in connection with depression even in normative samples. So what are patients protected against by paternal love? Or put the other way: how does absence of paternal care lead to a negative view of psychotherapy? If some well-known symptoms or explanations of depression are considered and applied to the psychotherapeutic setting, connection between paternal love and attitude toward psychotherapy becomes understandable. First, feeling unpleasant in psychotherapy sessions can be paralleled with anhedonia – inability of experiencing joy (e.g. van Praag, de Kloet and van Os 2004). Second, negative perception of future as a cognitive distortion and part of the negative cognitive triad (Beck, Rush, Shaw and Emery 1979) can result in less hope for recovery, as function of an imagined negative future with problems still lasting. Hopelessness, as negative expectancy (Abramson, Metalsky and Alloy 1989) for results of psychotherapy can also be considered as an explanation. Third, learned helplessness (Seligman 1975) can be interpreted as loss of agency, leading patients to attribute even advances to chance and not to psychotherapy work itself. So, paternal love – preventing depressive symptoms and presumably underlying cognitive and affective processes in adolescents – prevents negative attitude toward psychotherapy this way. Next, effects of duration of psychotherapy and paternal love on therapeutic attachment avoidance are considered.

Effect of duration of psychotherapy on attitude is mediated by the relational variable, attachment avoidance in psychotherapy. It means that not being in therapy for a longer period is responsible for a more positive attitude in itself, but with increase of time spent in therapy, a more secure (i.e. less avoidant) attachment is formed. As discussed earlier this relation of a quality not – or to a lesser chance – experienced before by patients leads to a more positive attitude toward psychotherapy. This result is in accordance with the suggestion of Obegi (2008) who proposed a stage theory of psychotherapy relation development parallel to the normative development of attachment in infancy and childhood. In this theoretical model formation of patient-therapist attachment is conceived of as a process. Development of the therapeutic bond begins with a formal and superficial relating of patient to therapist, where therapist is perceived as wiser and stronger. It is the helpless state of the patient which motivates relating. In this early stage perception of therapist is strongly influenced by former attachment experiences. In the next two stages of attachment-in-the-making and clear-cut attachment therapist becomes an attachment figure in his own right. Perception of and relating to therapist are governed by observations of the relationship of new quality. According to Riggs, Jacobvitz and Hazen (2002) avoidant adult attachment predicted lowest participation rate in psychotherapy in a normative female sample. Results in this study suggest that attachment avoidance can not only predict psychotherapy motivation, but can be predictive of patients' ability to use psychotherapy for their own good.

Results showing the effect of paternal but not maternal care on therapeutic attachment are in accordance with the studies of Mallinckrodt (1991) and Mallinckrodt and colleagues (1995). In the studies mentioned possible explanations for this selective paternal effect is missing. In explaining this result, firstly functions of father are to be observed. Winnicott (1987) lists three areas where role of father is of great value: relationship between father and mother, father supporting mother, and being himself distinguishable from mother. It is clear from these areas that in Winnicott's terms father is representing the outside world for the infant. Later on father becomes a representative of social norms, and paternal prohibition (le nom / non du père = the name / no of the father) is what prevents the child from merging with mother in fantasy (Lacan 1993). It means that while experiences of infant-mother symbiosis (in the sense of strong interrelatedness) are rather formative for representation of self (i.e. attachment anxiety), paternal contributions effect rather child's representation of outside world and significant others (i.e. attachment avoidance). For many cultures, including Hungarian, being stronger and wiser remain masculine attributions. These are characteristics of the psychotherapist as attachment figure. These culturally and professionally predetermined characteristics of therapist can also explain the paternal effect.

Although interpretations of results presented in this chapter are plausible, some limitations of the study have to be mentioned. First, pathway model tested and presented here is based on theoretical considerations. In case of duration of therapy predicting therapeutic attachment avoidance it was proposed that with time passing in psychotherapy attachment to therapist becomes more and more secure. But the study not being longitudinal it is also highly presumable, that patients with persistent avoiding mode of bonding simply drop out from psychotherapy. The same applies for relation between therapeutic attachment avoidance and attitude toward psychotherapy. In tested model it has been proved that less avoidance of therapist by patient leads to more positive attitude toward psychotherapy. But again since directions of causation were predetermined to best fit into an attachment-informed model of psychotherapy process and the study was not of longitudinal nature in this case direction of causation could be reversed as well. So not patient's attachment to therapist would affect attitude, but a more positive attitude would lead to a less avoiding relation to therapist. It is simply conceivable in terms of rewarding in learning theory. If psychotherapy has positive effects on everyday life, if time spent with therapist is convenient, if psychotherapeutic work leads to hope for recovery and all these positive results are associated with the person of the therapist, patient will seek the closeness and presence of therapist. In light of these limitations the study should be repeated in a longitudinal setting.

Another limitation is that only therapeutic attachment avoidance was measured. Although Haves, Wilson, Gifford, Follette and Strosahl (1996) describe the general phenomenon of experiential avoidance – which in my opinion includes attachment avoidance among many other forms of avoidance – as a potent candidate for functional diagnostic dimension, the other secondary strategy to decrease anxiety resulting from lack of a secure bond, namely that of therapeutic attachment anxiety has been ignored. This study is ignorant whether the effects of attachment anxiety would modify, and if they would in what direction the evaluation of psychotherapy and attitude toward it. It remains an open question whether mediated by attachment anxiety any of the maternal components of parental bonding would have an effect. Further research in the area should lift these limitations.

REFERENCES

Abramson, L. Y., Metalsky, G. I., and Alloy, L. B. (1989). Hopelessness Depression: A Theory-Based Subtype of Depression. *Psychological Review, 96*(2), 358-372.

Ainsworth, M. S. D., and Bowlby, J. (1991). An Ethological Approach to Personality Development. *American Psychologist, 46*(4), 333-341.

Alexander, F. G. (1935). Concerning the Genesis of the Castration Complex. *Psychoanalytic Review, 22*, 49-52.

Amato, P. R. (1994). Father-Child Relations, Mother-Child Relations, and Offspring Psychological Well-Being in Early Adulthood. *Journal of Marriage and Family, 56*(4), 1031-1042.

Asay, T. P., and Lambert, M. J. (1999). The empirical case for the common factors in therapy. In M. A. Hubble, B. L. Duncan, and Miller, S. D. (Eds.): *The heart and soul of change: What works in therapy* (pp 33-55).Washington, DC: American Psychological Association.

Barrera, M., and Garrison-Jones, C. (1992). Family and peer social support as specific correlates of adolescent depressive symptoms. *Journal of Abnormal Child Psychology, 20,* 1-16.

Barclay, C. R., and Smith, T. (1992). Autobiographical Remembering: Creating Personal Culture. In M. A. Conway, D. C. Rubin, H. Spinnler, and W. Wagenaar (Eds.): *Theoretical Perspectives on Autobiographical Memory* (pp. 75-97). Dordrecht: Kluwer Academic.

Beck, A. T., Rush, A. J., Shaw, B. F., and Emery, G. (1979). *Cognitive Therapy of Depression.* New York: The Guilford Press.

Beebe, B., and Lachmann, F. M. (2002). *Infant Research and Adult Treatment.* London: The Analytic Press.

Bowlby, J. (1977). The Making and Breaking of Affectional Bonds. *British Journal of Psychiatry, 130*, 210-210 and 421-431.

Cole, D., and McPherson, A. E. (1993). Relation of family subsystems to adolescent depression: Implementing a new family assessment strategy. *Journal of Family Psychology, 7,* 119-133.

Davanloo, H. (2005). Intensive Short-Term Dynamic Psychotherapy. In H. Kaplan, and B. Sadock (Eds): *Comprehensive Textbook of Psychiatry* (8th Edition, pp. 2628-2652). Philadelphia: Lippincot Williams and Wilkins.

Denis, P. (2005). Transference. In A. De Mijolla (Ed.): *International Dictionary of Psychoanalysis.* Detroit: Thomson Gale.

Dozier, M., Stovall-McClough, K. C., and Albus, K. E. (2008). Attachment and Psychopathology in Adulthood. In Cassidy, J. and Shaver, P.R. (Eds.): *Handbook of Attachment: Theory, research, and clinical applications* (2nd Edition, pp. 718-744). New York: The Guilford Press.

Farber, B. A., Lippert, R. A., and Nevas, D. B. (1995). The Therapist as Attachment Figure. *Psychotherapy, 32*(2), 204-212.

Fonagy, P., and Target, M. (2003): *Psychoanalytic Theories: Perspectives from Developmental Psychopathology.* London: Whurr Publishers.

Freud, S., and Breuer, J. (1895). Studies on hysteria. *The Standard Edition of the Complete Psychological Works of Sigmund Freud, 2*, 48–106.

Gelso, C. J., and Carter, J. A. (1994): Components of the Psychotherapeutic Relationship: Their Interaction and Unfolding During Treatment. *Journal of Counseling Psychology, 41*(3), 296-306.

Green, A. (2005). *Key Ideas for a Contemporary Psychoanalysis.* London and New York: Routledge.

Haves, S.C., Wilson, K.G., Gifford, E.V., Follette, V.M., and Strosahl, K. (1996). Experiential Avoidance and Behavioral Disorders: A Functional Dimensional Approach to Diagnosis and Treatment. *Journal of Consulting and Clinical Psychology, 64*(6), 1152-1168.

Haynal, A. (1993). Ferenczi and the Origins of Psychoanalytic Technique. In L. Aron, and A. Harris (Eds.): *The Legacy of Sándor Ferenczi* (pp. 53-74). Hillsdale, NJ: The Analytic Press.

Holmes, J. (1999): Defensive and Creative Uses of Narrative in Psychotherapy: An Attachment Perspective. In G. Roberts, and J. Holmes (Eds.): *Healing Stories* (pp.49-66). Oxford: Oxford University Press.

Kohut, H. (1971). *The Analysis of the Self.* New York: International Universities Press.

Kohut, H. (1977). *The Restoration of the Self.* New York: International Universities Press.

Lacan, J. (1993). *The Psychoses. The Seminar of Jacques Lacan.* London: Routledge.

Láng, A., Péley, B., Barlay, M. L., and Bernáth, L. (2011). A páciens-terapeuta kötődés hatása a terápiás attitűd alakulására – A Kötődési Elkerülés a Terápiában (KET) kérdőív kidolgozása és összefüggése a terápiás attitűddel. *Lélekelemzés, 6*(1), 22-51. (in Hungarian)

Luborsky, L., Mellon, J., Alexanser, K., van Ravenswaay, P., Chidress, A., Levine, F. J., Frits-Christof, D., Cohen, K. D., Hold, A. V., and Ming, S. (1985). A verification of Freud's grandest clinical hypothesis: the transference. *Clinical Psychology Revue, 5*, 231–46.

Lyons-Ruth, K. (1998). Implicit Relational Knowing: Its Role in Development and Psychoanalytic Treatment. *Infant Mental Health Journal, 19*(3), 282–289.

Mallinckrodt, B. (1991). Clients' Representations of Childhood Emotional Bonds With Parents, Social Support, and Formation of the Working Alliance. *Journal of Counseling Psychology, 38*(4),401-409.

Mallinckrodt, B., Coble, H. M., and Gantt, D. L. (1995). Working Alliance, Attachment Memories, and Social Competencies of Women in Brief Therapy. *Journal of Counseling Psychology, 42*(1), 79-84.

Modell, A. H. (1998). Review of Infant Mental Health Papers. *Infant Mental Health Journal, 19*(3), 341–345.

Obegi, J. H. (2008). The Development of the Client-Therapist Bond Through the Lens of Attachment Theory. *Psychotherapy: Theory, Research, Practice, Training, 45*(4), 431-446.

Parker, G., Tupling, H., and Brown, L. B. (1979). A Parental Bonding Instrument. *British Journal of Medical Psychology, 52*, 1-10.

Riggs, S. A., Jacobvitz, D., and Hazen, N. (2002): Adult Attachment and History of Psychotherapy in a Normative Sample. *Psychotherapy: Theory, Research, Practice, Training, 39*(4), 344-353.

Scharfe, E., and Bartholomew, K. (1994). Reliability and stability of adult attachment patterns. *Personal Relationships, 1*, 23-43.

Seligman, M. E. P. (1975). *Helplessness: On Depression, Development, and Death.* San Francisco: W.H. Freeman.

Stern, D. N. (1998). The Process of Therapeutic Change Involving Implicit Knowledge: Some Implications of Developmental Observations for Adult Psychotherapy. *Infant Mental Health Journal, 19*(3), 300–308.

Stolorow, R. D., and Atwood, G. E. (1996). The Intersubjective Perspective. *Psychoanalitic Review, 83*, 181-194.

Tóth, I., and Gervai, J. (1999). Szülői Bánásmód Kérdőív (H-PBI): A Parental Bonding Instrument (PBI) magyar változata. *Magyar Pszichológiai Szemle, 54*(4), 551-566. (in Hungarian)

Ursano, R. J., Sonnenberg, S. M. and Lazar, S. G. (2004): *A Concise Guide to Psychodynamic Psychotherapy*. Washington, DC: American Psychiatric Publishing.

van Praag, H. M., de Kloet, E. R., and van Os, J. (2004). *Stress, the Brain and Depression.* Cambridge: Cambridge University Press.

Wallin, D. J. (2007): *Attachment in psychotherapy*. New York: The Guilford Press.

Waters, E., Merrick, S., Treboux, D., Crowell, J., and Albersheim, L. (2000). Attachment Security in Infancy and Early Adulthood: A Twenty-Year Longitudinal Study. *Child Development, 71*(3), 684-689.

Winnicott, D. W. (1987). *The Child, the Family, and the Outside World.* New York: Perseus Publishing.

Woodhouse, S. S., Schlosser, L. Z., Crook, R. E., Ligiéro, D. P., and Gelso, C. J. (2003): Client Attachment to Therapist: Relations to Transference and Client Recollections of Parental Caregiving. *Journal of Counseling Psychology, 50*(4), 395–408.

In: Psychotherapy
Editors: A. J. Lancaster, and O. Sharpe

ISBN 978-1-61942-611-5

Chapter 6

How to Conduct the Short-Term Life Review Interview for Terminally Ill Patients

Michiyo Ando[1]*, and Tatsuya Morita[2]
[1]Faculty of Nursing, St. Mary's College, Kurume City, Fukuoka, Japan
[2]Seirei Mikatahara General Hospital, Japan

Introduction

Terminally ill patients sometimes experience depression, anxiety, or psycho-existential suffering. Psycho-existential suffering is defined as pain caused by extinction of being and extinction of meaning of self due to the loss of relationships with others, loss of autonomy, or loss of a future[1.] In this model, psycho-existential suffering has the sense of meaning as a core concept. Because psycho-existential suffering is related to quality of life, good death, depression[2], desire for hastened death, hopelessness, and suicidal ideation[3], it is important to palliate psycho-existential suffering.

Reminiscence therapy is an intervention used to palliatepsycho-existential suffering.This was developed by Butler, R.to elevate the state of psychological well-being(e.g., life satisfaction)in elders[4]. We tested the efficacy of reminiscence therapy for palliation of psycho-existential suffering. About four weeks were required to complete the formal structured reminiscence therapy[5]in terminally ill cancer patients[6.] This study demonstrated a positive effect on spiritual well-being[7], but about 30% of the enrolled participants could not complete the study because of rapid physical deterioration. Then we developed a novel psychotherapy approach, the Short-Term Life Review, comprising two sessions over one week.

We explored its feasibility and efficacy using a pre–post study design[8]. This approach yielded a high completion rate of 83%, and there was a significant increase in the sense of meaning of self as measured by the Functional Assessment of Chronic Illness Therapy-

* Corresponding Author:Michiyo Ando.St. Mary's College, Tsubukuhonmachi 422.Kurume City, Fukuoka, Japan. E-mail: andou@st-mary.ac.jp.

Spiritual Well-Being Scale (FACIT-Sp)[9]. Moreover, when we compared the efficacy of the Short-Term Life Review with that of the supportive care approach used in our randomizedcontrol study, the Short-Term Life Review was found to be more effective[10]. In addition, Good Death items[11] such as"Hope,""Not being a burden to others," "Life completion," and "Preparation for death" showed a significant increase, and a significant amelioration in anxiety and depression was also observed.

That is, the Short-Term Life Review is effective on spiritual well-being, depression, anxiety, and good death. We think that it is need to present how to conduct this therapy to use correctly. The present study demonstrates a method of the Short-Term Life Review interviewsuch that it can be applied across various populations.

METHOD OF THE SHORT-TERM LIFE REVIEW

1. Participants' Criteria

The Short-Term Life Review is for elderly people, patients receiving medical treatment, and terminally ill cancer patients.

Inclusion criteria were as follows:

1) Participants must have the physical and mental strength to endure a session of 30 to 60 minutes.
2) Participants must beable to communicate.
3) Participants must be over 20 years old.

Exclusion criteria were as follows:

1) Participants havingsevere pain or other physical symptoms.
2) Participants havingcognitive impairments such as dementia or disturbance of consciousness.
3) Participants havingserious family problems such as issues regardinginheritance of property, conflicts about their funeral among family members, and reconciliation of past issues between them and their family members.

2. Conditionsfor Interviewers

2.1. Technique of Communication

Interviewers need to have adequate communicationskills to conduct theShort-Term Life Review interview. A desirable attitude to adopt is a client-centered counselingmethod suggested by Rogers, CR.,[12] which enables the interviewer to perceive the participants'feelings.The interviewer should have *genuineness*such that he can express his emotionsthat he feels, shows*acceptance* such that he accepts the participant's feelings without judging them as good or bad, and shows*empathic understanding*such that he understands what the participant feels.

2.2. Preparation

1) The interviewer explains the purpose and the method of the Short-Term Life Review. In addition, the interviewer needs to state clearly that the participant is required to review his life because some participantswould not be willing to do that.
2) The interviewer selects the best time in the daily schedule of the participant and a suitable place for a session in order to protect his privacy.
3) The interviewer needs to be aware of the ethical aspectsso as to protect the participant's privacy and not disclose his review.

3. Interventions

3.1. Period

Each interview session lasts between 30 and 60 minutes with a 1-week interval between the first and second sessions.

3.2. Consideration Points

1) The interviewershould use simple and clear words.

The interviewer should use simple and clear words and ask questionsafter taking into account the age, gender, and cognitive level of the participant.

2) The interviewer should consider the time schedule in a session.

Some participants review only one memory for a prolonged period of time.If it is important to review that particular memory, 3 or 4 question items pertaining to it are selected.

3) The interviewer helps participants to review both good and bad memories during the evaluation.

It is important for the participant to review both good and bad memories to integrate his life.

4) The interviewer needs to pay attention so that participantsdo not review too many bad memories.

If a participant reviews too manybadmemoriesthat would have otherwise stayed hidden,the interviewer needs to stop reviewing to maintain the participant's mental health.

3.3. Procedure

The following questions are used to review participants' lives so as to integrate their lives.

The interviewer asks the following questions in the first session.

First Session

(1)What is the most important thing in your life?

Some participants do not recognize an important thing.In such cases, the interviewer suggests family or children as examples.

(2) What are the most vivid or impressive memories in your life?

Some participantsfind it difficult to choose the most vivid or impressive memories because there are too many such memories. In these cases, the interviewersuggests birth of children or wedding as examples.

(3) In your life, what event or person has affected you most?

This question is about a turning point in the participants' lives, and the participants usually recognize one.

(4) What is the most important role you have played in your life?

This question pertains to the participants' identity and is useful for them to find the meaning of theirexistence.

(5) What is the proudest thing in your life?

Some participants hesitate to answer this question. It is helpful if the interviewer clarifies that it is not only related to socialpride but also self-pride.

(6) Are there things you want to tell some important people or your family?

This question is a moderately difficult one about the participants' legacy and they usually do not knowwhat they want to say.

(7) What advice or words of guidance do you have for the important people in your life or for the younger generation?

This question recognizes the continuity of the participants' lives and makes them understand the relationships betweentheir present and future.

After The First Session

The participants' narratives are recorded and the interviews are transcribed verbatim.

The sample of an album

(1) What is the most important thing in your life?

(2) Whant are the most vivid or impressive memories in your life?

(3)In your life, what event or person has affected you most?

(4) What is the most important role you have played in your life?

(5) What is the proudest thing in you life?

(6) Is there anything which you want to tell to important people or your family?

(7) What advice or words of guidance do you have for the important people in your life or for the younger generation ?

The interviewer creates a simple album that includes key words from the answer to each question; these key words are selected after a discussion between the participantsand interviewer. Key words include both positive and negative elements from the interview. The interviewer then pastes pictures or drawings from books or magazines that were related to the participants' words or phrases to make the album beautiful and memory provoking. We present a sample of album to make (Figures).

Second Session

The participantsand interviewer view the album together and the participant confirms the contents of the album. The interviewer tries to encourage the participants to feel the continuity of self from the past to the present, to accept life completion, and to be satisfied with their lives. After the second session, the interviewer presents the album to the participants.

DISCUSSION

The present study demonstrated the method of conducting Short-Term Life Review interviews. This intervention was implemented in Korea and the United States, and it was feasible to conduct it in both locationsdespite the cultural differences[13]. Thus, its efficacy has beenproved and it will be useful for people from other cultures. Some questions might be difficult for elderly people with low cognitive ability. Thus, we can select questions from the interviews conducted in our previous study[14] that focused on important questions about "important things,""impressive memories," and "roles in life." These questions might be easier to answer.

I believe that the Short-Term Life Review may be effective on psycho-existential sufferings and psychological distress of terminally patients over cultural differences.

REFERENCES

[1] Murata H. Morita T. Conceptualization of psycho-existential suffering by the Japanese Task Force: the first step of a nationwide project. *Palliat Support Care* 2006; 4: 279-285.

[2] Nelson CJ, Rosenfeld B, Breitbart W, Galietta M. Spirituality, religion, and depression in the terminally ill. *Psychosomatics*2002; 43: 213-220.

[3] McClain CS, Rosenfeld B, Breitbart W. Effect of spiritual well-being on end-of-life despair in terminally-ill patients. *Lancet*2003; 361: 1603-1607.

[4] Butler R. The life review: An interpretation of reminiscence in the aged. *Psychiatry* 1963; 26: 65-76.

[5] Haight BK. Thetherapeutic role of a structured life review process in homebound elderly subjects. *J Gerontol*1988; 43: 40-44.

[6] Ando M, Tsuda A, Morita T. A preliminary study of life review interviews on the spiritual well-being of terminally ill cancer patients. *Supportive Care Cancer*2006; 15: 225-231.

[7] Wegberg BV, Bacchi M, Heusser P, Helwig S, Schaad R, Rohr, EV, Bernhard J, Hurny C, Castiglione M, Cerny T. The cognitive-spiritual dimension - an important addition to the assessment of quality of life: Validation of a questionnaire (SELT-M) in patients with advanced cancer. *Ann Oncol*1998; 9: 1091-1096.

[8] Ando M, Morita T, Okamoto T, Ninosaka Y. One week Short-Term Life Review interview can improve spiritual well-being of terminally ill cancer patients. *Psycho-Oncology* 2009; 17:885-890.

[9] Peterman AH, Fitchett G, Brady MJ, Pharm LH, Cella D. Measuring spiritual well-being in people with cancer: The Functional Assessment of Chronic Illness Therapy-Spiritual Well-Being Scale (FACIT-Sp). *Ann Behav Med*2002; 24: 49-58.

[10] Ando M, Morita T, Akechi T. Efficacy of Short-Term Life Review interviews on the spiritual well-being of terminally ill cancerpatients. *J Pain and Symptom Management*2010; 39: 993-1002.

[11] Miyashita m, Morita T, Sato K, et al. Good Death Inventory: a measure for evaluating good death from the bereaved family member's perspective. *J Pain Symtom Manage* 2008; 35: 486-498.

[12] Rogers CR. The necessary and sufficient conditions of therapeautic personality change. *J Counse Psycho* 1957; 21: 95-103.

[13] Ando M, Morita T, Ahn SH, et al. International comparison study on the primary concern of terminally ill cancer patients in Short-Term Life Review interviews among Japanese, Koreans, and Americans. *Palliative and Supportive Care* 2009; 7: 349-355.

[14] Ando M, Morita T, Akechi T. Factors in narratives to questions in the Short-Term Life Review interviews of terminally ill cancerpatients and utility. *Palliative and Supportive Care*(in press).

In: Psychotherapy
Editors: A. J. Lancaster, and O. Sharpe
ISBN 978-1-61942-611-5

Chapter 7

A HERMENEUTIC APPROACH TO CULTURE AND PSYCHOTHERAPY

John Chambers Christopher[1], Gary Foster[2], and Susan James[3]
[1] Health and Human Development
Montana State University; Bozeman, Montana, US
[2] Department of Philosophy; Wilfrid Laurier University;
Waterloo, Ontario, Canada
[3] Educational and Counselling Psychology and Special Education;
University of British Columbia; Vancouver, BC

ABSTRACT

Despite the growing awareness of culture within psychology, critics contend that understandings of culture remain largely superficial. Hermeneutics is a way of thinking interpretively about cultural meanings and discerning their specific manifestations that helps to remedy this situation. Hermeneutics offers a comprehensive theory of culture that (a) details how the self is embedded in culture, (b) highlights culture's inherently moral nature, and (c) provides conceptual tools for approaching culture in specific encounters. It can be utilized by psychotherapists not only to help understand clients from different cultural backgrounds but also to better recognize how the dominant Western cultural outlook, individualism, influences psychotherapy theory, research, and practice. These concepts are applied to cross-cultural cases.

INTRODUCTION

Psychology and the practice of psychotherapy and counseling, according to many critics, have failed to fully address the challenges of working with minority group members, immigrants, and those dwelling in non-Western societies. Sue and Sue (1990) unequivocally maintain that when counseling theories are uncritically applied to ethnic minorities and non-Western peoples they contribute to portraying them as pathological. Mental health services and interventions are "frequently antagonistic or inappropriate to the life experiences of the culturally different client" (Sue and Sue, 1990, p. 7). Concepts, interventions, and measures developed in Western cultures are regularly extended to persons in and from non-Western cultures and research findings are interpreted at face value often resulting in an *imposed etic* and a perpetuation of the socio-political status quo (Pedersen, 1991; Prilleltensky, 1994; Sue and Sue, 1990). Not surprisingly, research indicates that groups such as African Americans have a considerable amount of distrust of the fields of counseling and psychotherapy and of Anglo psychologists (Nickerson, 1994). Research on underutilization and premature termination of mental health services by ethnic minorities lend strong support to these claims (Brinson and Kottler, 1995; Vandervert, 1995; Vernon and Roberts, 1982; Whaley, 2001).

Given this state of affairs, Sue and Sue (1990) offer a challenge to counselors and psychologists. They write:

> As mental health professionals, we have a personal and professional responsibility to (a) confront, become aware of, and take actions in dealing with our biases, stereotypes, values, and assumptions about human behavior, (b) become aware of the culturally different client's world view, values, biases, and assumptions about human behavior, and (c) develop appropriate help-giving practices, intervention strategies, and structures that take into account the historical, cultural, and environmental experiences/influences of the culturally different client. (p. 10)

Pursuing such an agenda, however, is enormously difficult when conducted within the reigning dualistic presuppositions of Western culture. Western thought tends to dichotomize life into opposing pairs such as mind/body, fact/value, good/bad, subject/object, self/other, and individual/society. These dichotomies pervade psychology as well as popular thought. For instance, academic and professional psychology have long seen themselves as objective, neutral, and culture-free enterprises dedicated to the discovery of universal and ahistorical facts and laws (Bernstein, 1978; Braginsky, 1992; Giorgi, 1970; Richardson and Christopher, 1993; Richardson, Fowers, and Guignon, 1999; Taylor, 1985a, 1985b). Western social science, shaped by positivism and more generally, empiricism, has held fast to a sharp metaphysical separation of facts and values with values seen as undesirable subjective emotional intrusions into the scientific process (Bernstein, 1978). From this mainstream view of social science, theory and practice should not be informed by cultural values.

This dualistic outlook has been largely overturned by a variety of post-positivist theorists who have considered how the pursuit of objectivity and neutrality have impeded the social sciences from understanding their own ethical and cultural roots (Christopher, 1996; Gergen, 1995; Hoshmand, 2006; Martin and Thompson, 1997; Prilleltensky, 1989; Richardson and Christopher, 1993; Richardson, Fowers, and Guignon, 1999; Slife, Reber, and Richardson, 2005; Slife, Williams, and Barlow, 2001). There is a history of seminal theorists such as Ellis (1973), May (1967), and Wachtel (1977) declaring that values and assumptions strongly shape the theory and practice of counseling and psychotherapy. In Wachtel's (1977) words, the counseling theories "that guide contemporary psychotherapeutic efforts both reflect and shape the culture's view of human potential and the good life" (p. 3). In her APA presidential address, Spence (1985) concludes that, "...whatever their intentions, scientists are the products of their society and time, and their construction of social reality is shaped by the world view and values of the culture in which they were reared" (p. 1285). Yet despite these observations, Sue and Sue (1990) are accurate when they note, "For too long we have deceived ourselves into believing that the practice of counseling and the data base that underlie the profession are morally, ethically, and politically neutral" (p. 24). It is little wonder that we have been left conceptually impoverished to identify cultural influences and deal with the moral dimension that many theorists are now saying is necessarily present in any scientific endeavor, especially those in the human sciences (Bellah, 1983; Bellah, Madsen, Sullivan, Swidler, and Tipton, 1985; Bernstein, 1978; Christopher, 1996, 2004; Cushman, 1990; Doherty, 1995; Richardson and Christopher, 1993; Sugarman and Martin, 1995; Taylor, 1989; Tjeltveit, 1989; Walsh, 1995). Consequently the role of individualism has remained disguised within the social sciences because "cultural influences may be quite pervasive, widespread, and powerful in forming the basis of "being" for ordinary people and, yet, remain elusive for those researchers who have sought to understand them" (Kitayama and Markus, 2000, p. 122).

To adequately respond to the challenge of Sue and Sue, we are faced with finding some point of leverage to understand the cultural values and assumptions of not only others but ourselves while we are situated within a cultural outlook that doesn't see itself as being a cultural outlook. Americans frequently assume that either we don't have a culture or that culture refers to superficial variations in clothing, food, and holiday customs. In a somewhat similar way, psychologists and counselors have assumed they were doing value-free and culture-free therapy. Part of the difficulty is that the definitions of culture provided in much of the cross-cultural and multicultural literature are often brief and tend to lack substantive value (Adams and Markus, 2001; Cole, 1996; Jahoda, 2002; Ratner, 2000). Another, as Maruyama (1992) makes clear, is that psychology has not generated the cognitive structures that would allow us to think contextually when we encounter diversity (see also Shweder, 1991). Instead, Sampson (1993) trenchantly argues that psychology has hastily responded to diversity with what he calls add-on eclectic strategies. So we are faced with two challenges: the first, to define culture in some way that doesn't trivialize it and assists us in discerning how we are culturally embedded and second, to learn to think culturally.

Our aim in this chapter is sketch out a hermeneutic account of culture. Philosophical hermeneutics provides a non-dualistic model of culture and the self. It is also a means of thinking interpretively about cultural meanings and discerning their specific manifestations. As a metatheory for psychology, hermeneutics can deepen our understanding of how we are shaped by culture and how much of psychological theory, research, and practice is influenced by individualism, our dominant cultural outlook. Hermeneutics is a framework for thinking about the world of our clients and the ways culture permeates every dimension of this world. This framework goes beyond just making global generalizations about what culture is. In addition to needing a comprehensive understanding of the nature of culture and its relationship to the self, psychotherapists must be able to think culturally. As Seeley (2000), following Devereaux (1958) argues, "Rather than learning about the stereotypical characteristics of particular cultures, psychotherapists need to become familiar with the general characteristics, categories, and functions of culture per se" (p. 72).

The term hermeneutics derives from the Greek word for interpretation and is related to Hermes, god of communication who ferried messages between the gods and humans. More recently, during the Protestant Reformation, hermeneutics was the theory and method of interpretation that emerged as a means of interpreting the Bible. Friederich Schleiermacher, at the turn of the eighteenth century, ushered in the contemporary understanding of hermeneutics, when he established a general interpretive methodology for uncovering the original intent of all forms of human communication, not just written texts like the Bible or legal statures. This version of hermeneutics, sometimes called *romantic hermeneutics* (Palmer, 1969; Richardson, et al., 1999) currently influences qualitative research methods (Benner, 1994; Fischer, 1980; Michrina and Richards, 1996; Packer and Addison, 1989; Ratner, 1997; Rennie, 1999; Tappan, 1997; Van Manen, 1990), theories of epistemology and clinical interpretation in psychodynamic therapies (Barclay, 1992; Bouchard and Guerette, 1991; Chessick, 1990; Eagle, 1986; Gentile, 1998; Schaefer, 1976; Spence, 1982, 1993), and narrative approaches to psychotherapy (Frank, 1987; Gergen, 1994; McNamee, 1996; Neimeyer and Mahoney, 1995; Schaefer, 1993). Following Schleiermacher in the tradition of romantic hermeneutics, Wilhelm Dilthey (1989) developed a critique of the natural science approach to the human sciences. Dilthey argued that the distinct subject-matter of the human sciences required a distinct methodology, one that acknowledged the role of interpretation in understanding the history, society and the individual. Less well known within psychology, Martin Heidegger's work in the 1920's instigated the most recent turn in hermeneutic thought, *philosophical* or *ontological hermeneutics*. Philosophical hermeneutics goes beyond methodology to consider the broader ontological questions about human nature that arise when we acknowledge that interpretation is central to human existence. This iteration of hermeneutic thought is highly influential in contemporary philosophy and social theory but is largely unknown within psychology except for a few notable exceptions (e.g., Messer, Sass, and Woolfolk, 1988; Richardson, et al., 1999; Woolfolk, 1998).

We believe that philosophical hermeneutics has numerous important contributions to make to psychology. In this chapter we outline a hermeneutic model of the self and its relationship to culture. Integrating the writings of philosophers Martin Heidegger, Hans-Georg Gadamer, Charles Taylor, and Paul Ricoeur, and the cultural anthropologist Clifford Geertz throughout the chapter, we begin by considering how the reigning Western understanding of the person, ontological individualism, makes it especially difficult to grasp how thoroughly we are shaped by culture. We then outline a hermeneutic theory of culture. Heidegger's notion of *being-in-the-world* is then reviewed as offering an alternative non-Cartesian ontology of the human agent that complements an interpretive view of culture. We also introduce Taylor's claim that culture is a moral framework that orients us to the good. We then explore how the hermeneutic notion of dialogue can provide a framework for engaging with those from different cultural backgrounds. Finally, we apply these concepts to a cross-cultural case study.

Ontological Individualism and the Challenge of Recognizing Culture

The dominant cultural outlook in the West is Individualism. In individualism, the self is the primary social reality, the basic building block of society. Individuals are seen as independent, and self-contained. They should be authentic, unique, responsible, expressive, rational. Anthropologists such as Geertz (1973), Lutz (1988), and Shweder, (1991; Shweder and Bourne, 1984) have explored how individualism may be a "peculiar idea" within human history and cross-cultural psychologists Harry Triandis (1989) estimates that individualism is the cultural outlook for only 30% of the world's population.

In the United States individualism is taken for granted as being "the way things are." The individualistic interpretation of the self is regarded as a scientific, rational, or as 'common sense' self-understanding instead of as one self-interpretation among a myriad of others. Ontological individualism casts the individual and culture as distinct and separable from each other, making it particularly difficult for us to grasp how we are shaped by culture. In ontological individualism the person is regarded in atomistic terms that render the person metaphysically separate from others, society, and nature (Bellah, Madsen, Sullivan, Swidler, and Tipton, 1985; Dumont, 1986; Lukes, 1973). Richardson, Fowers and Guignon (1999) describe this further, "We tacitly view human beings atomistically as discrete centers of experience and action concatenated in various ways into social groups, struggling to reduce inevitable conflicts with others through negotiations and temporary alliances" (p. 71). Such a self should ideally be "self-defining" (Taylor, 1975), refusing to rely upon the beliefs, values, and outlooks of others but seizing responsibility for coming to one's own identity.

Taylor (1975) contends that the emergence of this "self-defining subject" was accompanied by a new view of the universe as a brute physical domain of objects open to free and objective scientific investigation. Such a universe was best understood in mechanistic and materialistic terms as a neutral arena for the course of human history. While such an outlook makes good sense to most of us today it was a radical break with the history of ideas. Prior to the European Enlightenment beginning in the 17th century and still today in most non-Western parts of the world humans being were seen as situated in an ordered and inherently meaningful cosmos in which the individual had a defined place and role. Since the Enlightenment, this meaningful cosmos gave way to what Max Weber evocatively called the "disenchanted" world of modernity. This disenchanted perspective relies upon a sharp split between external objects and subjective experience. After this split, meanings and values are thought to reside in the realm of subjective experience. At the time this subject-object division was the kind of dramatic intellectual and cultural breakthrough that Isaiah Berlin (Berlin, Hardy, and Hausheer, 1998) would refer to as a "great liberating idea." The new view of the self as discrete and the world as disenchanted were ideological tools to liberate both scientific inquiry and the individual from the authoritarian and dogmatic excesses and oppressiveness of church, state, and society.

Taylor (1995) suggests, that the modern, disengaged, "punctual" self is as much a moral as a scientific ideal. In his writings (1975, 1989) he thoroughly documents how this individualism with its emphasis on autonomy and self-responsibility gradually evolved through many centuries of Western history (cf., Baumeister, 1986, 1987; Cushman, 1995). The modern self confronting a natural and social world to which it has no essential or defining ties "connects with ...central moral and spiritual ideas of the modern age," such as the modern ideal of "freedom as self-autonomy...to be self-responsible, to rely on one's own judgment, to find one's purpose in oneself" (1995, p. 7). This self is well-positioned to freely and rationally treat both itself and the outside world instrumentally, to alter them in desired ways, or, in later permutations of the modern self, to resist social pressure to conform and pursue self-actualization or personal authenticity as it sees fit. Culture, then, can come to be seen as a potential external threat that can somehow diminish the individual's autonomy. Critics suggest that our contemporary individualistic outlook has purchased valuable freedoms at the price of much alienation, stressing mastery and control over nature and ourselves to the detriment of other kinds of social, moral, or spiritual values in living.

Individualism functions, as Bernstein (1978) trenchantly argues, as the "disguised ideology" of the social sciences in the United States and much of Western Europe. Within psychology recent years have witnessed an increasing number of critiques of how individualism influences in unrecognized ways various fields of psychology (Christopher, 1999; Christopher, Nelson, and Nelson, 2004; Cirillo and Wapner, 1986; Cushman, 1990, 1991; Fowers and Richardson, 1993; Frank, 1978; Hogan, 1975; Kanfer, 1979; Kirschner, 1996; Perloff, 1987; Sampson, 1981, 1985, 1988, 1989; Smith, 1978; Spence, 1985; Waterman, 1981; Wolszon, 1998).

A powerful example of this underlying individualistic influence comes from what Geertz (1973) identified as the "stratigraphic" concept of the human being that dominates the social sciences. Like Bronfenbrenner's (1977) ecological model of the person, stratigraphic approaches portray the human being as a set of onion-like concentric circles, each layer of which is complete and irreducible in itself (Geertz, 1973). The innermost circle is biological, which is encircled successively by the psychological, social, and cultural domains. As Geertz puts it:

> Strip off the motley forms of culture and one finds the structural and functional regularities of social organization. Peel these off in turn and one finds the underlying psychological factors—"basic needs" or what-have-you—that support and make them possible. Peel off psychological factors and one is left with biological foundations—anatomical, physiological, neurological—of the whole edifice of human life. (p. 37)

The implication is that the psychologist can focus exclusively on the psychological "circle," leaving the levels of social and cultural organization to sociologists and anthropologists.

While these stratigraphic approaches do provide accounts in which culture is addressed, the downside is that culture can become mere extraneous context. Models and theories that take this approach adopt and reinforce the supposition that the individual is ontologically prior to the social; that it somehow makes sense to think of the individual as a biological entity existing independently of society and culture. Geertz (1973) challenges the notion that it is possible to understand the human being stripped of "the trappings of culture." In his view, which we shall turn to next, culture permeates human existence so thoroughly that the attempt to separate individuals and culture is incoherent and distorts our understanding of human nature.

A Hermeneutic View of Culture: Webs of Significance

Jackson and Meadows (1991) alert us to the fact that culture is a vague concept that most individuals never think about in any precise manner. Nevertheless, they think it essential that counselors engaged in multicultural counseling have a clear understanding of what this notion means. There is no shortage of definitions of culture in the cross-cultural and multicultural literature but these definitions are often not substantive and rarely help to bridge the gap between theory and practice (Christopher, 2001; Cole, 1996; Jahoda, 2002; Ratner, 2000).

Viewed from a hermeneutic perspective, culture is constituted by the shared meanings that make human interactions possible. These meanings form a common framework for helping people to make sense of the social (and physical) world. They form a background set of assumptions and values that not only shapes our understanding of the world but guides us practically through that world. Geertz (1973) claims that culture is a universal requirement of life, it is that which puts a particular order or structure on the lives of a people in a particular place.

Geertz (1973, 1983) makes a distinction between the notions of world view and ethos – two interdependent aspects of culture. The idea of a world view or *weltanschauung* denotes the more cognitive aspect of culture, that which describes or defines one's conception of reality. To hold a particular worldview is to have a framework for understanding the way that the world or reality works – its causal relations, various dimensions, the nature of its objects and so on. An *Ethos*, on the other hand, characterizes the more normative aspect of human existence. *Ethos* is concerned with the moral, aesthetic and affective dimensions of human life. As Geertz puts it, "A people's *ethos* is the tone, character and quality of their life, its moral and aesthetic style and mood; it is the underlying attitude towards themselves and their world that life reflects" (Geertz, 1973, p. 127).

Geertz (1973) characterizes culture, and in particular the notions of world view and *ethos* in terms of "webs of significance". These are what give meaning and coherence to our life activities. By "significance" Geertz implies something similar to what Heidegger (1962) means by the term *signification*. Heidegger characterizes the most fundamental aspects of our being-in-the world in terms of signification, care and concern. Our thoughts, feelings and actions reflect deep-seated presuppositions about what is real, important or valuable. The notion of care used by Heidegger is not simply that of a sympathetic emotional response, but refers to what we value, what consumes our energy and focus in life. These presuppositions reveal themselves to us and others through our actions, through how we actually spend our time and energy. The things through which a culture expresses itself in terms of the collective use of time and energy reveal the webs of significance or the webs of care of that culture. The actions of people from a particular culture reflect this 'caring.' Actions are embodiments of values and tell us something about what is significant in a culture (Christopher and Bickhard, in press).

These structures permeate and express themselves through the institutions and social practices of a particular culture. If we do an ethnography of everyday life, it becomes clear that this is so. For instance we ask our counseling students to write down everything they do for the first fifteen minutes after they get up in the morning. What we find is that American students often report hitting the snooze button on their alarm clocks, taking hot showers, and attending to pets. Each of these mundane behaviors may reveal to us certain aspects of our world view and *ethos*. Hot showers, for instance, require a rich background of understanding. The possibility of hot showers relies on knowledge of physics, hydrology, electricity, sanitation, and so on. This knowledge must also be applied or translated to technology including pipes, valves, boilers, etc… When we turn on the shower in the morning anticipating a stream of hot water we are relying on a vast body of knowledge – both theoretical and applied – accumulated and understood in terms of our culture's worldview which, can generally be characterized as mechanistic and materialistic. Hot showers tells us something about core cultural values. When we ask "why do we shower?" and "why do many shower one or more times daily?" these values begin to be revealed. Students tell us that evidence of odor, dirt and sweat evokes negative feedback from others. Evidence of eliminative body functions in our society is expected to be neutralized or eliminated. There is a social cost to not doing so. We still believe, along with Francis Bacon and John Wesley that "Cleanliness is next to Godliness." We associate cleanliness with responsibility, health, and wellness. It is an assumption or presupposition implicit in our cultural ethos. We take a negative view of those below a certain level of cleanliness. One characteristic of schizophrenia is a dysfunction in self-care, which many understand as a dysfunction in hygiene. Our assumptions about cleanliness then influence our understanding of what is meant by wellness, maturity and mental health. This gets expressed in the American way of life as a form of self-care, a form which sees millions of dollars spent each year on bath products. This type of self-care through cleanliness suggests the influence our Romantic heritage and its characteristic form of expressive individualism (Bellah, Madsen, Sullivan, Swidler, and Tipton, 1985; Taylor, 1985b).

This kind of ethnographic "fieldwork in familiar places" (Moody-Adams, 1997) helps us recognize the extent to which culture pervades our lives. Simple, everyday actions display an abundance of cultural presuppositions and values. Social practices like hot showers reveal to us how connected facts and values, world view and *ethos* are in our collective experience. Most of the time we do not consciously recognize these implicit values and assumptions when we engage in our everyday practices (practices such as bathing). Identifying these implicit cultural themes via an interpretive approach is illustrative of hermeneutics as a method. The implications of the interpretive approach lead to some of the core tenets of philosophical hermeneutics—for instance, that the individual is largely constituted by cultural assumptions and practices (see critiques by Cole, 1996; Shweder, 1990; Kashima, 2000, and Poortinga, 1997). And this in turn may help provide an important corrective to the dominant tendency within psychology to view culture as external to the individual.

Being-in-the-World: A Hermeneutic View of the Person

Heidegger characterizes the dominant western view of the person as based on a fundamental error. Western individualism characterizes persons as autonomous, atomistic, and independent of the world of objects and social structures. This individualistic view of humans, according to Heidegger, is itself a creation of culture, one that is derivative of a more primordial way of being that he terms *being-in-the-world* (Heidegger, 1962; cf., Campbell, Christopher and Bickhard, 2002; Christopher, 2004). Being-in-the-world refers to the way human beings are always fundamentally engaged in life or the world and do not experience the self as a separate *cogito* or thinking subject in the manner made famous by Descartes (Heidegger, 1962).

In his characterization of being-in-the-world, Heidegger wants to show the derivative nature of our experience of a subject-object duality or what Taylor (1991) calls the "reification of the disengaged first-person-singular self" (p. 306). Heidegger illustrates this by having us consider the simple task of hammering. When using tools such as a hammer, we do not normally experience this as a discrete object. Our phenomenological experience of 'hammering' is one in which the hammer is treated as part of our self. The actual experience is more unified than the abstract characterization we may give of it upon reflection (where we separate our self from the object). Normally we only come to notice the hammer as an object when something goes wrong (we hit our finger or the hammer breaks, etc…). When engaged in the task of hammering we also lose our awareness of 'I' or of our subjectivity. Such engagement eliminates the subject-object or mind-body distinction that we often posit by way of abstraction when we characterize our experience in the world intellectually. Heidegger sees our engagement in life as a more fundamental experience than this aforementioned understanding which highlights our separation from the world..

Heidegger characterizes our being-in-the-world in terms of what he calls "throwness." That is, we are thrown into this world, we do not choose to be born, that choice was made for us. Due to the nature of our throwness, we already experience the world in a certain unified way before we come to distinguish our self from objects. Even after we have recognized this separation we still experience most of our everyday activities in a more unified manner. We live our everyday life outside of the awareness of this distinction. We live as expressions of our culture and world. As Heidegger (1962) puts it:

> Ontically, of course, Dasein is not only close to us—even that which is closest: we *are* it, each of us, we ourselves. In spite of this, or rather for just this reason, it is ontologically that which is farthest. p. 36

The view that has been attributed to Descartes characterizes the "I' as the reflective or conscious part of our being, a part that is somewhat independent of our various beliefs, presuppositions and ideas. The hermeneutic view of the person suggests that these ideas and beliefs have already become part of what we mean by self or "I" by the time we become conscious of self. This learning of culture is illustrated by simple things such as a trip to McDonald's. In our culture we learn from a young age what is expected from the various participants of the McDonald's experience. When we awaken to consciousness, we find that we have already developed habits and understandings of the world that are part of how we experience the world. We find our self to be a participant in a drama that we have not constructed (Camus, 1983) or as Heidegger puts it, when we become aware of our 'self' and the world, we find that it is a world that is publicly constituted and interpreted. It is the world of the 'they' (Heidegger, 1962, p.296). We participate in this publicly interpreted world of the 'they' when eating a meal at McDonald's and reinforce cultural themes such as "time is money." We become part of the process of perpetuating and reinterpreting these cultural themes.

We can become partially aware of the effect of our cultural embeddedness, characteristic of our being-in-the-world through reflective abstraction (Bickhard and Christopher, 1994; Campbell and Bickhard, 1986; Campbell and Christopher, 1996). This may mean, however, that we will best come to understand our self, "not by inward-turning and introspection" (the Cartesian way) "but by catching sight of ourselves as we are engaged and preoccupied in everyday contexts" (Guignon, 1984, p. 232). Cognitive researchers who are recognizing the enormous role played by implicit cognitive functioning or the "adaptive unconscious" are similarly concluding we may need to "look outward to know ourselves" (Wilson, 2002). As Wilson writes, "No amount of introspection, however, can illuminate the contents of the adaptive unconscious, no matter how hard I try" (p. 163).

Our attempt to develop perspectives for reflecting on culture will always be partial and provisional. The perspectives that we develop will always be constituted through what Gadamer (1975) calls our 'prejudices' or pre-judgments. These are the beliefs and ideas that we inherit by virtue of growing up in a particular culture. Any distance that we get from culture through abstraction or critical reflection is always temporary and provisional (Gadamer, 1975). We can never fully follow the Cartesian model of detaching our self from culture. They provide a framework or horizon that enables us to make sense of the world. While we can develop partial, provisional perspectives that allow us to reflect on our culture, we unavoidably take on the meanings implicit in these practices prior to awareness. We are partly constituted by our cultures, which means that it is not possible to fully detach ourselves. Any distance that we get from our culture is always temporary and provisional (Gadamer, 1975). This does not mean, however, that we are all the same by virtue of our cultural constitution. Our individual life history or story is unique, but it develops through the shared background beliefs and meanings of our culture. As Charles Taylor puts it, this individual uniqueness consists largely of variations or various combinations of cultural themes and aspirations as expressed in an individual life. (Taylor, 1989; cf., Sugarman and Martin, 1995). The desire to separate this individual life from culture is a fairly modern phenomenon, one that we have characterized simply as individualism.

Moral Visions

Given the dualistic predilection in Western thought to bifurcate facts and values, we use the term *moral visions* to recapture the centrality of the moral, ethical, value-related dimension of our existence. Values and morals from the hermeneutic perspective are not subjective "things" that human beings tack onto their representations and perceptions. Instead values are intersubjective, unavoidable, and inextricably intertwined with facts. "Care" is presupposed in our most basic ways of being-in-the-world (Heidegger, 1962). What we do, how we allocate our time and energy, what we focus on, all reveal a structure of care. Thoughts, emotions, and behavior presuppose deeper distinctions of what is important and valuable.

This point becomes clearer if we consider the notion of folk psychologies. Every culture possesses certain presuppositions concerning human nature. The *folk* or *indigenous psychology* of a culture embodies these presuppositions and attempts to give an account of the human subject accordingly. Bruner (1990, p. 35) defines a folk psychology as:

> a set of more or less connected, more or less normative descriptions about how human beings 'tick,' what our own and other minds are like, what one can expect situated actions to be like, what are possible modes of life, how one commits oneself to them, and so on. (p. 35)

These folk psychologies tell us about the nature of emotions, motivation, psychopathology and self as understood by the culture in question. These understandings are sometimes well developed as with the various Buddhist or Hindu theories of the self. These exist and inform our conceptions of self and other at a pre-conscious level and guide our interactions regardless of whether they have been explicitly articulated. They make our understandings and interactions with others possible, drawing as they do upon both the culture's world view and its *ethos*.

A world view tells us what a person *is* according to the culture in question. It explains a culture's conception of what capabilities, characteristics, faculties and resources a person is said to possess. It also tells us about the boundaries of personhood – whether persons are conceived of as atomistic or social beings. *Ethos* characterizes the ethical dimension of a culture. *Ethos* tells us what norms or standards are appropriate to live by or what is desirable for human life. It tells us what is right and wrong and how we should behave, think, interact or feel.*Ethos* tells us what constitutes the good life as well as the mature, healthy or successful life. The world view tells what human nature is like according to a particular culture while ethos tells us how a person 'should' develop – 'what' one should become.

Folk psychologies draw on elements of a culture's world view and *ethos* not only to provide an account of what a person *is* but also what a person *should be*. Just as world view and *ethos* are always intertwined within the webs of meaning and significance that make up culture, so do they intertwine in our understandings of human nature and of our own identity. A folk psychology accordingly "summarizes not simply how things are but (often implicitly) how they should be" (Brunner, 1990, pp. 39-40). One implication is that the 'moral' or 'ethical' is entailed by our understanding of the self. Taylor (1989) even argues that "Selfhood and the good, or in another way selfhood and morality, turn out to be inextricably intertwined themes" (p. 3). Paul Ricoeur (1992) developed a hermeneutical account of selfhood which employs the notion of narrative identity, a notion which not only illustrates the social nature of selfhood but also shows how the descriptive aspects of selfhood are inseparable from the evaluative dimensions. He sees the fact value distinction as problematic when we try to examine or characterize the human subject. Ricoeur's work provides a useful complement to the sociological-historical account of selfhood that we find in Taylor (1989).

*Moral visions*refer to the constellations of cultural values and assumptions that constitute our understanding of the nature of the person and of the good life. Moral visions establish our sense of what the self*is* and what the self *should be*. Moral visions operate both implicitly and explicitly to orient us to what is deemed higher, deeper or more worthy; those things that give us strength, integration, wholeness, vitality, dignity, and goodness (Taylor, 1989). At the same time, moral visions delineate what we should avoid, resist, or oppose, both internally and externally. As used here, moral does not mean simply what is seen as right or wrong, but our deepest understanding of what is good, worthy, and desirable (Brinton, 1987). And these matters can vary dramatically across cultures. In traditional Chinese society, for instance, the defining moral virtue is *filial piety*, being a dutiful to one's parents. The good person is one who follows the relationships established and codified by Confucius and in this way demonstrates proper respect and maintains harmony. In Anglo-American society the good or ideal person is defined in more circumscribed and individualistic terms; rationality, autonomy, and authenticity are cardinal virtues.

Taylor (1989) describes these moral visions held by cultural groups as *inescapable moral frameworks* that orient us to what is worthy and provide direction in approaching those ideals. Like Heidegger's notion of care, moral visions are always present, even if, and perhaps especially when, they are unrecognized. As Taylor (1985a) writes, "these deepest evaluations are the ones which are least clear, least articulated, most easily subject to illusion and distortion. It is those which are closest to what I am as a subject, in the sense that shorn of them I would break down as a person, which are among the hardest for me to be clear about"

(p. 40). These evaluative frameworks form a *moral topography* or moral space within which our identities take shape and our aims and ideals are intelligible (Taylor, 1987; see also McLeod and Lynch, 2000; Sugarman and Martin, 1995). A sense of the "good" person and the "good" life is implicit in all our day-to-day events. Even such apparently amoral or anti-social individuals as gang members can be shown to be animated by moral visions (Christopher, 1996; Schmitz and Christopher, 1997).

Taylor (1987) utilizes a *via negativa*—using an example of what something *is not* to help make clear what it *is*—to help us experience the moral space or topography in which we are embedded. He alleges we all have a sense of what it means to feel "out-of-joint:"

> This is conceptually expressed in a host of ways: as being lost, or condemned, or exiled, or unintegrated, or without meaning, or insubstantial, or empty, to name some categories. Corresponding to each of these descriptions of breakdown is some notion of what it would be to overcome it, to have integration, or full being, to be justified, or found, or whatever. But more, there is a notion of 'where' this integration, fullness, etc., might come from, what might bring it about. . . . In other words, these different, often indefinite and tentative senses of what integration consists of incorporate notions of where it might be found, in the sense of where the strength lies, where the sources or resources are situated, which could bring integration, or fullness about. (pp. 300-301)

In his own work Taylor is primarily interested in explicating the moral sources of Western culture. However, his framework is a powerful tool for thinking about cultural differences. It reminds us that different cultures have not only different understandings of what the person or self is but also different understandings of the good or ideal person. The coordinates of the moral topographies in which the self is situated are marked out by a diversity of goods.

Taylor believes the spatial metaphor that lies at the heart of his notion of moral topography illuminates the manner in which these inescapable moral frameworks provide a sense of identity and orientation. Our identity, in his view, is based on one's sense of location in one or more moral visions. "To define my identity," he observes, "is to define what I must be in contact with in order to function fully as a human agent, and specifically to be able to judge and discriminate and recognize what is really of worth or importance, both in general and for me" (1985b, p. 258). Orientation in and to life comes from our relative position in this moral space that allows us to situate ourselves to the goods established by our culture's *ethos*. We can sense the direction we must pursue in order to more closely approach the good life and we can discern how far we are from it.

CULTURES AS MORAL VISIONS

A fundamental ontological assumption of western culture is expressed in the way that we view the relation between facts and values. Facts, representative of empirical states of affairs, are afforded more certainty or reality than values. Values are seen as subjective possessions which people choose to adopt, but are generally not seen as constitutive of who or what we are. We assume that the self is something autonomous from values and culture. Heidegger challenges this notion by claiming that "we do not, so to speak, throw a 'signification' over some naked thing which is present-at-hand, we do not stick a value on it" (1962, p. 190). According to Heidegger values are already a part of the world of facts in which we participate. The separation of facts from values is an abstraction from the everyday world in which we live. This abstraction presupposes a self that is autonomous in relation to values, but again according to Heidegger our selfhood is shaped by the meanings and social practices that precede us and which we participate in during our self-formation (Heidegger, 1962). Shweder, Mahapatra, and Miller (1987) express the way that our cultural values and assumptions are communicated implicitly through our social interactionsin the following:

> [M]orally relevant interpretations of events by local guardians of the moral order (e.g. parents) are typically presented and conveyed to young children in the context of routine family life and social practices. Those moral premises are carried by the messages and meanings implicit in the emotional reactions of others (anger or disappointment or "hurt feelings" over a transgression). They are carried by the verbal exchanges--commands, threats, sanction statements, accusations, explanations, justifications, excuses--necessary to maintain routine social practices." (p. 73).

As humans we are beings whose selves are formed by the values and assumptions of our culture. It is not just that culture influences who we are, it is rather that who or what we are is reflected in our cultural answers to questions such as "what does it mean to be a person?" or "what kind of person should one become?" Heidegger expresses this condition by telling us a human being (*Dasein*) is a being who "in its very Being, that Being is an *issue* for it" (p. 32) These questions are fundamentally ethical questions, they have to do with what we value most dearly in a particular culture. Our lives exist in the space of these moral questions (Taylor, 1989). Society or culture presents us with possible answers to these questions, but our identity itself is formed by the cultural dialogue that generates both these answers as well as the questions themselves.

As we discussed on pages 5-7, American culture is defined by a predominantly individualistic moral vision. Individualism, like any cultural vision, presents answers to the aforementioned questions of what the self is and what is should be. A number of authors have tried to show how this moral vision has shaped and permeated psychology (Christopher, 1992, 1999; Christopher, Christopher, and Dunnagan, 2000; Cirillo and Wapner, 1986; Cleary, 1999; Cushman, 1991, 1995; Fowers and Richardson, 1993, 1996; Frank, 1978; Greenberg, 1994; Kirschner, 1996; Lambeth, 1994; Richardson, 1989; Richardson and Guignon, 1988; Roland, 1996; Rubin, 1997; Sampson, 1977, 1988, 2000; Spence, 1985; Sue and Sue, 1990; Sullivan, 1986; Taylor, 1985a; Waterman, 1981, 1984; Wolszon, 1998; Woolfolk and Richardson, 1984).

Most non-western cultures embrace a very different form of self-understanding based on a collectivist rather than an individualist worldview and *ethos* (Hui and Triandis, 1986; Kim, Triandis, Kagitçibasi, Choi, and Yoon, 1994; Triandis, 1989, 1995). Such cultures tend to have a more interdependent or social view of the self (Geertz, 1973, 1983; Moore, 1968; Munro, 1969). Individualistic moral visions, characteristic of western views of selfhood tend to focus on independence, separation, personal discovery, etc., whereas collectivist views stress social harmony and family relations as well as one's role within these institutions (Hui, 1984, 1988; Hui and Triandis, 1986; Kim et al., 1994; Markus and Kitayama, 1991; Triandis, 1995). It should be noted that terms such as individualism and collectivism are meant as general characterizations. They do not capture the degrees of difference between various cultures that may fall under one or the other of these characterizations.

This is an important point to remember. Moral visions are such that they do not form a single coherent perspective on life in the way that a moral, religious or political theory might. Moral visions, embodied as they are in societies, take different forms. Individualism for instance, varies in form and expression in modern pluralistic societies. Two predominant forms of individualism, as labeled by Bellah and his colleagues are utilitarian and expressive individualism (Bellah et al., 1985). Utilitarian individualism personifies the confidence in science and technology characteristic of the sixteenth century Enlightenment and the emergence of the Utilitarian moral and political doctrine of Jeremy Bentham and John Stuart Mill. This view emphasizes rationality, rational self-interest, efficiency and individual initiative. Utilitarian individualism "takes as given certain basic human appetites and fears and sees human life as an effort by individuals to maximize their self-interest relative to their given ends" (Bellah et al., 1985, p. 336). In contrast to the scientific orientation of utilitarian individualism is the humanistic emphasis of expressive individualism. Following the Romantic reaction to the scientific dominance of the Enlightenment spirit, expressive individualism emphasizes the creative and artistic potential of the individual. This form of individualism views the good life as a life "rich in experience, open to all kinds of people, luxuriating in the sensual as well as the intellectual, above all a life of strong feeling" (Bellah et al., 1985, p. 34). Each individual "has a unique core of feeling and intuition that should unfold or be expressed if individuality is to be realized" (Bellah et al., 1985, p. 333). Bellah et al. note that contemporary American society brings together both forms of individualism in a precarious union. Utilitarian individualism tend to be the predominant way of understanding the world of industry and business, but for many people, expressive individualism characterizes the goals and desires of their personal or family life (Taylor, 1985b). Neither of these approaches takes the form of dogma, but both operate implicitly in this culture and strongly influence identity formation.

Hermeneutic Conceptual Tools for Approaching Cross-Cultural Interactions and Conflict

At this point we would like to introduce four ideas that we see as helpful in working with culture in psychotherapy. These four ideas, the hermeneutic circle, effective historical consciousness, hermeneutic dialogue, and *phronesis* are presented as optimal ways of grappling with the differences in moral visions that occur when working across cultures.

The Hermeneutic Circle and the Reconciliation of Culture-General and Culture-Specific Approaches to Multicultural Counseling

Hermeneutics helps resolve a dichotomy in the theories of multicultural counseling literature (Bezanson and James, 2005). Over the last few decades multicultural counseling theories have evolved into two categories: cultural general (etic) theories and cultural specific (emic) theories. Culture general theories of multicultural counseling provide a universal or etic approach to conceptualizing mental health issues with people of a culture other than the dominate one by examining the key issues that cut across humanity. Examples of this framework are Vontress' (1979) existential approach to cross-cultural counseling, Patterson's (1996) universal system of counseling and Fisher and colleagues' (Fischer, Jome, and Atkinson, 1998) 'common factors' perspective. Critics of these approaches suggest that they rely on a strong therapeutic relationship but this could be sabotaged if the therapist is not aware of the complexities of the group with whom he or she is working. These universal approaches can also be seen as simply facilitating acceptance of the ways of the dominate culture (Bezanson and James, 2005).

Culture specific approaches to multicultural therapy, on the other hand, emphasize the necessity of being knowledgeable about an ethnic group in order to provide suitable counseling services. Racial and ethnic differences become the basis for theories and models, and as such a counselor must gain an in-depth understanding of the particular group that he or she is working with (Sue, 1981, Pedersen, 1997; Tatman, 2004, Trimble, 2003). Critics of this approach suggest that making culture the focus of the practice may propagate that which Shweder (2004) calls "the ethnography of difference" or "disparagement" (p. 4). Thus, defining differences between groups can result in misleading generalizations that might not be useful when working with actual clients whose backgrounds are more complex than the theories acknowledge (Bezanson and James, 2005).

The debate over the usefulness of either approach has caused theorists and practitioners to focus their energy on defending their position, possibly at the expense of developing an integrated approach that would benefit the profession. We suggest that the dichotomy implied by the 'universal' versus 'specific' debate is not an either/or situation but may become the building blocks for a multidimensional framework (Bezanson and James, 2005) when understood from a hermeneutic perspective. Necessary to the hermeneutic process of interpretation is knowledge of the relationship between *the part* and *the whole,* or what is called the hermeneutic circle. As an interpretive process, hermeneutics provides a way of understanding the cultural influences that help create the self and thus is a useful framework for developing culturally sensitive practices. When applied to psychotherapy, this approach requires the delicate task of understanding the individual in the context of their culture and understanding the culture from the perspective of the client. This view does not privilege *the part* (the individual) over *the whole* (the culture) or visa versa but rather attempts to provide a true convergence of culture specific and culture general approaches. Christopher (1996, 2001), Foster and James (2004), James and Foster (in press) and Bezanson and James (2005) provide detailed accounts of a hermeneutic approach and its applicability to psychotherapy and cultural psychology.

The most obvious critique of culture-specific approaches focuses on the numerous possibilities for stereotyping when practitioners rigidly adhere to some abstract notion of a culturally influenced concept of the individual (Bezanson and James, 2005). For instance, the therapist may expect that client behave in a certain way because they are from a particular group, rather than seeing how the sessions unfold. Consideration of *the part* (the client) and *the whole* (the culture) promotes an understanding of the interaction between the two and discourages the idea that culture can be considered separate from individuals that collectively manifest the behaviors, beliefs and values of that culture. As such, racial and ethnic differences inform practice rather than becoming the sole basis for theories and models. The individual is situated within his or her local world but an understanding of culture-specific knowledge is still valued and utilized if appropriate.

Rather then the map becoming the territory, therapy requires striking a balance by moving back and forth in order to refine the notion of the part and the whole. The process is not about having information, the specifics or the universals, but more of creating a dynamic process where neither culture-specific nor general cultural theories alone hold the means for the therapist to understand the client's world (Bezanson and James, 2005). To the degree that broad generalizations like individualism and collectivism are important it is as a starting point in the hermeneutic circle that helps to delineate a range of possibilities of human functioning. Such a preliminary view of the whole can then be critically assessed to determine the degree to which it helps to illuminate a specific client's life and experience, which in turn refines our notion of what such broad concepts as collectivism actually entail.

Counseling psychology developed out of a temporally specific *zeitgeist* of Western thought, thus it provides a specific form of culture with its own value system and beliefs that we impose on clients of different ethnicities. Culture-general theories attempt to transcend any specific culture in order to access a body of knowledge that privileges individualism and choice. Consideration of this 'counseling' culture is imperative for understanding our beliefs concerning well-being and mental health. Hermeneutics offers a framework for considering this paradigm in which therapists work. In this case, the part (the practitioner) and the whole (the helping culture) are considered and the influence of these cultural institutions as well as the values and assumptions they imply are addressed simultaneously as we work with people of different ethnicities (Bezanson and James, 2005).

The Idea of Effective Historical Consciousness

The phrase "effective historical consciousness" was coined by Hans-Georg Gadamer (1975), a major figure in the modern hermeneutics movement. This notion implies an awareness by individuals of the role that "effective history" plays in human life. Effective history is the notion that the past shapes our understanding and outlook in the present and the present provides the framework for understanding the past. Our modern notions of virtue as well as our ideas of dignity, honor and respect are shaped by their history in the context of western religious, philosophical and political dialogue. Other cultures with a different religious, philosophical and political history will understand the virtues differently. Effective historical consciousness denotes an awareness of these historical influences on our thinking, understanding and beliefs, an awareness that Gadamer sees as crucial to our own self-understandings.

Due to the fact that our identity and self-understandings are shaped by history in this way, we believe that the awareness implied in the notion of "effective historical consciousness" should help inform counseling practices. We need to find a way to communicate or teach such awareness to our clients. Such teaching would aim at making both clients and therapists aware of the influence and limitations of these historical traditions on our thinking. These traditions provide us with our moral sources and shape our sense of self. We need to preserve these traditions, but we must preserve them in a critical manner. That is, we must not see these traditions as static with an intractable authority, but rather as living, growing and in need of scrutiny. What emerges from this is a kind of critical dialogue between the client or therapist and the cultural, historical tradition that they are part of. The individual comes to understand their self, not as an isolated or atomistic being, but as part of the historical struggle of preserving what is valuable in a tradition and challenging or opposing that which is at odds with human well-being.

Hermeneutic Dialogue

Two defining aspects of culture are reflected in a particular culture's answer to the questions: "What does it mean to be human?" and "What is the good life of human beings?" The answers to these questions divide cultures by presenting what seem to be irreconcilable and fundamental differences. What makes matters worse is the apparent lack of an objective standard through which to judge the validity or soundness of a culture's answers to these questions. This would seem to suggest that these answers will be culture-bound, lacking validity outside of the framework of the particular culture in which they are created. The conclusion that we are forced to draw from this situation is that these answers will be culturally-relative (Bernstein, 1983).

Our day to day lives, however, are not normally experienced as relative in this way. Typically, our experience of life confirms the contention of Heidegger, Geertz and Taylor that the form of life we share is of fundamental importance to us and we are shaped and motivated by our social practices and cultural meanings. As North Americans, we tend to experience ideals such as individual autonomy and rights, authenticity and tolerance, not merely as possible ways of living, but as valid, legitimate or true ways of being. We often forget that people from other cultures view their own ideas about the relation between the individual and culture for instance as obvious and true as well. We often fail to recognize or we mis-recognize the nature of the moral vision of another culture when we view that culture's practices, forms of life, or cultural meanings as inferior. This does not imply that we should never disagree with the views or moral values of another culture, but before we can authentically do so we should, following Gadamer (1975), engage in a form of dialogue that recognizes (provisionally) the legitimacy of these views as claims to truth.

Dialogue, for Gadamer, allows us to genuinely attempt to understand the horizon of understanding of another cultural group. Understanding the horizon of another group (or individual) allows for the possibility of a *fusion of horizons*. Gadamer uses the metaphor of a horizon in order to illustrate the limitations inherent in human understanding. Our attempts at understanding another culture, according to Gadamer, will always be determined or shaped by our pre-judgments or prejudices. These pre-judgements consist of the various assumptions or presuppositions that we develop throughout our life by way of our participation in a particular culture or form of life. This implies that human knowledge and understanding is always partial, perspectival and fallible as we always come to understand the world within a particular horizon or from a particular vantage point (Gadamer, 1975). We ought not to view this horizon as fixed or static but as something that evolves through the ongoing dialogue in which we participate both within our culture and while engaging with other cultures. The dynamic nature of cultural horizons implies that they are never closed. We may only have one particular vantage point for making judgments at a particular time in our history, but that vantage point changes with the change and growth of our horizon. Gadamer sees this limitation not merely as a comment on the incomplete nature of our understanding but as a defining feature of the human condition.

To attain a fusion of horizons in the manner that Gadamer advocates requires an openness to the horizon or perspective of others, even granting their values a kind of provisional authority through which to judge our own values. This means that we must bracket or suspend the authority of our own views or values creating a kind of Hegelian dialectic where ideas or concepts are only fully understood when they have been challenged by opposing theses. This approach attempts to avoid the pitfall of trying to understand the perspective of others superficially by making foreign ideas fit into our own conceptual framework. This process, when successfully carried out will inevitably change our own horizon and alter our perspective on our own deeply held beliefs and values. This dialogical approach and the openness it involves creates an authentic way of relating to others according to Gadamer. It moves us from an I-It way of relating to an I-Thou relationship (Buber, 1970).

None of this implies, however, that we adopt a position of unqualified relativism. We may still hold standards and ideals but this sort of dialogical exploration moves us towards a transforming of our standards (Taylor, 1992). Our standards are altered or transformed as we come to realize the ways in which elements of other cultures may enhance or renew aspects of our own tradition or way of life. We come to realize that our own worldview and *ethos* are incomplete. They represent one possibility among many. This does not diminish the value of our own way of life, but allows us to be open to having our perspective enriched by the perspective of others. Incorporating elements of another culture may lead to qualitative growth in our own. We see this already to some degree in modern multi-cultural nations, but in such contexts, we also see the struggle involved in overcoming the tendency to reduce dialogue to monologue. The dominant culture of any society often tends to resist change from the outside as part of its own struggle for survival.

This approach does not imply that we indiscriminately accept and adopt the views or practices of others into our way of life. Gadamer introduces the process of *application*as a way of tempering the work of dialogue. The knowledge that we gain through dialogue with another culture is tested by way of critical reflection in order to see if it really does help us clarify or improve our understanding of our own situation. What we gain from the other will be tested, applied and modified according to our own concrete situation and in our own historical context. Even in this application, however, it is important to maintain an openness so that we do not apply this newfound understanding too narrowly.

Hermeneutics and Aristotle's "Phronesis"

Hermeneutic philosophers have noted the manner in which Aristotle's concept of *phronesis* resembles a hermeneutic approach to philosophy and understanding (Gadamer, 2001; Ricoeur, 1992). *Phronesis* has been generally translated into English as 'practical wisdom'. This form of practical wisdom involves the correct application of general or universal rules (theoretical) to particular, concrete circumstances. What is distinct about phronesis is the manner in which Aristotle viewed this relationship between the universal and the particular. It is not simply a matter of applying the general to the concrete in terms of a 'top-down' approach, but it involves a two-way reflection similar to that implied by the hermeneutic relationship between the part and the whole. The person who possesses the virtue of practical wisdom does not mechanically apply universal rules to concrete situations, but through experience and the gaining of wisdom learns how to apply the right rule in the correct way in a particular situation. This means that the rule itself, the universal or theoretical principle is not fully understood or does not gain its full measure of truth until one has understood it through the application. The 'part' here, as in a hermeneutic approach, helps inform the 'whole' (or the general rule) and the whole guides us in dealing with the part. For instance, to be benevolent or to possess the virtue of benevolence does not mean that we simply are generous with our money or time. The true virtue of benevolence is expressed by the person who knows who to give what in a concrete situation of need.

What this implies for psychotherapists, particularly in a pluralistic or multicultural context, is that counseling and making good decisions regarding clients who hold different values or perspectives will involve more than applying general or universal principles. Aristotle's form of practical wisdom suggests that we need to work to understand the context or concrete circumstances of a client, including their cultural, social or religious background in order to understand not only which principles should be applied but also 'how' these principles should be applied. This approach once again takes a more dialogical (as opposed to monological) view of the relation between the therapist and the client whose culture may be foreign.

Multiculturalism and Intercultural Contact

The moral visions framework outlined in the chapter provides a powerful vantage point for discerning what is at stake in cross-cultural interactions. Moral visions influence counseling theory, but they also influence practice by shaping case conceptualization, diagnoses and diagnostic systems, the direction of cure, treatment goals, and the choice of interventions. According to Szasz (1961) the "socio-ethical orientations" of the psychiatrist will "influence his [or her] ideas on what is wrong with the patients, what deserves comment or interpretation, in what possible directions change might be desirable, and so forth" (p. 116). The underlying moral visions of therapy differ to some degree across theoretical orientations. Generally, however they all draw on some variant of individualism (Christopher, 1996; Richardson, 1989). For instance, behaviorism, cognitive-behaviorism, reality therapy and psychoanalytic ego therapy all are consonant with the version of individualism that Bellah et al., refer to as *utilitarian individualism,* that encourages using reason to control the emotions and thereby achieve self-defined goals. Other approaches to therapy including humanistic and transpersonal theories, self-psychology, and certain schools of object-relations theory like that of Winnicott, as well as many feminist orientations have their roots in Romanticism and what Bellah et al. term *expressive individualism.* Expressive individualism emphasizes authenticity, spontaneity, the importance of turning inward and making contact with one's inner life, and of identifying and expressing feelings in order to attain intimacy and reconnect with humanity and nature (see Richardson, 1989.

Cross-cultural interactions entail the intersection of multiple cultures. The culture of therapy is influenced by Western culture but is not synonymous with it. Psychology as a profession and an academic field reinterprets the moral sources of Western culture and these reinterpretations in turn influence Western folk psychology. A good example of this is the psychoanalytic notion of defense which is now part of the North American folk psychologies. Furthermore, the values and assumptions underlying professional theory and practice are situated within and exist along side the cultural values and assumptions manifested in different parts of society. This results in a kind of dialectical relation between professional psychology and folk psychology. Moreover there is a dynamic tension for the psychotherapist between their professional theoretical commitments and their cultural orientation as shaped by their own family and socio-economic group. This complex intertwining and tension between different strands of Western culture results in a heterogeneous complexity of moral sources that underlie the therapist. Consequently, all counseling even when the counselor and client are of the same ethnicity is cross-cultural. Inviting in a client from a widely different culture adds exponentially to this complexity. It is this overwhelming complexity that we face, consciously or not, when engaging in multicultural counseling and intercultural contact.

Some examples of the complexity of these issues are provided by research conducted with Portuguese immigrants in Canada and the United States (James, 2002, Morrison and James, 2006). These examples raise questions about the applicability of Murray Bowen's notion of differentiation across cultures. In Bowen's work, differentiation plays a significant role in marriage and family therapy. Differentiation relies on a highly individualistic understanding of identity. Bowen defines *differentiation of self*as "the difference between people in the proportion of life energy prone to be invested and bound in relationships" (Kerr and Bowen, 1988, p. 68). According to this view, individual identity is not well developed where more energy is invested in preserving or maintaining relationships. Individuality is better developed in the more highly differentiated individual who focuses on his or her own functioning. A lack of differentiation leads to higher levels of emotion and anxiety resulting from concern for others.

> Trying to achieve a higher level of differentiation or more solid (basic) self means increasing one's capacity for emotional detachment or neutrality. More detachment or neutrality depends on changes in thinking. Such changes are reflected in the ability to be in emotional contact with a difficult, emotionally charged problem and not feel compelled to preach about what others "should" do, not rush in to "fix" the problem, and not pretend to be detached by emotionally insulating oneself. Improving one's ability to contain these emotionally driven urges is contingent on developing a way of thinking that can counterbalance them. (p.108)

The notion of differentiation, as attractive as it may be in our culture, relies on a particular, culture-bound moral vision. This reliance limits the applicability of this notion when it comes to cross-cultural psychology. For instance, our research with Portuguese immigrants indicates that they handle differentiation differently (Morrison and James, 2006). A father from the community stated,

> It's my way or no way. (Laughing) It is my way or the highway. It's one table, one plate on the table . ... That's the way it goes (laughing). And no complaints, my older son is 27 years old. . . . And he is still here.

This communal moral vision had a number of important implications for the Portuguese community. This vision of a "good" family can be misunderstood by therapists. A number of therapists who work with Portuguese immigrants were interviewed and said that the Portuguese families were enmeshed. The interdependence can be misunderstood and rashly pathologized if it is not understood from the moral visions of the family.

Looking at the concept of the person from the perspective of the Portuguese community highlights a very different way of thinking. The dominant Western way of dividing reality into subjects and objects or self and other does not accord with the folk psychology of Portuguese immigrants. This community relies on a different conception of selfhood, one that is not primarily dualistic. Markus and Kitayama (1991) have called this the *interdependent* sense of self in which "the self is viewed as *inter*dependent with the surrounding context, and it is the "other" or the "self-in-relation-to-other" that is focal in individual experience" (p. 225). This interdependent sense of self is illustrated by an example taken from the fieldwork of Fajans (1985) among the Baining in New Guinea. She writes, "the social actor is not a rigidly defined and delimited entity" for "the boundaries of the individual and the definition of the person are neither permanent nor immutable, but alter and adapt in specific contexts" (p. 381). A Portuguese woman's description of suffering highlights this notion as well (James, 2002). "You need to suffer to redeem yourself and others. In a Catholic Church suffering is not only for yourself but also for others and for the world." Another woman concurred, "Someone, after all, has to carry the cross like Jesus Christ carried the cross for everyone. Some of us, are chosen by God to care for others and pay for their sins."

Here we see a very different sense of self, one where the sharp distinctions characteristic of the independent sense of self do not exist. Suffering, helping and meeting needs is understood in more communal terms and less in voluntary, individualistic terms. The suffering of others and the duty to help relieve suffering is part of the conception of self by virtue of being part of the community. Suffering is not divided into "my" suffering or "their" suffering. Without realizing this characteristic of a Portuguese sense of identity, a North American counselor could easily pathologize the experience of a Portuguese immigrant.

A different sense of self also affects our understanding and experience of emotions. For example, Portuguese children mentioned struggling with guilt around their desire to be more independent. Typically North American psychotherapists would attempt to make sense of guilt within the dualistic framework consistent with an independent self-construal (Christopher and Smith, 2006). In this sense, emotion terms have been understood as having a two-dimensional scaling solution (Russell, 1980); along the first dimension they can be mapped as pleasant/good versus unpleasant/bad or along the second dimension as active/high energy versus inactive/low energy. This same two dimensional pattern of results can be found in Non-Western cultures. In collectivist cultures however, a third dimension has been identified which is not found in the United States. (Markus and Kitayama, 1991). In these cultures we see other-centered emotions which stand in contrast with ego-centered ones. In Portugal other-centered emotions include suffering as we mentioned already. In addition, *saudade* refers to a mixture of sadness, love, compassion, and longing that has a real similarity to a term, *fago*, used in Micronesia for the same qualities (Lutz, 1988). Another other centered emotion used In Palau, *ta rengrir* denotes the other-centered emotion of getting along or being of one mind (Smith and Smith, 1995). *Awumbuk*, a term used by the Baining of Papua New Guinea to indicate a kind of social hangover, is an especially vivid example of interpersonal emotion.

> ...a lassitude that people feel after the departure of visitors, friends, or relatives who have resided with them....When the social group disbands, these connections are severed. The extended persona is destroyed and individuals must reconstitute their boundaries.... The departure induces a loss of social vitality and leaves the home party feeling relatively weakened and diminished, experienced as an additional weight or burden.... (Fagans, 1985, p. 380)

These other-centered or social emotions, we should add, are often neither exclusively positive nor negative. They may often include both connotations much like our idea of sweet sorrow.

The concept of other-centered emotions poses a difficult challenge to western approaches to counseling and psychotherapy. We tend to view emotions as personal and private, something that comes from our interior being (Taylor, 1989; Dreyfus and Rabinow, 1983). We see emotions as something one 'has' or 'possesses' (cf. Macpherson, 1962). By contrast, collectivist cultures often interpret emotional experiences externally, by looking to the environment or to relations with other people. These other centered emotions do not play such an important role in individualist cultures. We do often not even have a name in English for such emotions. Western society operates as if such emotions are unimportant or perhaps not even real. Mesquita (2001) tells us: "Emotions in collectivist cultures are expected to stress and reproduce the self in relation to others or the self in relation to the world, whereas emotions in individualist cultures are assumed to underline and amplify a bounded, subjective self" (p. 68). This raises an important question for counselors, namely, "how should we deal with other centered emotions?" The presence of other centered emotions may even suggest a pathological condition when viewed from an individualistic perspective. A self experiencing such emotions may appear to be divided or co-dependent.

We have noticed that the Portuguese immigrant children struggle when they try to differentiate from their parents. Portuguese parents may characterize their 'differentiated' children as "*falta de orgulho*" which roughly translates as "having no pride in one's family or culture". Parents may also feel an intense emotion with that differentiation. It is sometimes described as *agonias,* literally translated as "the agonies" (James, 2002). For instance, the community Priest said,

> Children can give people *agonias* because they are not living with faith or they are doing things that are forbidden like divorcing. And for the people it's certainly a weight on them and it gives them a tightening feeling, like claustrophobia.... *Agonias* is really anxiety about sins, the sins of your children.

In this example *agonias* seems to carry a different connotation than guilt—it has more of an interpersonal quality. We seem to have no way of representing this interpersonal dimension within the folk psychology of North American culture therefore we view it as something negative such as "co-dependency" or as being "enmeshed." From a Portuguese perspective, however, the guilt of the children and the agonies of the parents are appropriate. They are a testament to the fact that the Portuguese sense of self is interdependent, that is, it is understood as involving the hopes, aspirations and desires of one's family members. Pathology in this case would involve being detached and disconnected and not experiencing *agonias*. If a therapist working with Portuguese clients were to attempt to reduce the guilt they would demonstrate a lack of understanding for the Portuguese sense of self.

An understanding of emotion as well as its expression is also shaped by cultural norms as a number of researchers have observed (Lebra, 1976; Markus and Kitayama, 1994; Menon and Shweder, 1994; Mesquita, Frijda, and Scherer, 1997). Noting these differences, multicultural counselors have warned against drawing premature conclusions. An example of the cultural influence on emotions is expressed in interviews (James, 2002) that we conducted with therapists who treat Portuguese clients,

> A lot of them ... don't exactly say what they want so it takes forever to get information from them and they go about it in a round about way and they don't directly ask what they're looking for.

Thus, the way that Portuguese negotiate seeking help can be misunderstood if therapists have different ideals and expectations of how a client should act.

Resolving these cultural differences and addressing the personal conflicts they engender will not be an easy or straightforward task. Rather than applying such hermeneutic notions as effective historical consciousness, hermeneutic dialogue, phronesis, and the hermeneutic circle, it would be much easier to try to make the problems fit into a counseling framework that we are familiar with. To do so, we believe, would fail to adequately address the problems that immigrants face. Clients who are struggling with the stress of culture shock or enculturation may be helped by our recognition of the complexity of their situation. The recognition of these cultural differences and divergent moral visions (including different assumptions about the nature of the self, the good person and the good life) can help the client to understand and deal with the social stresses better, in part by helping them recognize the enormity of what's at stake. For instance, Christopher and Smith (2006) explored how educating clients about the moral visions involved can help clients develop self-acceptance and compassion. Thus, a sensitivity to "what's at stake" may allow counselors to better help clients through a potentially traumatizing transition to a new culture. Such sensitivity may be nurtured by recognizing the significance and influence of historical factors that make up the tradition of the client. The consciousness or self of the client is shaped by this history as well as the meanings and symbols of a particular tradition. In light of this, deciding an appropriate way to help a client will involve a kind of practical wisdom that resembles Aristotle's *phronēsis*. It will not be a simple matter of applying principles of counseling theory algorithmically to the client's situation, but of making a judgement about which principles are appropriate given the concrete circumstances and historical factors involved. This is something that mature and sensitive counselors may often do intuitively as a response to problems that they encounter in cross-cultural counseling. We see this sensitivity as an important dimension of counseling that should be nurtured among therapists.

For Portuguese immigrants, negotiating the divide between family obligations and individuation is conceivably a lifelong process. In order to find a balance between the sometimes conflicting cultural influences we may need to recognize this as a process and attribute moral meaning to it. This avoids the simple and insensitive solution of assuming that the family has problems and recognizes the fact that we live in a time where moral visions are confronting each other more and more. We must recognize the implications of a more global world and of more inter-cultural societies. We must seek to help those who attempt to live bi-culturally (or even multi-culturally) understand the role of the moral visions that make up their world.

Portuguese immigrants who seek therapy are faced with a challenge. To some degree American culture and the therapies that uncritically build upon it may lack the resources to help the Portuguese immigrants cope with a situation that does not have readily apparent solutions. The emancipatory thrust of the American *ethos* emphasizes the elimination of suffering and even freedom from unhappiness, as is promised in much of the popular psychology literature. Some critics have suggested that this cultural outlook can result in a kind of tyranny of happiness (Held, 2002). A one-sided emphasis on emotional satisfaction and happiness tends to neglect, according to Frank (1973), other, more traditional, but often worthwhile values or virtues such as "the redemptive power of suffering, acceptance of one's lot in life, adherence to tradition, self-restraint and moderation" (p. 7). We see this emphasis on redemptive suffering in the Portuguese immigrant community. Instead of emphasizing liberation from pain and suffering, Portuguese culture regards this ability to suffer for others as the mark of a virtuous person.

The moral visions framework we've described was put to the test in some of our work cross-culturally in Micronesia, although the examples that follow need not be strictly cross-cultural. Our work with gang members and inmates who had been diagnosed with conduct disorder, oppositional defiant disorder, and antisocial personality disorder raised questions about what could possibly be moral in the lives of those widely regarded as immoral and antisocial. In exploring the lives of this population we found that their lives, like ours,' are clearly informed by a conception of the good (Christopher, 1996; Schmitz and Christopher, 1997.

For instance gang members indicated a commitment to such virtues as honor, respect, and dignity. Recognizing this raised our awareness of the critical distinction between certain moral sources and the interpretation and application of these moral sources in particular situations. Even if we reject the moral visions of these gang members, it is important to identify and understand the values that inform it, values that are worthwhile. Honor, dignity and a general sense of virtue are implicit in most value systems. Identifying such values may serve as an ally to the counselor in dealing with the more problematic aspects of a client's life. We do not have to discredit the whole person, but we can start with affirming the positive values contained in that person's moral vision.

Discovering and acknowledging the client's orientation towards the 'good' can have a number of therapeutic benefits. Rather than feeling that they are simply bad people, outcasts of society, or pathological, clients can feel that something very important to their sense of self has been recognized. This may open the door for a bond of communication and understanding between counselor and client. Helping the client to understand their own moral vision and the way that it influences their sense of identity (as well as their actions) may help them to think through with the counselor, alternative strategies for attaining their idea of the good life. Proceeding in this way allows the client to see change in terms of an alteration of their own moral vision rather than in terms of having a foreign moral vision imposed on them from the outside. Given the intimate connection between moral visions and one's sense of self, this would seem to be an important step in overcoming the barriers between counselor and client, especially in a cross-cultural context.

The encounter between the moral vision of the counselor and that of the client parallel's, to a large extent, the encounter between horizon's advocated by Gadamer and discussed earlier in this chapter. Just as a fusion of horizon's required an openness to the horizon of the other and a provisional granting of the truth or legitimacy of that horizon, so the encounter between counselor and client requires an initial working within the client's moral vision and a refusal to impose one's ethnocentric view of the good on the client. This in itself does not solve the problem when it comes to counseling. We have admitted that the counselor possesses his or her own moral vision or horizon and can only make sense of the world and the client (initially) through this. Not only does this vision allow us to make sense of the client, but it also helps us to prescribe a solution to the problem. If we did not think that we could help find such a solution, or if the client did not think that we could, then the therapeutic encounter would be useless. A totally neutral stance towards the client's moral vision (which in itself reveals a particular moral vision – one based on a particular view of scientific or philosophical reason) would give us nothing to prescribe. It would seem therefore, that we need to allow our moral visions to play some role in our judgments concerning a client's condition and our proposals for treating this condition without negating or disrespecting her or his moral vision.

Gadamer's (1975) "fusion of horizons" would once again seem to offer a possible solution. In order to respect the moral vision of our client, while at the same time making discriminations or judgments about what is good or healthy behavior, requires a dialogical situation not unlike the one Gadamer proposes. As we discussed earlier in the paper, hermeneutic dialogue requires a dialectic between openness and application. As counselors we need to be open to the horizon of the client and allow that horizon provisional authority in terms of our understanding of their situation. Until we openly attempt to understand the client's situation as they understand it, we are not in an authentic position to work towards a solution. Even when we have made a sincere, reflective and critical attempt at understanding this horizon, we must remember the fallible nature of our undertaking. Once we have gained insight into our client's situation or horizon, it is important to remember the second part of Gadamer's dialectic which involves a critical application of the insights attained. Applying these insights in order to make sense of the client's concrete situation helps us to avoid an uncritical or superficial understanding or adoption of the perspective of the client. Such an adoption may allow for an understanding of the client that is deeply empathetic, but not terribly useful in helping the client work through an understanding of their moral vision in a way that aids them in overcoming the confused or negative aspects. This is why the interaction between counselor and client is best understood in terms of dialogue. A true fusion of horizons will indeed be a dialogue between the two parties that leads to greater understanding on both parts. The counselor may not (and probably will not) know how he or she can help the client in their particular concrete situation until he or she has engaged in the process of dialogue involving the dialectic between openness and application.

Implications: Beyond Objectivism and Relativism

Bellah et al. (1985) have made us aware of the fact that social science makes assumptions about the nature of persons, the nature of society, and the relation between persons and society. It also, whether it admits it or not, makes assumptions about good persons and a good society and considers how far these conceptions are embodied in our actual society. (p. 301)

Should we be troubled by this condition? Should the aim of the social sciences be to eradicate such biases in order to attain a more neutral or objective understanding of the subject-matter of counseling, psychology or the social sciences in general as has been recommended by Spence (1985)?

Proponents of philosophical hermeneutics (Gadamer, 1975; Richardson and Christopher, 1993; Richardson and Woolfolk, 1994; Taylor, 1985a, 1985b; Ricoeur, 1981), social constructionism (Cushman, 1990; Gergen, 1985), and interactivism (Bickhard, 1980; Campbell and Bickhard, 1986), among others, contend that attempts to gain objective, value-free, ahistorical knowledge are both futile and misguided. These attempts presuppose the questionable subject-object and fact-value dichotomies that have been conceptual hallmarks of Western culture. Bickhard (1980) has argued that "the concept of knowledge as objective, to which we then attach values, purposes, goals, and so forth is mistaken. Objective knowledge is a myth. All knowledge is motivationally structured" (p. 33). Knowledge is a product of interpretations. These interpretations can never be purely objective due to our inescapable historicity (see Hiley, Bohman, and Shusterman, 1991; Rabinow and Sullivan, 1987). This implies that we are always situated within a particular historical horizon of understanding, one which contains its own moral vision, and we always try to make sense of the world through the cultural and personal presuppositions that this horizon gives rise to.

Gadamer (1975) called these presuppositions prejudices. He speaks of the Enlightenment spirit as one which displays a prejudice against prejudice. This prejudice against prejudice (or presuppositions) has given rise to what Bernstein (in discussing the social sciences) (1978) called the ideal of the disinterested observer "who explains, understands, interprets, or simply describes, what is" (p. xix). Hermeneutic thinkers such as Gadamer (1975) and Taylor (1989) oppose the notion of the disinterested observer telling us that it is not possible to fully remove ourselves from the prejudices of our traditions. The very ideas of objectivity and value-neutrality according to Taylor are "connected with some of the most important moral and spiritual ideals of our civilization" such as individualism (Taylor, 1987, p. 472; also see Bernstein, 1986; Cirillo and Wapner, 1986). A hermeneutic view tells us that ironically this objective or neutral approach is itself the product of a particular moral vision.

The counselor can never take the stance of a detached observer neutrally evaluating different interpretations. We are always speaking from within a set of presuppositions; thus, our understandings and interpretations can only be criticized from the base of other prejudices not in question at the moment. Of course, this does not mean that we should not attempt to be more careful and rigorous in our thinking. But, if we assume we are being neutral, unbiased, or value-free, then we are simply failing to recognize the prejudices from which we operate.

Bellah and his colleagues, recognizing the impossibility gaining objectivity and value neutrality in the social sciences, have proposed that we think in terms of *social science as moral inquiry* or *social science as public philosophy* (Bellah et al, 1985; Haan, Bellah, Rabinow, and Sullivan, 1983). Applied to counseling, this approach recognizes the fact that we are always working within the space of moral visions or cultural horizons. This means that we would have to recognize that counseling is "a tradition, or set of traditions, deeply rooted in the philosophical and humanistic (and, to more than a small extent, the religious) history of the West" (Bellah et al., 1985, p. 301). Acknowledging this fact about counseling may remind us that our beliefs about what it means to be a person and our normative assumptions about what a person should be are "contestable and that the choice of assumptions involve controversies that lie deep in the history of Western thought" (p. 301). As a form of public philosophy, counseling "would make the philosophical conversation concerning these matters its own" (p. 301).

A consequence of viewing counseling as a largely moral activity or enquiry is that we must acknowledge with Prilleltensky (1989) that our current conception of the role of ethics in counseling is too narrow. If counseling involves the encounter of moral visions between counselor and client that we have claimed, then ethics cannot merely play the role of providing ethical procedures or guidelines as outlined in our professional ethics manuals. The role of morality in the counseling is more substantive. Bickhard (1989), for instance, maintains that:

> Therapy is not just an activity to which ethical considerations can be applied, nor just an activity which makes use of moral considerations in selecting its instrumental goals. Psychotherapy is a very special kind of intrinsically ethical relating to another person. (p. 163)

This more substantive understanding of the role of ethics will also extend beyond counseling. Moral visions not only affect counseling practice, but counseling theory and research as well. This suggests that counselors should: (a) acknowledge our cultural embeddedness, (b) seek to continually clarify and question the moral visions that motivate us, (c) relentlessly attempt to discern how moral visions affect our work as counselors, and (d) regularly engage in public discourse on the nature and appropriateness of our moral visions.

This article has tried to outline a meta-theoretical account of culture by focusing on the way that moral visions permeate culture. The aim of such an account is to help counselors to acknowledge and explore their moral visions in order to have a better grasp of the role that they play in their own understanding as well as the self-understanding of their clients

The meta-theoretical account provided here aims at furthering the effort to find an account of understanding the human subject that is "beyond objectivism and relativism" (Bernstein, 1985). Such an account will acknowledge that there are no ahistorical, neutral or truly objective criteria to adopt as counselors. On the other hand, this does not lead us to adopt a fruitless relativism that suggests that all moral visions are equally good or useful. There are grounds for criticizing moral visions that exist within cultural and historical traditions. Their culture-bound nature does not render them illegitimate. Historically we have developed judgments that condemn racism, sexism, and oppression from within the context of cultural communities (MacIntyre, 1988; Ricoeur, 1981). Many of these critiques have gained currency beyond their original cultural setting and have been recognized on a more universal level. This move from a specific cultural starting point to a widening and more universal perspective suggests one possibility for defining a middle way between objectivism and relativism, a path which the authors of this article seek.

The previous example illustrates the more general attempt to move beyond objectivism and relativism implied in philosophical hermeneutics. This approach aims at truth but recognizes that the finite nature of human understanding limits us to truths that will never have complete certainty. The middle ground is found in the recognition that our moral visions are neither fully objective nor arbitrarily relative. We must acknowledge and take responsibility for our actions and their consequences, especially the effect that our judgments or prescriptions will have upon our clients. We must make choices about the source of the problem and the direction of the cure and intervene accordingly, but we must not allow ourselves or our clients to believe that these judgments are not influenced by our moral visions. Maturity in counseling, much like the maturity implied in Aristotle's practical wisdom (*phronesis)* is expressed in our capacity for making good judgments regarding the implications of our moral visions and the application of well-reasoned and critically evaluated counseling prescriptions.

Part of this maturity consists in the recognition that our judgment is fallible, our theories, conceptualizations, diagnoses and interventions are uncertain. We must make the best judgments that we can based on our experience and the best reasons and arguments we have available (Taylor, 1989). These judgments mature through thoughtful dialogue with clients, colleagues and through life experience.

Our judgments and prescriptions themselves will reflect a stance that we are taking, a moral vision by which we live. Such a vision presupposes a conception of the good which we aim to live by and which will inevitably influence our interaction with clients, even if we do not explicitly urge them to adopt our view. Counseling ultimately engages us in a discussion of the good life with the client, one which ideally leads to a dialogical conclusion or solution.

Conclusion

Moral visions are essential to human life as we have emphasized throughout this paper. The idea of culture itself is that of a web which is imbued with one or more moral visions. Contrary to certain modern conceptions of individualism, the individual and culture are not radically separate entities. Individuals live a certain culture by defining personhood and the concept of the good life in culture-specific terms. The intersubjective nature of cultural ideals is expressed in social practices that are often unique to particular cultures and which help create the identity of its inhabitants. We gain this identity through growing up in or participating in the practices of a particular culture. The identity that we gain through our culture is often involuntary and largely unacknowledged, at least until we begin to reflect upon who we are or contrast our identity with a different cultural group. Our encounter with other cultures allows us to understand more clearly the presuppositions inherent in our own. These presuppositions include our conception of what it means to be a person and what it means to live a good life.

We sometimes make the mistake of categorizing the behavior of others, especially those from a different culture as pathological, distorted, crazy or even evil. We often do this because we do not acknowledge the fact that our perspective is limited by our cultural horizon and the presuppositions that compose it. Understanding a particular behavior through a different set of presuppositions and background assumptions – namely those inherent in the horizon of a different culture, may change our assessment and the way that we interpret a particular behavior. As Pederson (1991) tells us, we can only avoid being "culturally encapsulated" if we allow our cultural "givens" to be questioned through dialogue so that our differences might be bridged.

This type of intercultural dialogue may not radically transform either culture's horizon. It is difficult to change something that has been deeply ingrained in us well before we were even conscious of it. What such dialogue does offer, however, is the chance to reflect on the assumptions and beliefs that we take for granted by virtue of growing up in a particular culture and adhering to a particular view of the good. This kind of dialogue may deepen, enhance and even modify our own conception of the good and the good life. This kind of transformation paralleling what Gadamer has called a fusion of horizons, may lead to cultural and personal advancement and enrichment.

REFERENCES

Adams, G., and Markus, H. R. (2001). Culture as patterns: An alternative approach to the problem of reification. *Culture and Psychology, 7*(3), 283-296.

Barclay, M. W. (1992). The utility of hermeneutic interpretation in psychotherapy. *Theoretical and Philosophical Psychology, 12*, 103-118

Baumeister, R. F. (1986). *Identity: Cultural change and the struggle for the self.* New York: Oxford University Press.

Baumeister, R. F. (1987). How the self became a problem: A psychological review of historical research. *Journal of Personality and Social Psychology, 52*, 163-176.

Bellah, R. N. (1983). The ethical aims of social inquiry. In N. Haan, R. N. Bellah, P. Rabinow and W. M. Sullivan (Eds.), (pp. 360-381). New York: Columbia University Press.

Bellah, R. N., Madsen, R., Sullivan, W. M., Swidler, A., and Tipton, S. M. (1985). *Habits of the heart: Individualism and commitment in American life.* New York: Harper and Row.

Benner, P. (1994). *Interpretive phenomenology: Embodiment, caring, and ethics in health and illness*. Thousand Oaks, CA: Sage Publications.

Berlin, I., Hardy, H., and Hausheer, R. (1998). *The proper study of mankind : An anthology of essays*. London: Pimlico.

Bernstein, R. J. (1978). *The reconstructing of social and political theory*. Philadelphia: University of Pennsylvania Press.

Bernstein, R. J. (1983). *Beyond objectivism and relativism: science, hermeneutics, and praxis*. Philadelphia: University of Pennsylvania Press.

Bickhard, M. H. (1980). *Cognition, convention, and communication*. New York: Praeger.

Bickhard, M. H. (1989). Ethical psychotherapy and psychotherapy as ethics: A response to Perrez. *New Ideas in Psychology, 7*(2), 159-164.

Bickhard, M. H., and Christopher, J. C. (1994). The influence of early experience on personality development. *New Ideas in Psychology, 12,* 229-252.

Bouchard, M. and Guerette, L. (1991). Psychotherapy as a hermeneutical experience. *Psychotherapy: Theory, Research, Practice, Training, 28*, 385-394.

Braginsky, D. D. (1992). Psychology: Handmaiden to society. In S. Koch and D. E. Leary (Eds.), *A century of psychology as science*(pp. 880-891). Washington, DC: American Psychological Association.

Brinson, J. A., and Kottler, J. A. (1995). Minorities' underutilization of counseling centers' mental health services: A case for outreach and consultation. *Journal of Mental Health Counseling, 17*, 371-385.

Brinton, C. (1987). *A history of Western morals.* New York: Paragon House. (Original work published 1959).

Bronfenbrenner, U. (1977). Toward an experimental ecology of human development. *American Psychologist, 32*, 513-531.

Bruner, J. (1990). *Acts of meaning.* Cambridge, MA: Harvard University Press.

Buber, M. (1970). *I and Thou*. New York: Charles Scribner's Sons.

Campbell, R. L., and Bickhard, M. H. (1986). *Knowing levels and developmental stages*. Basel: Karger.

Campbell, R. L., Christopher, J. C., and Bickhard, M. H. (2002). Values and the self: An interactivist foundation for moral development. *Theory and Psychology*, *12*, 795-823.

Camus, Albert. (1983). *The Myth of Sisyphus*. Markham, ON: Penguin Books, Ltd.

Chessick, R. D. (1990). Hermeneutics for psychotherapists. *American Journal of Psychotherapy, 44*, 256-273.

Christopher, J. C. (1996). Counseling's inescapable moral visions. *Journal of Counseling and Development*, *75,* 17-25.

Christopher, J. C. (1999). Situating psychological well-being: Exploring cultural values and assumptions underlying theory and research on psychological well-being. *Journal of Counseling and Development*, *77*, 141-152.

Christopher, J. C. (2001). Culture and psychotherapy: Towards a hermeneutic approach. *Psychotherapy, 38*, 115-128.

Christopher, J. C. (2004). Moral visions of developmental psychology. In B. Slife, J. S. Reber, and F. C. Richardson (Eds.), *Critical thinking about psychology: Hidden assumptions and plausible alternatives*(pp. 207-231). Washington, D. C.: APA Press.

Christopher, J. C., and Bickhard, M. H. (in press). Culture, self, and identity: Interactivist contributions to a metatheory for cultural psychology. *Culture and Psychology*.

Christopher, S., Christopher, J. C., and Dunnagan, T. (2000). Culture's impact on health risk appraisal psychological well-being questions. *American Journal of Health Behavior, 24*, 338-348.

Christopher, J. C., Nelson, T., and Nelson, M. D. (2004). Culture and character education: Problems of interpretation in a multicultural society. *Journal of Theoretical and Philosophical Psychology*, *23*, 81-101.

Christopher, J. C., and Smith, A. (2006). A Hermeneutic Approach to Culture and Psychotherapy. InR. Moody, and S. Palmer (Eds.), *Race, culture and psychotherapy: Critical perspective in multicultural practice* (pp. 265-280). New York: Brunner/Routledge.

Cirillo, L., and Wapner, S. (1986). *Value presuppositions in theories of human development*. Hillsdale, NJ: Lawrence Erlbaum.

Cleary, R. J. (1999). Bowlby's theory of attachment and loss: A feminist reconsideration. *Feminism and Psychology, 9*, 32-42.

Cole, M. (1996). *Cultural psychology: A once and future discipline*. Cambridge, MA: Harvard University Press.

Cushman, P. (1990). Why the self is empty: Toward a historically situated psychology. *American Psychologist, 45*(5), 599-611.

Cushman, P. (1991). Ideology obscured: Political uses of the self in Daniel Stern's infant. *American Psychologist,46,* 206-219.

Cushman, P. (1995). *Constructing the self, constructing America: A cultural history of psychotherapy*: Addison-Wesley.

Devereaux, G. (1958). Cultural factors in psychoanalytic therapy. *Journal of the American Psychoanalytic Association*, *1*, 629-655.

Dilthey, W. (1989). *Introduction to the Human Sciences* (R.A. Makkreel, and F. Rodi, Trans. and Ed.), Princeton, NJ: Princeton University Press.

Doherty, W. J. (1995). *Soul searching: Why psychotherapy must promote moral responsibility*. New York: Basic Books.

Dreyfus, H. L., and Rabinow, P. (1983). *Michael Foucault: Beyond structuralism and hermeneutics*. Chicago: The University of Chicago Press.

Dumont, L. (1986). *Essays on individualism*. Chicago: University of Chicago Press.

Eagle, M. N. (1986). Psychoanalysis a hermeneutics. *Behavioral and Brain Sciences, 9*, 231-232.

Ellis, A. (1973). Humanistic psychotherapy. New York: McGraw-Hill.

Fajans, J. (1985). The person in social context: The social character in Baining "psychology." In G. M. White, J. Kirkpatrick and et al. (Eds.), *Person, self, and experience: Exploring Pacific ethnopsychologies.* (pp. 367-397). Berkeley, CA, USA: University of California Press.

Fischer, A. R., Jome, L. M., and Atkinson, D. R. (1998). Back to the future of multicultural psychotherapy with a common factors approach. *Counseling Psychologist, 26*, 602-606.

Fischer, C. T. (1980). Phenomenology and psychological assessment: Re-presentational description. *Journal of Phenomenological Psychology, 11*, 79-105.

Foster, G. and James, S. (2004). Narratives of hope and reconciliation: A hermeneutic approach to cultural therapy. *Constructivism and the Human Sciences, 9*, 67-76.

Fowers, B. J. and Richardson, F. C. (1993). Individualism and aggression: A hermeneutic analysis of Huesmann and Eron's cognitive theory of aggression. *Theory and Psychology,3,* 353-377.

Fowers, B. J. and Richardson, F. C. (1996). Individualism, family ideology, and family therapy. *Theory and Psychology,6,* 121-151.

Fowers, B. J., and Richardson, F. C. (1994). Why is multiculturalism good? *American Psychologist, 51*, 609-621.

Frank, J. (1978). *Psychotherapy and the human predicament.* New York: Schocken.

Frank, J. D. (1973). *Persuasion and healing: A comparative study of psychotherapy*. New York: Schocken Books.

Frank, J. D. (1987). Psychotherapy, rhetoric, and hermeneutics: Implications for practice and research. *Psychotherapy: Theory, Research, Practice, Training, 24*, 293-302.

Gadamer, H.-G. (1975). *Truth and method.* New York: Crossroad.

Gadamer, H.-G. (2001). *Reason in the Age of Science*. Cambridge, MA: The MIT Press.

Geertz, C. (1973). *The interpretation of cultures.* New York: Basic Books.

Geertz, C. (1983). *Local knowledge: Further essays in interpretive anthropology*. New York: Basic Books.

Gentile, J. (1998). Listening for deep structure: Between the a priori and the intersubjective. *Contemporary Psychoanalysis, 34*, 67-89.

Gergen, K. J. (1985). The social constuctionist movement in modern psychology. *American Psychologist, 40*, 266-275.

Gergen, K. J. (1994). *Realities and relationships: Soundings in social construction.* Cambridge, MA: Harvard University Press.

Gergen, K. J. (1995). Postmodern psychology: Resonance and reflection. *American Psychologist, 50*, 394.

Giorgi, A. (1970). *Psychology as a human science: A phenomenologically based approach.* New York: Harper and Row.

Greenberg, G. (1994). *The self on the shelf: Recovery books and the good life*. Albany: State University of New York Press.

Guignon, C. B. (1984). *Heidegger and the problem of knowledge.* Indianapolis: Hackett.

Haan, N., Bellah, R. N., Rabinow, P., and Sullivan, W. M. (1983). *Social science as moral inquiry*. New York: Columbia University Press.

Held, B. S. (2002). The tyranny of the positive attitude in America: Observation and speculation. *Journal of Clinical Psychology, 58*, 965-992.

Hegel, G.W.F. (1977). *Phenomenology of Spirit.* New York: Oxford University Press.

Heidegger, M. (1962). *Being and time* (J. Macquarrie and E. Robinson, Trans.). New York:

Hiley, D. R., Bohman, J. F., and Shusterman, R. (Eds.). (1991). *The interpretive turn: Philosophy, science, culture*. Ithaca, NY: Cornell University Press.

Hogan, R. (1975). Theoretical egocentrism and the problem of compliance. *American Psychologist, 30*, 533-540.

Hoshmand, L. T. (Ed.). (2006). *Culture, psychotherapy, and counseling.* Thousand Oaks, CA: Sage.

Hui, C. H. (1988). Measurement of individualism-collectivism. *Journal of Research in Personality, 22,* 17-36.

Hui, C. H., and Triandis, H. C. (1986). Individualism-collectivism: A study of cross-cultural researchers. *Journal of Cross-Cultural Psychology,17,* 225-248.

Jackson, A. P., and Meadows, F. B., Jr. (1991). Getting to the bottom to understand the top. *Journal of Counseling and Development, 70*, 72-76.

Jahoda, G. (2002). The sifting sands of culture. In F. J. R. v. Vijver and A. M. Chodynicka (Eds.), *New directions in cross-cultural psychology* (pp. 91-106). Warsaw, Poland: Polish Psychological Association.

James, S. and Foster, G (in press). *Reconciling Rules with Context: A Hermeneutic Approach to Cultural Psychotherapy*.

James, S. (2002). *Agonias*: The social and sacred suffering of Azorean immigrants. *Culture, Medicine and Psychiatry, 26*, 87-110.

Kanfer, F. H. (1979). Personal control, social control, and altruism: Can society survive the age of individualism? *American Psychologist, 34*, 231-239.

Kashima, Y. (2000). Conceptions of culture and person for psychology. *Journal of Cross-Cultural Psychology, 31*, 14-32.

Kerr, M. E., and Bowen, M. (1988). *Family evaluation: An approach based on Bowen theory*. New York, NY: W. W. Norton.

Kim, U., Triandis, H. C., Kagitçibasi, C., Choi, S.-C., and Yoon, G. (Eds.). (1994). *Individualism and collectivism.* Thousand Oaks, CA: Sage.

Kirschner, S. R. (1996). *The religious and romantic origins of psychoanalysis.* New York: Cambridge University Press.

Kitayama, S., Markus, H. R., and Lieberman, C. (1995). The collective construction of self esteem: Implications for culture, self, and emotion. In J. A. Russell and J.-M. Fernâandez-Dols (Eds.), *Everyday conceptions of emotion: An introduction to the psychology, anthropology and linguistics of emotion.* (pp. 523-550). Dordrecht, Netherlands: Kluwer Academic Publishers.

Lambeth, G. S. (1995).Psychoanalytic theories of narcissism: An historical and critical analysis. Unpublished doctoral dissertation, The University of Texas at Austin.

Lebra, T. S. (1976). *Japanese patterns of behavior*. Honolulu: University of Hawaii Press.

Lukes, S. (1973). Individualism. Oxford: Basil Blackwell.

Lutz, C. A. (1988). *Unnatural emotions: Everyday sentiments on a Micronesian atoll and their challenge to Western theory*. Chicago: University of Chicago Press.

MacIntyre, A. (1988). *Whose Justice? Which Rationality?* Notre Dame, IN: University of Notre Dame Press.

Markus, H. R., and Kitayama, S. (1991). Culture and the self: Implications for cognition, emotion, and motivation. *Psychological Review,98,* 224-253.

Markus, H. R., and Kitayama, S. (1994). The cultural construction of self and emotion: Implications for social behavior. In *Emotion and culture: Empirical studies of mutual influence* (pp. 89-130). Washington, DC: American Psychological Association.

Martin, J., and Thompson, J. (1997). Between scientism and relativism: Phenomenology, hermeneutics and the new realism in psychology. *Theory and Psychology, 7*, 629-652.

Maruyama, M. (1992). *Context and complexity: Cultivating contextual understanding*. New York: Springer-Verlag.

May, R. (1967). *Psychology and the human dilemma*. Princeton, NJ: D. Van Nostrand.

McLeod, J., and Lynch, G. (2000). 'This is our life': Strong evaluation in psychotherapy narrative. *European Journal of Psychotherapy, Counselling and Health, 3*, 389-406.

McNamee, S. (1996). Psychotherapy as a social construction, *Constructing realities: Meaning-making perspectives for psychotherapists* (pp. 115-137). San Francisco, CA: Jossey-Bass.

Menon, U., and Shweder, R. A. (1994). Kali's tongue: Cultural psychology and the power of shame in Orissa, India. In S. Kitayama and H. Markus (Eds.), *Emotion and culture* (pp. 241-284). Washington, DC: American Psychological Association.

Mesquita, B. (2001). Emotions in collectivist and individualist contexts. *Journal of Personality and Social Psychology, 80*, 68-74.

Mesquita, B., Frijda, N. H., and Scherer, K. R. (1997). Culture and emotion. In J. W. Berry, P. R. Dasen and et al. (Eds.), *Basic processes and human development (2nd ed* (Vol. 2, pp. 255-297). Needham Heights, MA: Allyn and Bacon.

Messer, S. B., Sass, L. A., and Woolfolk, R. L. (1988). *Hermeneutics and psychological theory: Interpretive perspectives on personality, psychotherapy, and psychopathology*. New Brunswick, NJ: Rutgers University Press.

Michrina, B. P., and Richards, C. (1996). *Person to person: Fieldwork, dialogue, and the hermeneutic method*. Albany, NY: State University of New York Press.

Moody-Adams, M. M. (1997). *Fieldwork in familiar places: Morality, culture, and philosophy*. Cambridge, MA: Harvard University Press.

Moore, C. A. (1968). *The status of the individual in East and West*. Honolulu: University of Hawaii Press

Morrison, M. and James, S. (2006). Portuguese Immigrant Families: The Impact of Acculturation. (Manuscript submitted for publication).

Munro, D. J. (1969). *The concept of man in early China*. Stanford, CA: Stanford University Press.

Neimeyer, R. A., and Mahoney, M. J. (Eds.). (1995). *Constructivism in psychotherapy*. Washington, DC, USA: American Psychological Association.

Packer, M. J., and Addison, R. B. (Eds.). (1989). *Entering the circle: Hermeneutic investigation in psychology*. Albany, NY: State University of New York Press.

Palmer, R. E. (1969). *Hermeneutics*. Evanston, Illinois: Northwestern University Press.

Patterson, C. H. (1996). Multicultural counseling: From diversity to universality. *Journalof Counseling and Development, 74*, 227-231.

Pedersen, P. B. (1991). Multiculturalism as a generic approach to counseling. *Journal of Counseling and Development, 70*(1), 6-12.

Pederson, P. B. (1997). The cultural context of the American Counseling Associations code of ethics. *Journal of Counseling and Development*, *76*, 23-28.

Perloff, R. (1987). Self-interest and personal responsibility redux. *American Psychologist, 42*, 3-11.

Poortinga, Y. H. (1997). Towards convergence. In J. W. Berry, Y. H. Poortinga and J. Pandey (Eds.), *Handbook of cross-cultural psychology (2nd): Volume One, Theory and method* (pp. 347-387). Needham Heights, MA: Allyn and Bacon.

Prilleltensky, I. (1989). Psychology and the status quo. *American Psychologist, 44*(5), 795-802.

Prilleltensky, I. (1994). *The morals and politics of psychology: Psychological discourse and the status quo*. Albany, NY: State University of New York Press.

Rabinow, P., and Sullivan, W. M. (1987). *Interpretive social science: A second look.* Berkeley, CA: The University of California Press.

Ratner, C. (1997). *Cultural psychology and qualitative methodology: Theoretical and empirical considerations*. New York, NY: Plenum Press.

Ratner, C. (2000). Outline of a coherent, comprehensive concept of culture: The problem of fragmentary notions of culture. *Cross-Cultural Psychology Bulletin, 34*, 5-11.

Rennie, D. L. (1999). Qualitative research: A matter of hermeneutics and the sociology of knowledge, *Using qualitative methods in psychology* (pp. 3-13). Thousand Oaks, CA: Sage Publications.

Richardson, F. C. (1989). Freedom and commitment in modern psychotherapy. *Journal of Integrative and Eclectic Psychotherapy,8,* 303-319.

Richardson, F. C., and Christopher, J. C. (1993). Social theory as practice: Metatheoretical options for social inquiry. *Theoretical and Philosophical Psychology, 13*, 137-153.

Richardson, F. C., and Guignon, C. (1988). Individualism and social interest. *Journal of Individual Psychology,44,* 13-29.

Richardson, F. C., Fowers, B. J., and Guignon, C. B. (1999). *Re-envisioning psychology: Moral dimensions of theory and practice*. San Francisco, CA: Jossey-Bass.

Ricoeur, P. (1981). *Hermeneutics and the Human Sciences.* Cambridge, UK: Cambridge University Press.

Ricoeur, P. (1992). *Oneself as Another*. Chicago: The University of Chicago Press.

Ritzer, G. (1996). *The McDonaldization of society.* Thousand Oaks, CA: Pine Forge Press.

Roland, A. (1996). The influence of culture on the self and selfobject relationships: An Asian-North American comparison. *Psychoanalytic Dialogues, 6*, 461-475.

Rubin, J. B. (1997). Psychoanalysis is self-centered, *Soul on the couch: Spirituality, religion, and morality in contemporary psychoanalysis* (pp. 79-108). Hillsdale, NJ: The Analytic Press.

Sampson, E. E. (1977). Psychology and the American ideal. *Journal of Personality and Social Psychology,35,* 767-782.

Sampson, E. E. (1981). Cognitive psychology as ideology. *American Psychologist, 36*(7), 730-743.

Sampson, E. E. (1985). The decentralization of identity: Toward a revised concept of personal and social order. *American Psychologist, 40*, 1203-1211.

Sampson, E. E. (1988). The debate on individualism: Indigenous psychologies of the individual and their role in personal and societal functioning. *American Psychologist, 43,* 15-22.

Sampson, E. E. (1989). The challenge of social change for psychology: Globalization and psychology's theory of the person. *American Psychologist, 44*, 914-921.

Sampson, E. E. (1993). Identity politics: Challenges to psychology's understanding. *American Psychologist*, *43*, 1219-1230.

Sampson, E. E. (2000). Reinterpreting individualism and collectivism: Their religious roots and monologic versus dialogic person-other relationship. *American Psychologist*, *55*, 1425-1432.

Schafer, R. (1976). *A new language for psychoanalysis*. New Haven: Yale University Press.

Schafer, R. (1993). Narration in the psychoanalytic dialogue. In E. Berman and et al. (Eds.), *Essential papers on literature and psychoanalysis.* (pp. 341-368). New York, NY: New York University Press.

Schmitz, S. E., and Christopher, J. C. (1997). Trouble in Smurftown: The moral visions of youth gangs on Guam. *Child Welfare, 76,* 411-428.

Seeley, K. M. (2000). *Cultural psychotherapy*. Northvale, NJ: Jason Aronson.

Shweder, R. A. (1990). Cultural psychology: What is it? In J. W. Stigler, R. A. Shweder and G. Herdt (Eds.), *Cultural psychology: Essays on comparative human development* (pp. 1-43). New York: Cambridge University Press.

Shweder, R. A. (1991). *Thinking through cultures: Expeditions in cultural psychology*. Cambridge, MA, US: Harvard University Press.

Shweder, R. A. (2003). Why do men barbecue? *Recipes for cultural psychology*. Cambridge, MA: Harvard University.

Shweder, R. A., and Bourne, E. J. (1984). Does the concept of the person vary cross-culturally? In R. A. Shweder and R. A. LeVine (Eds.), *Culture theory: Essays on mind, self, and emotion* (pp. 158-199). New York: Cambridge University Press.

Shweder, R., Mahapatra, M., and Miller, J. G. (1987). Culture and moral development. In J. Kagan and S. Lamb (Eds.), *The emergence of morality in young children* (pp. 1-83). Chicago: University of Chicago Press.

Slife, B. D., Reber, J. S., and Richardson, F. C. (Eds.). (2005). *Critical thinking about psychology: Hidden assumptions and plausible alternatives*. Washington, DC: American Psychological Association.

Slife, B. D., Williams, R. N., and Barlow, S. H. (Eds.). (2001). *Critical issues in psychotherapy: Translating new ideas into practice*. Thousand Oaks, CA,: Sage Publications.

Smith, B. M. (1978). What it means to be human. In R. Fitzgerald (Ed.), (pp. 3-24). Australia: Pergamon Press.

Smith, S. T., and Smith, K. D. (1995). Turkish emotion concepts: A prototype approach. In J. A. Russell, J.-M. Fernandez-Dols and et al. (Eds.), *Everyday conceptions of emotion: An introduction to the psychology, anthropology and linguistics of emotion.* (pp. 103-119). Dordrecht, Netherlands: Kluwer Academic Publishers.

Spence, D. P. (1982). *Narrative truth and historical truth: meaning and interpretation in psychoanalysis*. New York: W. W. Norton.

Spence, D. P. (1993). The hermeneutic turn: Soft science or loyal opposition? *Psychoanalytic Dialogues, 3*, 1-10.

Spence, J. T. (1985). Achievement American style: The rewards and costs of individualism. *American Psychologist,40,* 1285-1295.

Sue, D. W. (1981). *Counseling the culturally different*. New York: John Wiley.

Sue, D. W., and Sue, D. (1990). *Counseling the culturally different.* New York: Wiley.

Sugarman, J., and Martin, J. (1995). The moral dimension: A conceptualization and empirical demonstration of the moral nature of psychotherapeutic conversations. *Counseling Psychologist, 23*, 324-347.

Sullivan, W. M. (1986). *Reconstructing public philosophy*. Berkeley: University of California Press.

Szasz, T. S. (1961). *The myth of mental illness*. New York: Hoeber-Harper.

Tappan, M. B. (1997). Interpretive psychology: Stories, circles, and understanding lived experience. *Journal of Social Issues, 53*, 645-656.

Tatman, A. (2004). Hmong history, culture and acculturation: Implications for counseling the Hmong. *Journal of Multicultural Counseling and Development, 32*, 222-234.

Taylor, C. (1975). *Hegel.* New York: Cambridge University Press.

Taylor, C. (1985a). *Human agency and language: Philosophical papers 1.* New York: Cambridge University Press.

Taylor, C. (1985b). *Philosophy and the human sciences: Philosophical papers, 2.* New York: Cambridge University Press.

Taylor, C. (1985c). Justice After Virtue. In M. Benedikt and R. Berger (Eds.), (pp. 23-48). Vienna.

Taylor, C. (1987). The moral topography of the self. In S. B. Messer, L. A. Saas, and R. L. Woolfolk, (Eds.). *Hermeneutics and psychological theory: Interpretive perspectives on personality, psychotherapy, and psychopathology*(pp. 288-320). New Brunswick, NJ: Rutgers University Press.

Taylor, C. (1989). *Sources of the self: The making of the modern identity.* Cambridge, MA: Harvard University Press.

Taylor, C. (1991). The dialogical self. In D. R. Hiley, J. F. Bohman and R. Shusterman (Eds.), *The Interpretive Turn* (pp. 304-314). Cornell, NY: Cornell University Press.

Taylor, C. (1992). *Multiculturalism and "the politics of recognition."* Princeton, NJ: Princeton University Press.

Taylor, C. (1995). *Philosophical arguments*. Cambridge, MA: Harvard University Press.

Tjeltveit, A. C. (1989). The ubiquity of models of human beings in psychotherapy: The need for rigorous reflection. *Psychotherapy, 26*, 1-10.

Triandis, H. C. (1989). The self and social behavior in differing cultural contexts. *Psychological Review, 96,* 506-520.

Triandis, H. C. (1995). *Individualism and collectivism.* Boulder, CO: Westview.

Trimble, J. E. (2003). Forward. In D. B. Pope-Davis, H. L. K. Coleman, W. M. Liu, and R. L. Toporek (Eds.), *Handbook of multicultural competencies in counseling and psychology* (pp. x-xiii). Thousand Oaks, CA: Sage.

Van Manen, M. (1990). *Researching lived experience: Human science for an action sensitive pedagogy*. New York: State University of New York Press.

Vandervert, L. R. (1995). Chaos theory and neurological positivism--clarifications: A reply to Newman, Bickhard, Alexander and Globus. *New Ideas in Psychology, 13*, 143-148.

Vernon, S. W., and Roberts, R. E. (1982). Prevalence of treated and untreated psychiatric disorders in three ethnic groups. *Social Science and Medicine, 16*, 1575-1582.

Vontress, C. E. (1979). Cross-cultural counseling: An existential approach. *The Personnel and Guidance Journal, 58*, 117-122.

Wachtel, P. L. (1977). *Psychoanalysis and behavior therapy*. New York: Basic Books.

Walsh, R. A. (1995). The study of values in psychotherapy: A critique and call for an alternative method. *Psychotherapy Research, 5*(4), 313-326.

Waterman, A. S. (1981). Individualism and interdependence. *American Psychologist, 36,* 762-773.

Waterman, A. S. (1984). *The psychology of individualism*. New York: Praeger.

West, W. (2000). *Psychotherapy and spirituality: Crossing the line between therapy and religion.* London: Sage.

Whaley, A. L. (2001). Cultural mistrust and mental health services for African Americans: A review and meta-analysis. *Counseling Psychologist, 29*, 513-531.

Wilson, T. D. (2002). *Strangers to ourselves: Discovering the adaptive unconscious.* Cambridge, MA: Belknap Press/Harvard University Press.

Wolszon, L. R. (1998). Women's Body Image Theory and Research: A Hermeneutic Critique. *American Behavioral Scientist, 41*, 542-557.

Woolfolk, R. L. (1998). *The cure of souls: Science, values, and psychotherapy.* San Francisco, CA: Jossey-Bass.

Woolfolk, R. L., and Richardson, F. C. (1984). Behavior therapy and the ideology of modernity. *American Psychologist,7,* 777-786.

In: Psychotherapy
Editors: A. J. Lancaster, and O. Sharpe

ISBN 978-1-61942-611-5

Chapter 8

DEVELOPMENT OF A NOVEL SPIRITUAL GROUP PSYCHOTHERAPY BASED ON THE FOURFOLDPATHS: HAPPY SCIENCE CLINIC GROUP PSYCHOTHERAPY

Yoichi Chida[*1, 2], *and Yoonja Kim*[1]
[1] Department of Medical Science
[2] Happy Science Clinic; Department of Public Health and Epidemiology,
Kanagawa, Japan
University College London

ABSTRACT

A large number of publications have previously shown spirituality/religiosity to crucially boosting the mental resilience and curing the psychiatric illness. Religiosity and spirituality can be defined broadly as any feelings, thoughts, experiences, and behaviors that arise from a search for the "sacred", with the former implying group or social practices and doctrines and the latter tending to refer to personal experiences and beliefs. The present study aimed to develop a novel spiritual group psychotherapy based on the Four True Paths; Love, Wisdom, Self-reflection, and Progress, and to evaluate the efficacy in a randomized controlled trial with 26 Japanese out-patients suffering from mood disorders or neurotic, stress-related, and somatoform disorders. The treatment participants (n=14) at 3-6 people per group took part in five 90-minutes sessions at one-week intervals, while the delayed-treatment control patients (n=12) only received a usual care including medication. Their mental status was assessed before and after the intervention by the Profile of Mood States and the Positive Negative Affect Schedulescale. We found that the depressive symptom was significantly improved in the trial group, compared with the control group. In conclusion, the currently developed group psychotherapy might have an unyielding effectiveness on thedepressive symptom, which further needs to be confirmed by a large randomized controlled trial.

[*]Address for corresponding: Yoichi Chida, West Canyon II 3F, 1-12-20Mizonoguchi, Takatsu-ku, Kawasaki city, Kanagawa 213-0001, Japan, TEL: +81-44-322-0787; FAX: +81-44-322-0788; E-mail: yoichi. chida@gmail.com

Keywords: Buddhism; Causality; Happy Science; Randomized controlled trial; Reincarnation; Spiritual group psychotherapy.

Abbreviations List

BMI	body mass index;
HSC	Happy Science Clinic;
PANAS	Positive Negative Affect Schedulescale;
POMS	Profile of Mood States;

Introduction

Religiosity and spirituality can be defined broadly as any feelings, thoughts, experiences, and behaviors that arise from a search for the "sacred", with the former implying group or social practices and doctrines and the latter tending to refer to personal experiences and beliefs [Hill et al, 2000]. The term sacred refers to a divine being, divine object, Ultimate Reality, or Ultimate Truth as perceived by the individual.There is an extensive literature relating religiosity/spirituality with mental and physical health [Chida et al, 2009; Grepmair et al, 2007; Grossman et al, 2007; Ano and Sanders,2005; Shreve-Neiger and Edelstein, 2004; Hackney and Vasconcelles, 2003]. For example, a meta-analysis on 49 relevant studies [Ano and Sanders,2005] concluded that positive and negative forms of religious coping were related to positive and negative psychological adjustment to stress, respectively. Furthermore, a meta-analysis on 147 studies demonstrated a robust but modest (r=–0.096) negative correlation between religiosity/spirituality and depressive symptoms, due in part to favorable effects on coping with stressful life events [Smith, 2003].

Regarding religious or/and spiritual psychotherapy, a number of clinical trials have so far been reported on psychiatric or physical patients [Masters and Spielmans, 2007; Bormann et al, 2006; Berry, 2002;]. There is, however, less evidence-base for the use of more specific eastern spiritual techniques such as Buddhist in psychotherapeutic practice [Kelly, 2008]. The original nature of the soul is divine, and if you perceive the law of "Causality" (i.e., cause and effect) and lead the best possible life in accordance with the law, you can become a being of higher spiritual level [Allen, 2006; Okawa, 2004]. In connection with any discussion of the meaning of cause and effect, the idea of "Reincarnation" is very important. Other major religions, namely, Christianity, Islam, Judaism, Confucianism, Taoism, do not describe the concept of reincarnation as clearly as Buddhism does, so it is one of the major features, of Buddhism [Okawa, 2007 (a)]. Indeed, reincarnation has also been argued in some recent western psychiatric practices such as the Past-Life therapy [Weiss, 1988].

The Happy Science Clinic (HSC) group psychotherapy is based not only on these Buddhism core teachings of "Causality" and "Reincarnation," but also on the Principles of Happiness which is the "Fourfold Paths" of Love, Wisdom, Self-reflection, and Progress as follows [Okawa, 2007 (b)].

Love

The first principle of happiness is "Love". This love is not the kind of love that you expect to receive from others. The love that the patients learn in the HSC group psychotherapy is "love that gives." Another word that expresses "love that gives" is compassion. Compassion is an emotion, and its magnitude is a function of personality characteristics. Generally, felt compassion evokes the desire to do something to relieve the sufferer(s) [Cassell, 2005].

We can logically infer that a person feeling grateful might be more inclined to feel loved and cared for by others [Shelton, 1990]. This is the following two reasons; The first is an interpersonal context, for gratitude is an interpersonal emotion, which precludes it from being directed toward oneself. Second, implicit in the experience of gratitude is the recipient's theory of mind from which he or she infers another's well-meaning intention, resulting in one's feeling loved and esteemed [Shelton, 1990]. From this more expansive perspective, gratitude is fundamentally a moral affect with empathy at its foundation: In order to acknowledge the cost of the gift, the recipient must identify with the psychological state of the one who has provided it. The benefactor's giving is interpreted by the recipient as freely offered, and with that comes the acknowledgement that such offering might prove costly to or incur hardship for the benefactor. Such an understanding blends fittingly with some object relations formulations of gratitude, where it is seen as a major derivative of the capacity for love [Klein, 1957]. Indeed, Naikan therapy, which is the Japanese Buddhist-based psychotherapy on psychiatric patients, essentially involves a programme of structured self-reflection on the benefactor's giving, eventually elevating participant's "love that gives" [Murase and Johnson, 1974]. In a previous Gallup [1998] survey of American teens and adults, over 90% of respondents indicated that expressing gratitude helped them to feel "extremely happy" or "somewhat happy."

Given these previous reports, the HSC group psychotherapy instructs the patients to boost the emotion of gratitude through the self-reflection that the givings prove(d) costly to or incur(red) hardship for the benefactors, eventually shifting from "love that takes" toward "love that give" and getting happier.

Wisdom

The second principle of happiness is "Wisdom." Wisdom could be viewed as a metaheuristic that activates and organizes knowledge about the fundamental pragmatics of life in the service of optimizing an integration between mind and virtue [Baltes and Staudinger, 2000]. A heuristic usually is defined as a highly automatized and organized strategy for directing search processes or for organizing and using information in a certain class of situations [Dawes, 1988]. The function of heuristics in judgment and decision making is to reach solutions under conditions of limited resources. Thus, if it is impossible to use the full information—and this is typical of most real-world situations—heuristics guide which and how much information is taken into account in making a decision. In other words, what Simon (1983) defined as bounded rationality (i.e., using realistic amounts of time, information, and cognitive resources in making decisions) and efficient use of a happy life seem to be operative when dealing with wisdom tasks. It is notable in this context that the term heuristic in the same positive sense as Gestalt psychologists [Gigerenzer et al, 1999; Simon, 1956]. Wisdom experts may have more elaborate, flexible, and efficient systems of heuristics available than people with low levels of wisdom-related knowledge. As a consequence, wisdom experts may achieve high levels of performance when working on problems concerning the fundamental pragmatics of life faster and with fewer cues (Hitano, 1988).

The HSC group psychotherapy makes wisdom available to the patients in order to shift from "Perfectionism" toward "Optimalism." Perfectionists are indeed at risk for a variety of psychiatric disorders such as depression, anxiety disorders, sexual dysfunction, and eating disorders [Wu and Gortesi, 2009; Bardone-Cone et al, 2006; Kirkcaldy et al, 2006]. The central and defining characteristic of perfectionism is the fear of failure [Ben-Shahar, 2009]. The Perfectionist is driven by this fear; his primary concern is to avoid falling down, deviating, stumbling, erring. He tries in vain to force reality (where some failure is unavoidable) to fit into her straight-line vision of life (where no failure is acceptable). The Optimalist does not like to fail either, but he understands that there is no other way to learn and ultimately succeed. For the Perfectionist, achieving his goal is the only thing that matters. The process of getting there—the journey—is meaningless to him. The Optimalist, by contrast, values the journey that takes him to his destination, and understands that along the way there will be detours—some pleasant and desirable, some not. As psychologist Pacht [1984] notes, "For Perfectionists, only the extremes of the continuum exist—they are unable to recognize that there is a middle grounds." This all-or-nothing approach leads to procrastination and, more generally, to inefficient use of time. In contrast, the Pareto principle (also, known as the 80/20 rule) is applied in order to use time efficiently; roughly 80% of the effects come from 20% of the causes [Koch, 2005]. Thus, in the HSC group psychotherapy, the patients are instructed to list up their problems without escaping from reality, to put the priority of them in order, to adopt the 80/20 rule for the purpose to invest their efforts in the most important 20 percent, and enjoy the journey while remaining focused on their destination.

SELF-REFLECTION

The third principle of happiness is "Self-reflection," which is based on the power of the self. Our souls inevitably collect dust and grime as we live in this world. We are supposed to refine our own souls, and this is actually our spiritual discipline. Of course there may be help from an outside power; it is like getting help from a specialist and sometimes we need such help. But basically, instead of simply doing nothing and waiting for help, we need to polish our own diamond. If we do not refine it ourselves, what is the meaning of spiritual discipline in this world? If we realize we had made a mistake, who can correct it apart from ourself? Although someone else could wash our physical bodies, only we can cleanse our own souls; we are responsible for polishing them.

The HSC group psychotherapy helps the patients to boost forgiveness by carrying out self-reflection. Previous reports have shown that (a) forgiveness is an emotion-focused coping process that can promote health; (b) forgiveness might have its major impact on health through reducing unforgiveness rather than creating positive emotional experiences; (c) forgiveness, especially when undertaken for altruistic motives, can affect both physical and mental health; and (d) forgiveness interventions are appropriate for but infrequently used in medical settings [Worthington et al, 2007]. All of the definitions on forgiveness are built on one core feature: When people forgive, their responses (i.e., what they feel and think about, what they want to do, or how they actually behave) toward people who have offended or injured them become less negative and more positive—or prosocial—over time [McCullough, 2000]. The HSC group psychotherapy applies a modified method of "REACH" intervention which was developed by Worhington [Seligman, 2003a]. First, the patients are instructed to recall the hurt, in as objective a way as they can, but not to think of the other person as evil and not to wallow in self-pity. Take deep, show, and calming breaths as they visualize the event. Second, they are asked to try to understand from the perpetrator's point of view why this person hurt them. This is not easy, but make up a plausible story that the transgressor might tell if challenged to explain. Third, they are instructed to recall a time they transgressed, felt guilty, and were forgiven. This was a gift they were given by another person because they needed it, and they were grateful for this gift. Finally, they write a "certificate of forgiveness," write a letter of forgiveness to the offender, write it in their diary, write a poem or song, or tell a trusted friend what they have done.

PROGRESS

Self-reflection precedes the fourth principle of happiness, "Progress." if people seek progress without the practice of self-reflection, they will most likely face difficulties before they attain success. It would be like plating metal before removing the rust, it would be in vain because you cannot plate metal with gold if the surface is rusted. Then, the last principle of happiness is progress, the development of the self, of others, and of society. Without the feeling of making progress we cannot feel truly happy.

In the HSC group psychotherapy, the patients are instructed to increase optimism and hopefulness, which have critical effects on making progress. Optimism and hopefulness indeed cause better resistance to depression when bad events strike, better performance at work, particularly in challenging jobs, and better physical health [Chida and Steptoe, 2008; Snyder et al, 2005; Nunn, 1996]. A short course of the ABCDE model is employed in the HSC group psychotherapy in order to increase optimism and hope [Seligman, 2003b]. A stands for adversity, B for the beliefs we automatically have when it occurs, C for the usual consequences of the belief, D for our disputation of our routine belief, and E for the energization that occurs when we dispute it successfully. By effectively disputing the beliefs that follow an adversity, we can change our reaction from dejection and giving up to activity and good cheer. Furthermore, sentence-completion technique, which was devised by the psychotherapist Branden [Ben-Shahar, 2007], is applied to the HSC group psychotherapy. This simple technique—generating some of endings to an incomplete sentence—often helps the patients come up with insights that bring about meaningful change in their lives; For instance, "If I have twice as much ability as I am, I am becoming aware ...." and "If you would die tomorrow, I am becoming aware ....".

Taken together, the purpose of the present study is to develop a novel spiritual group psychotherapy based on the Four True Paths; Love, Wisdom, Self-reflection, and Progress, and to evaluate the efficacy in a randomized controlled trial (RCT) with 26 Japanese out-patients suffering from affective disorders.

METHODS

Design and Study Participants

The study consisted of a two-group (intervention vs. a usual care delayed-treatment control) by two-time (pre-intervention and post-intervention) trial design. The study was conducted at the Happy Science Clinic in Kawasaki city, Kanawaga, Japan, between June and August 2010.

Criteria for enrollment were 1) 18 years or older; 2) Japanese-literate, 3) diagnosed with mood disorders (ICD-10 F30-39) or neurotic stress-related and somatoform disorder (ICD-10 F40-48); 4) none of psychotic symptoms; 5) no other medical conditions that precluded completion of the self-report questionnaire without assistance. Participants gave full informed consent to participate in the study and ethical approval was obtained from the Ethics Committees of Department of Medical Science, Happy Science Clinic. A total of 30 eligible patients were enrolled, and were randomly assigned to the intervention (n=15) and delayed-treatment control condition (n=15). Three (1 and 3 patients in the treatment and control groups, respectively) dropped form the study because of "bad psychological status", where therefore the dropping-out rate of the current trial was 13.3%.

Procedures and HSC Group Psychotherapy

During a visit to the clinic, the subjects were handed a set of questionnaires and a written consent form. Besides the psychological items, these questionnaires included questions regarding education years, smoking history, and alcohol consumption. The study participants completed the questionnaires and consent form there. Their body height and weight were measured by the nurses. Their mental status was assessed at pre-intervention and post-intervention from the 30 item profile of mood states(POMS) short form Japanese version and the 16 item positive affect negative affect schedule (PANAS) scale, which were validated previously [Sato and Yasuda 2001; Yokoyama et al, 1990]. The six subscales of POMS are tension-anxiety, depression, anger-hostility, vigor, fatigue, and confusion. The two subscales of PANAS are positive affect and negative affect.

As shown in Table 1, the 5-week (90 min/week) HSC group intervention consisted of orientation to symptoms from the view of Spiritual life lessons; especially Causality and Reincarnation (Session 1), and skills on how to shift from “a Love that takes” toward “a Love that gives” (Session 2), from “Perfectionism” toward “Optimalism” (Section 3), from “Anger, hatred, and grudge” toward “Forgiveness” (Session 4), from “Hopelessness” toward “Hopefulness” (Session 5). For the purpose of understanding better, the participants in the treatment group were provided with a brief booklet and were viewed some video films which demonstrated the stories related to each session topic. In addition, they were encouraged to carry out some homeworks until the next sessions. The detailed theories and skills of each session have already been described in the introduction section. The participants in the delayed-treatment control group continued with their usual medical care including either weekly or monthly case manager and/or psychiatrist visits. They also continued any medication management if applicable. They did not, however, have any group meetings during the 5-week intervention period. After completing post-intervention questionnaires, they received the 5-week intervention as courtesy for participating in the study.

Table 1. Content of HSC Group Psychotherapy

Session (90 min/session)	HSC Group Psychotherapy
1	Orientation from the view of Spiritual Life Lessons: Causality and Reincarnation
2	Love: Shift from a Love that Takes toward a Love that Gives
3	Wisdom: Shift from Perfectionism toward Optimalism
4	Self-reflection: Shift from Anger, Hatred, and Grudge toward Forgiveness
5	Progress: Shift from Hopelessness toward Hopefulness

Statistical Analysis

Descriptive statics were run on all variables to examine frequency distributions and identify missing data and outliers: namely, mood status (POMS and PANAS), behavioral risk factors (smoking, alcohol intake, body mass index [BMI], and education years), and medical treatment factors (antidepressant, minor tranquilizer, and/or sleep inducer). Descriptive data were compared between the control and treatment groups as categorical variables except for age, education years, BMI, mood status, and illness duration that wereentered as a continuous variable; current smoking and alcohol intakewere categorized into two groups (YES or NO); diagnosis (depression [ICD-10 F32-33], panic disorder [ICD-10 F40.01, F41.0], social anxiety disorder [ICD-10 F40.1], somatoform disorder [ICD-10 F45], and post-traumatic stress disorder [ICD-10 F43.1]); medication (antidepressant, minor tranquilizer, or sleep inducer).Group comparisons of descriptive data were done using *t*-tests or Chi-square tests. Group comparisons of pre-intervention to post-intervention mean change scores were conducted by an analysis of covariance, which controls for possible covariates and confounders. All analyses were performed using Statistical Package for the Social Science (SPSS, version 14.0) and alltests of statistical significance were based on two-sided probability.

Results

As shown in Table 2, all of the demographic factors except for age and current drinkers status did not significantly differ between the control and treatment groups.

The participants in the treatment group were significantly younger and less current alcohol drinkers than those in the control group. Notably, the major population (>70%) of the present trail was diagnosed with depression. Regarding the baseline mood status, there were no differences of the POMS and PANAS scores between the control and treatment groups.

Table 2. Descriptive characteristics of the participants

	Control group (*N*=12)	Treatment group (*N*=14)
Age, yrs	35.4±10.9	36.6±7.4*
Men, %	33.3	28.6
Education, yrs	15.1±2.3	14.3±1.9
Current smokers, %	25.0	35.7
Current drinkers, %	91.7	50.0*
Body mass index, kg/m^2	22.7±5.3	22.8±4.7
Diagnosis, %		
Depression	75.0	71.4
Panic disorder	8.3	0.0
Social anxiety disorder	0.0	14.3
Somatoform disorder	16.7	7.1
PTSD	0.0	7.1
Illness duration, yrs	3.0±4.3	5.3±4.7
Medication		
Antidepressant, %	83.3	85.7
Minor tranquilizer, %	75.0	64.3
Sleep inducer, %	66.7	71.4
POMS		
Tension-anxiety	12.2 ± 4.5	11.1 ± 4.6
Depression	9.5 ± 4.9	9.9 ± 5.1
Anger-hostility	6.4 ± 4.2	7.1 ± 5.5
Vigar	4.0 ± 3.8	4.1 ± 2.7
Fatigue	14.2 ± 4.4	13.0 ± 4.7
Confusion	12.1 ± 4.2	10.8 ±4.2
PANAS		
Positive affect	16.6 ± 6.8	20.1 ± 7.2
Negative affect	26.9 ± 9.0	27.3 ± 8.4

Values are mean ± SD, unless indicated otherwise; PANAS, positive negative affect schedule; POMS, profile of mood states; PTSD, post-traumatic stress disorder; * $p<0.05$ compared with the corresponding value in Control group.

Table 3. Comparison of pre-intervention to post-intervention mean change scores by group

	Control group (N=12)	Treatment group (N=14)	
	M ± SE	M ± SE	p
POMS			
Tension-anxiety	−1.42 ± 1.21	−4.22 ± 1.11	0.26
Depression	−0.36 ± 1.21	−4.76 ± 1.18	0.044
Anger-hostility	−0.73 ± 1.73	−2.23 ± 1.58	0.82
Vigar	2.50 ± 1.16	1.00 ± 1.07	0.79
Fatigue	−2.73 ± 1.40	−3.23 ± 1.28	0.53
Confusion	−1.11 ± 1.31	−3.41 ± 1.20	0.52
PANAS			
Positive affect	3.73 ± 2.26	2.40 ± 2.16	0.19
Negative affect	−1.47 ± 3.07	−6.45 ± 2.94	0.73

PANAS, positive negative affect schedule; POMS, profile of mood states; All mean changes scores were controlled for age and current drinkers which significantly differed between Control and Treatment groups (as shown in Table 2); *p*-values were compared with the corresponding value in Control group.

An evaluation of the impact of treatment on mood status adjusted for age and current alcohol drinkers' status which significantly differed between the control and treatment groups. As a result, the treatment group showed a significantly improved score of depression in POMS, compared with the control group, while the other score of POMS and PANAS did not differ between the control and treatment groups (Table 3).

DISCUSSION

The current study of a pilot RCT has confirmed that the HSC group psychotherapyhas the efficacy on depressive mood in Japanese out-patients suffering from mood disorders or neurotic, stress-related, and somatoform disorders. Furthermore, the other mood outcomes such as tension-anxiety (POMS), anger-hostility (POMS), confusion (POMS), and negative affect (PANAS), seemed to be ameliorated by the HSC group psychotherapy, but not significantly maybe because the detection power of this study was very poor due to the small number of participants.

Given that the HSC group psychotherapy was argued to have a spiritual power that boosts positive mood, it is unexpected that vigar (POMS) and positive affect (PANAS) were not improved in this study. This is becuase the participants' religious/spiritual background (e.g., Buddhist, Christian, atheist, etc.) might diminish an enhancing effect of treatment on positive mood. Clearly, the further research is needed to evaluate such a religious/spiritual confounder by the demographic questionnaire at the baseline, and then to control for it in the statistic analyses. Another possibility is that the effect of treatment on positive mood could be more slowly appeared in comparison with that on negative mood. Thus, measurement of the changes in positive mood status should be repeated at the next 3 months after the treatment.

Previous RCT studies have confirmed that cognitive-behavioural therapy has an efficacy on various psychiatric disorders (Cuijpers et al, 2010; Gibbon et al, 2010; Hetrich et al, 2010). It is, therefore, rather intriguing to compare the efficacies between cognitive-behavioural therapy and HSC group psychotherapy. In addition, considering that HSC group psychotherapy is based on religious/spiritual theory, terminally ill patients might show more efficacy of HSC group psychotherapy on psychiatric symptoms, compared with cognitive-behavioural therapy.

ACKNOWLEDGEMENT

This research was supported by a grant from the NOBUKO-DAIKOKU medical research funding.

Competing interest: None declared.

Ethical approval: Not required.

REFERENCES

Allen J: As a man thinketh. Tarcher Penguin, New York, 2006 (Original work published 1902).

Ano GG, Vasconcelles EB: Religious coping and psychological adjustment to stress: a meta-analysis.*J. Clin. Psychol.* 2005; 61: 461-480.

Baltes PB, Staudinger UM: Wisdom: A metaheuristic (pragmatic) to orchestrate mind and virtue toward excellence.*Am. Psychologist.* 2000; 55: 122-136.

Bardone-Cone AM, Wonderlich SA, Frost RO, Bulik CM, Mitchell JE, Uppala S, Simonich H: Perfectionism and eating disorders: current status and future directions. *Clin. Psychol. Rev.* 2007; 27: 384-405.

Ben-Shahar T: *The pursuit of perfect.* Mc Graw Hill, New York, 2009.

Ben-Shahar T: *Happier.* Mc Graw Hill, New York, 2007.

Berry D: Does religious psychotherapy improve anxiety and depression in religious adults? A review of randomized controlled studies. *Int. J. Psychiatr. Nurs. Res.* 2002; 8: 875-890.

Bormann JE, Gifford AL, Shively M, Smith TL, Redwine L, Kelly A, Becker S, Gershwin M, Bone P, Belding W: Effects of spiritual mantram repetition on HIV outcomes: A randomized controlled trial. *J. Behav. Med.* 2006; 29: 359-376.

Cassell EJ: Chapter 31 Compassion. In: *Handbook of positive psychology*(Ed: Snyder CR and Lopez SJ). Oxford University Press, New York, 2005: pp 434-471.

Chida Y, Steptoe A, Powell LH: Religiosity/Spirituality and mortality. *Psychother. Psychosom.* 2009; 78: 81-90.

Chida Y, Steptoe S: Positive psychological well-being and mortality: A quantitative review of prospective observational studies. *Psychosom. Med.*2008; 70: 741-756.

Cuijpers P, Smit F, Bohlmeijer E, Hollon SD, Andersson G: Efficacy of cognitive-behavioural therapy and other psychological treatments for adult depression: meta-analytic study of publication bias. *Br. J. Psychiatry.*2010; 196: 173-178.

Dawes RM: Rational choice in an uncertain world.*Harcourt Brace Jovanovich,* Orlando, FL, 1988.

Gallup GH Jr: Thankfulness: Amerca's saving grace. *Paper presented at the National Day of Prayer Breakfast.* Thanks-Giving Square, Dallas, TX, 1998.

Gibbon S, Duggan C, Stoffers J, Huband N, Völlm BA, Ferriter M, Liev K: Psychological interventions for antisocial personality disorder. *Cochrane Database Syst. Rev.* 2010; 6: CD007668.

Gigerenzer G, Todd PM, the ABC group: *Simple heuristics that make us smart.* Oxford University Press, New York, 1999.

Grepmair L, Mitterlehner F, Loew T, Bachler E, Rother W, Nickel M: Promoting mindfulness in psychotherapists in training influences the treatment results of their patients: a randomized, double-blind, controlled study. *Psychother. Psychosom.* 2007; 76: 332-338.

Grossman P, Tiefenthaler-Gilmer U, Raysz A, Kesper U: Mindfulness training as an intervention for fibromyalgia: evidence of postintervention and 3-year follow-up benefits in well-being. *Psychother. Psychosom.* 2007; 76: 226-233.

Hackney CH, Sanders GS: Religiosity and mental health: a meta-analysis of recent studies.*J. Sci. Study Religion.* 2003; 42: 43-55.

Hatano G: Social and motivational bases for mathematical understanding. *New Dir. Child Dev.* 1988; 41: 55-70.

Hetrick SE, Purcell R, Garner B, Parslow R: Combined pharmacotherapy and psychological therapies for post traumatic stress disorder (PTSD).*Cochrane Database Syst. Rev.* 2010; 7: CD007316.

Hill PC, Pargament KI, Hood RW, McCullough ME, Swyers JP, Larson DB, Zinnbauer BJ: Conceptualizing religion and spirituality: Points of commonality, points of departure. *J. Ther. Soc. Behav.* 2000; 30: 51-77.

Kelly BD: Buddhist psychology, psychotherapy and the brain: A critical introduction. *Transcult. Psychiatry*. 2008; 45: 5-30.

Kirkcaldy BD, Siefen GR, Urkin J, Merrick J: Risk factors for suicidal behavior in adolescents. *Minerva Pediatr.* 2006; 58: 443-450.

Klein M: Envy and gratitude: *A study of unconscious sources. Basic Books,* New York, 1957.

Koch R: Living the 80/20 way: work less, worry less, succeed more, enjoy more.*Nicholas Brealey Publishing,* London, 2005.

Masters KS, Spielmans GI: Prayer and health: review, meta-analysis, and research agenda. *J. Behav. Med.* 2007; 30: 329-338.

McCullough ME, Pargament KI, Thoresen CT: The psychology of forgiveness: History, conceptual issues, and overview. In: *Forgiveness: theory, research, and practive* (Eds: McCulloufh, ME; Pargament KI; Thoresen CE). Guilford, New York, 2000: pp 1-14.

Murase T, Johnson F: Naikan, Morita, and Western psychotherapy. *Archiv. Gen. Psychiatry*. 1974; 31: 121-128.

Nunn KP: Personal hopefulness: A conceptual review of the relevance of the perceived future to psychiatry. *Br. J. Med. Psychol.* 1996; 69: 227-245.

Okawa R: Chapter 4 The idea of the void. In: *the essence of Buddha* (Ed: Okawa R). Sphere, London, 2007 (a): pp 99-126.

Okawa R: Chapter 1 the principles of happiness. In: *10 principles of universal wisdom* (Ed: Okawa R). Jaico Publishing House, Mumbai, 2007 (b): pp 1-25.

Okawa R: The essence of Buddhism: the concept of the law of causality. In: The challenge of the mind (Ed: Okawa R). *Time Warner Book,* London, 2004: pp 21-23.

Pacht AR: Reflections on perfection. *Am. Psychol.* 1984; 39: 386-390.

Sato A, Yasuda A: Development of the Japanese version of positive and negative affect schedule (PANAS) scales.*Seikaku Shinrigaku Kenkyu.* 2001; 9: 138-139.

Seligman MEP: Chapter 5 Satisfaction about the past. In*: Authentic happiness*(Ed: Seligman MEP). Nicholas Brealey, London, 2003a: pp 62-82.

Seligman MEP: Chapter 6 Optimism about the future. In: *Authentic happiness*(Ed: Seligman MEP). Nicholas Brealey, London, 2003b: pp 83-101.

Shelton CM: *Morality of the heart: A psychology for the Christian moral life. Crossroad,* New York, 1990.

Shreve-Neiger AK, Edelstein BA: Religion and anxiety: a critical review of the literature. *Clin. Psychol. Rev.* 2004; 24: 379-397.

Simon HA: *Reason in human affairs.* Stanford University Press, Stanford, CA, 1983.

Smith TB, McCullough ME, Poll J: Religiousness and depression: evidence for a main effect and the moderating influence of stressful life events. *Psychol. Bull.* 2003; 129: 614-636.

Snyder CR, Rand KL, Sigmon DR: Chapter 19 Hope theory. In: *Handbook of positive psychology* (Ed: Snyder CR and Lopez SJ). Oxford University Press, New York, 2005: pp 257-276.

Weiss BL: *Many lives, many masters: the true story of a prominent psychiatrist, his young patients, and the past-life therapy that changes both their lives. Fireside Books*, Alaska, 1988.

Worthington EL, Witvliet CVO, Pietrini P, Miller AJ: Forgiveness, health, and well-being: a review of evidence for emotional versus decisional for forgiveness, dispositional forgiveness, and reduced unforgiveness.*J. Behav. Med.* 2007; 30: 291-302.

Wu KD, Gortesi GT: Relations between perfectionism and obsessive-compulsive symptoms: examination of specificity among the dimensions. *J. Anxiety Disord*. 2009; 23: 393-400.

Yokoyama K, Arai S, Kawakami N, Takeshita T: Production of the Japanese edition of profile of mood states (POMS): Assessment of reliability and validity. *Nippon Koshu Eisei Zasshi*. 1990; 37: 913-918.

INDEX

D

E

F

G

H

I

O

P

Q

R

S

T

U

V

W

Y

Z